JN197206

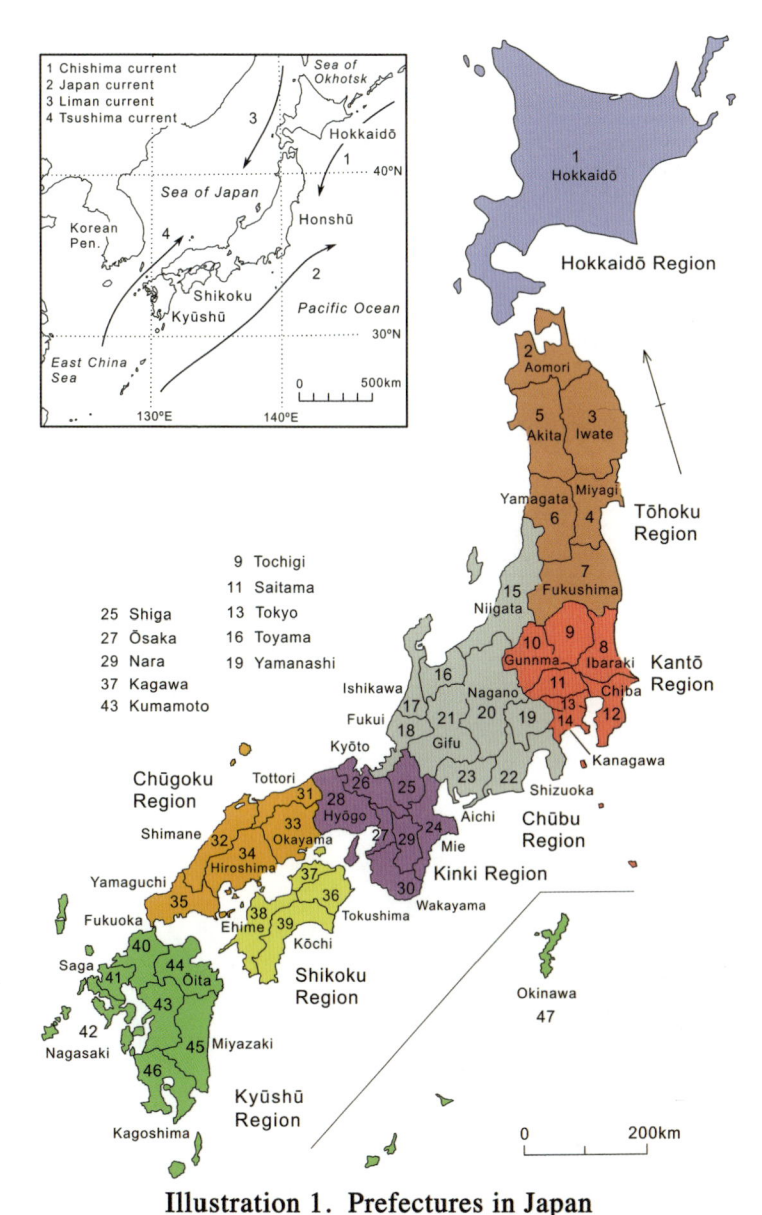

Illustration 1. Prefectures in Japan

Numbers on prefectures correspond with the sections of this book.

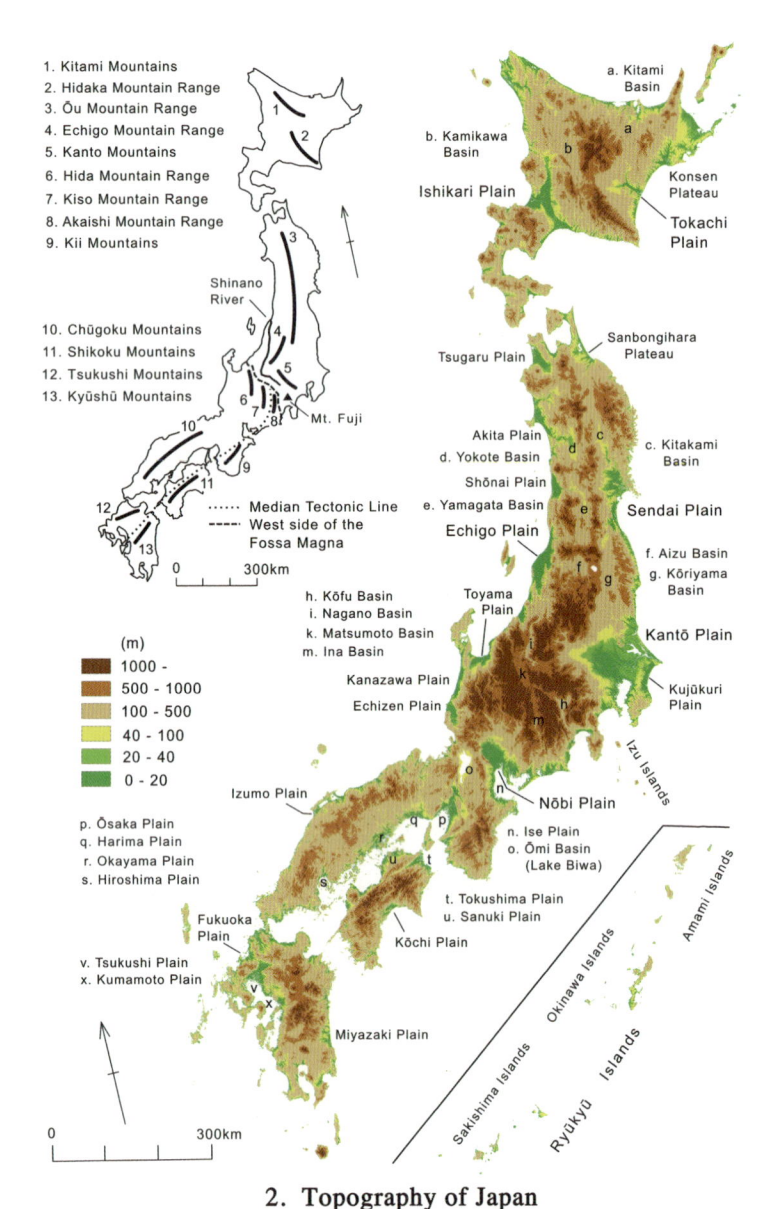

2. Topography of Japan

Made by the author with QGIS, Inkscape, and SRTM 90m data.

3. Tôya caldera lake and Mt. Yôtei (May 2015)

4. Rice harvest in Sendai Plain (October 2008)

5. Kusatsu hot spring (August 2006)

6. Kappabashi (Januray 1998)

7. Kamikôchi (May 2009)

8. Tea cultivation in Makinohara (March 2009)

9. Kiyomizu temple (November 1998)

10. Cape Shiono (March 1996)

11. Farm with *tsuiji-matsu* and Sekishû roofing tiles (August 2009)

12. Dispersed settlement in Sanuki Plain and Mt. Iino (August 1995)

13. Kusasenri (May 1998)

14. Shuri castle (December 2002)

All photographs were taken by the author.

THE REGIONAL GEOGRAPHY OF JAPAN

Takaaki Nihei

The Regional Geography of Japan

Hokkaido University Press

For Saito

The author is associate professor of human geography at Hokkaido University.

Published 2018
ISBN: 978-4-8329-0373-9

Printed in Japan
Published by Hokkaido University Press
North 9 West 8, Sapporo, 060-0808 Japan

Contents

Preface

A work on Japanese geography in English is worthy of publication since a considerable number of foreign visitors come to Japan not only to sightsee but also for study and work. Although their background information on Japanese geography is not always sufficient, they are interested in the country because of the archipelago that stretches northeast to southwest for 3,000 km, which brims with geographical diversity.

Another motive for writing this work is that the number of Japanese who have not studied geography in high school or at university has increased. The situation may be attributed to education policy and university entrance examinations, both of which focus on history in social studies. Nonetheless, as geographical studies play a significant role in international relations and the prevention of natural disasters, a considerable number of students have come to be aware of the discipline. Among the subjects dealing with geography, the regional geography of Japan *(Nihon no chishi)* provides basic information for people living in the country. The "close to home" information offered by regional geography will help those who frequently move for work or study, who create branded products in business or devise policies, and who have to introduce themselves in English. As to branding, according to Nihei (2010), the proper naming of commodities relevant to place is important.

However, since we can access copious amounts of information about regional geography on the Internet nowadays, it is difficult to choose a specific topic. For instance, if we search for information about a region on a free encyclopedia, we will encounter a lengthy list of historical figures or interminable comparisons with multiple other topics.

To address those issues, the author attempts to present the regional geography of Japan at the prefectural *(to-dô-fu-ken)* scale. The reason for selecting such a scale is that prefectural topics prevail in our daily conversation. For instance, new recruits in the workplace and students will mention their home prefectures in their introductions on themselves, rather than municipalities *(shi-chô-son)* and regions *(chihô)*. Prefectural topics are so neutral that they can be mentioned as easily as weather topics. Moreover, if sightseers and business people have some brief information on a prefecture they are visiting, their trips will be all the more enjoyable.

*

In this work, prefectural information is described in the order of nature, history, culture, population, transportation, and industry. Although the order is in compliance with the previous regional geography, the author seeks to imply a correlation between those topics with reference to the "cultural stratigraphy" *(bunka sôjo)* viewpoint advocated by Saito (2006). Cultural stratigraphy signifies that "cultures of certain ages leave traces up to the present like stratums." The amount of information per prefecture is confined to between 1,600 and 2,000 characters in Japanese for readability purposes. Japanese place names written in Chinese characters are difficult to pronounce. Sometimes, even the Japanese do not recognize them, and so, long vowels in Japanese words are basically described with circumflex in the main body (macron in maps). Japanese words are also written in italic in this book except for proper nouns and the common nouns listed in the New Oxford American Dictionary.

The contents of the topics are based on the author's experiences in fieldwork, field excursions, reading of re-prints, and writings of book chapters. Regarding the writings, they comprise a series of *Regional geography of Japan* (Yamamoto et al., 2006; Fujita and Tabayashi, 2007; Saito et al., 2009), a series of *Figures of Japan* (Teikoku Shoin, 2013), and a series of *Regional geography of world* (Kikuchi, 2011). The author also participated in the writing of textbooks for high schools and junior high schools (for instance, Arai et al., 2013; Taniuchi and Kagami, 2016). Regarding the re-prints of academic articles, the basic information, such as the authors, titles, journals, and pages, is provided via a database on the Internet (Nihei, 2004).

Numerical data is quoted from government statistics, namely, the 2010 Population Census, the 2010 Census of Agriculture and Forestry, statistics on agricultural income produced for 2013, the Annual Statistics of Fishery and Fish Culture for 2013, industrial statistics for 2012, and the Report on Prefectural Accounts for 2012. Those were the latest volumes when the author started to writing. Place names are cited from Teikoku's atlas (Teikoku Shoin, 2010). The domestic climate classification used is based on a study by Inoue and Matsumoto (2005), and numerical climatic data are cited from *Kakushu data—shiryô* (various data and material: http://www.jma.go.jp/jma/menu/menureport.html) produced by the Japan Meteoro-logical Agency. In the primary sector of industry, the seed varieties of rice referred to are from the Beikoku Data-bank (2014).

The order of prefectures is arranged from north to south, as well as government statistics, which are referred to the prefecture code of Japanese Industrial Standards. It starts from Hokkaidô and ends in Okinawa. The order of atlases and textbooks is the opposite, so the author sometimes received questions in geography courses, such as "Why is the entry on Hokkaidô printed at the end of the book?" The answer is that atlases contain illustrated prefectures from west to east since they have been published as books that open from left to right after the war. That is to say, if you make an atlas by folding a large map, the westernmost part is on the first page.

A simple map was interposed in each prefectural description. Although more information was added to the maps following the publisher's proofreading, the design still represents a simple drawing with lines and symbols. The initial maps are released from the author's website in scalable vector graphics format ("Base maps of prefectures in Japan" http://www.labo-geo.jp/nihei/paper/japan/). Not only the atlases published in Japan but also the latest maps provided by the internet, such as Google Maps and GSI maps (Geospatial Information Authority of Japan, 2013), are filled with information; nonetheless, even a map pared down to its essence will stir the reader's imagination. The author came to this conclusion during fieldwork in foreign countries looking at local maps that had simple and cogent renderings.

Acknowledgments

This work was supported by a grant from the Graduate School of Letters, Hokkaido University.

An outline of Japan

Location

Japan is located to the east of the Eurasian continent. The country stretches lengthwise north to south. It is surrounded by the Pacific Ocean, the Sea of Japan, East China Sea, and the Sea of Okhotsk, as shown in Illustration 1. At the north end of the territory is Etorofu (Iturup) Island (45°3'N, 147°50'E), while to the south is Okinotori Island (20°26'N, 136°5'E), to the east is Minamitori (Marcus) Island (24°17'N, 153°59'E), and to the west is Yonaguni Island (24°28'N, 123°0'E). Japan spreads 25 degrees in latitude (2,800 km) and 30 degrees in longitude (3,100 km at 24°N). Etorofu Island is included in the Northern Territories that Russia has effectively controlled since the end of World War II. The terrain extends 380,000 km^2 and consists of four main islands: Honshû, Hokkaidô, Kyûshû, and Shikoku. There are also many small islands. Japan's area is about 25 times smaller than the United States and China. However, compared to European countries, Japan is almost the same size as Germany and larger than the United Kingdom.

Nature

In terms of topography, mountains and forests occupy approximately 70 percent of the land (Illustration 2). All the mountains belong to young orogenic belt. The high mountains that exceed 3,000 m altitude are positioned in the central part of Honshû Island, including the highest, Mt. Fuji, with an altitude of 3,776 m. The Shinano River is the longest river; it flows for 367 km from the Echigo Plain into the Sea of Japan. The second longest river is the Tone

River, which flows through the Kantô Plain, while the third longest is the Ishikari River in the Ishikari Plain. Many rivers are short in length, and have steep riverbeds. In order to prevent floods, flow courses were straightened and riverbanks were artificially concreted. However, fishways and open-spaces for visitors were created in some rivers. Plains were created from the rivers' sedimentation, accumulated volcanic ash, and upheaved seabed, during the Holocene of the Quaternary. Alluvial plains, alluvial fans, and deltas are included in that category. Large plains such as Kantô, Ishikari, Tokachi, Echigo, Nôbi, and Sendai are located in the east and central parts of the country.

The climate varies from continental to tropical, although the majority of the land is a temperate climate in which people enjoy the benefit of four distinct seasons. In winter, the weather contrasts between the Sea of Japan side and the Pacific Ocean side. To be specific, snow falls predominantly in the Sea of Japan side, beside the north of Japan and mountainous areas. Indeed, more than 50 percent of the land is classified as "heavy snowfall zones," as per the Act of Special Measures for Heavy Snowfall Areas. The original vegetation is roughly divided into mixed forests of evergreen and deciduous broad-leaved trees in the south (temperate climate zone), and mixed forests of conifers and deciduous broad-leaved trees in the north (continental climate zone). The vegetation is closely connected with regional agriculture and cultures.

For a particular condition in geology, the whole territory is subject to natural disasters including earthquakes, tidal waves (tsunami), volcanic eruptions, typhoons, torrential downpours, and snow storms. Based on the author's observations, there are fewer high-rise buildings in central business districts in Japanese cities and towns as compared with the United States and Brazil. One of the reasons for less high-rises in Japan are the legal restrictions on buildings, such as the Building Standards Act that was enacted due to colossal earthquakes and fires. Considering those natural disasters and the history of wars, it seems such a calamitous condition may have led to the Japanese people's preference for being fond of new things. For instance, the rebuilding cycle for general houses is less than 30 years, which is about one third of that in the United Kingdom.

Culture

Japanese computer games, animation, and manga are popular with young people worldwide. The Japanese nature of enjoying miniatures and imaginary things may be linked to the products, as can be observed in traditional bonsai (potted dwarf trees). In the food culture, Japanese food such as sushi and green tea are also recognized internationally. Some Westerners who visited Japan during the Meiji period (from the late nineteenth to the early twentieth century) advised that the Japanese were so poor that they even ate seaweed. Nevertheless, the food, which is low in calories and subtle in flavor, came to be accepted in advanced countries.

Population and Traffic

The country's population has reached 128 million, although there is a noteworthy variation between the prefectures. The population rose during the two baby booms: one shortly after the war and one in the early 1970s. Consequentially, the population pyramid formed a peculiar shape. The current condition of an aging population and declining birthrate casts a shadow over the matters of successors at small industries and nursing for the aged. Foreign staff has increased not only in manufacturing plants, farms, and retail stores, but also in medical services, listed companies, and academic institutes.

With regard to transportation systems, the connecting cities for national highways and JR railroads (the Japan Railway Group: formerly the Japanese National Railways) were constructed along old roads *(kaidô)*. Expressways and high-speed railroads (Shinkansen) were constructed after the breakthroughs in civil engineering, and so, they run through mountains and valleys for which land prices were inexpensive. With regard to air transportation, since the country is long and narrow and consists of many islands, more airports have been constructed than one would expect for a population or area of this size.

Primary Sector of Industry

Depending on the regional resources available, the primary sector of industry has evolved based on the local environment, in particular its topography. The main forms of products are livestock based on gross product and horticultural crops per cultivated area. This is followed by forestry, paddy rice, and pastures by area alone. Paddy fields still provide a distinctive landscape in rural Japan, although they were consolidated and shaped rectangular to cope with mechanization. In other commercial crop production, there is a tendency for large-scale producing centers to move from markets to remote areas as the transportation systems develop. The former feudalistic landlord and tenant system was completely revised by an agricultural land reform after the war. Since then, agricultural land development is regulated by the Agricultural Land Act.

Forestry has declined and less working people enter the

mountains as compared to several decades ago. Subsequently, agriculture and forestry damage from wild animals such as wild boars and deer has increased. Fisheries have flourished because the country is surrounded by ocean currents, although more recently they have been affected by economic changes, available stock, international relations, and public awareness of the environment.

Secondary Sector of Industry

The manufacturing industry imports raw materials and exports products developed in Japan. The energy supply also depends much on overseas countries. The main industrial products in terms of gross production are automobiles, medicines, gasoline, machinery, and sheet steel. Since trade friction and personnel expenses have increased, Japanese factories have expanded overseas into the United States, China, and other countries in Southeast Asia, Europe, and Latin America. With regard to domestic production, following the rise of semiconductor production in neighboring countries, automobile factories have spread to the Kyûshû and Tôhoku regions that were formerly alluded to as a "silicon island" and the "silicon road," respectively.

Tertiary Sector of Industry

At present, this category encompasses approximately 70 percent of the working population. In particular, the growing sectors are information technology, research and development, medical and welfare services, tourism, and higher education for foreign students. With regard to the commercial landscape, the number of family-owned stores in shopping districts facing railroad stations decreased as motorization progressed. Even large department stores near the stations, the buildings for which were typically constructed during economic growth periods around 1970 (the high economic growth period) and around 1990 (the bubble economy), withdrew from business in local cities following the deregulation of the Large-Scale Retail Stores Location Law. Department stores once observed the regular holidays stipulated by the law.

In contrast, nationwide businesses increased, such as shopping centers with huge parking lots, chain restaurants in suburbs, and 24-hour convenience stores. This resembles the backdrop from which suburbs were created. However, reflecting on the author's study of field trips in Canada, the terms "locality" or "regionality" will apply in Japan, too, since people in Canada began to appreciate local goods, the close connections between vendors and visitors, health, and the natural environment (Tabayashi et al., 2016).

Regional Divisions

In Japan, more than 300 prefectures appeared with the abolition of the domain system in 1871 (Meiji 4). They were merged into 47 prefectures in 1890 (Illustration 1). The existing prefectural borders relatively coincide with the ancient provincial borders, in particular, the Ritsuryô code, which was a legal system in existence from the late seventh to the tenth century.

Prefecture groups have been commonly divided into eight regions: Hokkaidô, Tôhoku, Kantô, Chûbu, Kinki, Chûgoku, Shikoku, and Kyûshû. Hokkaidô was not included in the Ritsuryô code and forms a region by an isolated prefecture. In the Chûbu and Chûgoku regions, the prefectures located along the Sea of Japan side are also known as the Hokuriku and San-in regions respectively. Prefectures consist of the municipalities that have assemblies, i.e., city *(shi)*, town *(chô* or *machi)*, and village *(son* or *mura)*. In 2002, there were 3,218 municipalities.

6

However, due to the great merger of municipalities during the Heisei period, this number decreased to 1,727 in 2010. In the plain where the population is concentrated, it is complicated to distinguish municipality boundaries from landscapes.

The regional geography of Japan

1. Hokkaidô

Hokkaidô is located in the northernmost part of the country, facing the Pacific Ocean, the Sea of Okhotsk, and the Sea of Japan (Figure 1).

Nature

The highest peak is Asahidake (2,291 m) on Mt. Taisetsu (Daisetsu). It is a volcanic complex that is composed of part of the Chishima (Kuril) volcanic belt from a geographic point of view. It was designated as Daisetsuzan National Park in 1934. Tôya Caldera and Usu Volcano Geopark are included in the Nasu volcanic belt (Illustration 3). It was listed as a UNESCO's Global Geopark in 2009, the first time an area in the country received such a designation, along with Unzen Volcanic Area Geopark and Itoigawa Geopark.

The Ishikari Plain is the second-largest plain in the country. Peatland spreads through the lower reaches of the Ishikari River in the south of the plain. The plain was changed to an extensive paddy-field complex as a result of drainage works. For instance, Shinotsu Canal was constructed between the late 1950s and the early 1960s as a World Bank-supported project. The Tokachi Plain in the east was changed into the largest upland-field area in the country after farmers improved the volcanic ash soil.

Blakiston's Line is a zoological boundary positioned on the Tsugaru Strait. It divides the flora and fauna between the islands of Hokkaidô and Honshû. To the north of the

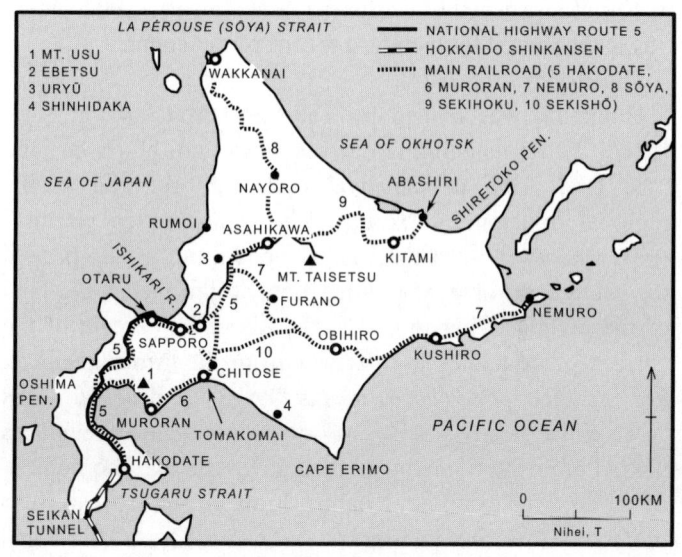

Figure 1 Hokkaidô

line, boreal subspecies are to be found, such as Ezo brown bears *(Ursus arctos yesoensis)*, Ezo sika deer *(Cervus nippon yesoensis)*, Eurasian red squirrels *(Sciurus vulgaris orientis)*. The main vegetation comprises mixed forests of conifers and deciduous broad-leaved trees. It retains an undergrowth of bamboo grasses and spring cicadas *(Terpnosia nigricosta)* that chirp unceasingly from late May. Shiretoko National Park in the east was listed in the UNESCO World Heritage Site in 2005 for its unique food chain between the land and the sea.

According to the Köppen climate classification system, an extensive area has a Dfb climate (humid continental-mild summer). The Sea of Japan side is covered with deep snow in winter, while the Pacific Ocean side receives relatively low snowfalls. A temperature of -41.0 °C observed at Kamikawa weather station in Asahikawa in 1902 (Meiji 35) is the lowest temperature record of the country.

History and Culture

Hokkaidô was named by Takeshirô Matsuura in 1869 (Meiji 2). Its meaning is derived from "north" *(hoku)* and "the land Ainu people live" *(kai)*. *Dô* referred to the regional division by "five provinces and seven circuits" *(goki shichidô)* under the Ritsuryô code. In the Edo period, the prefectural area was called Ezo, which means the land of the people living in the north. About 80 percent of the current place names are derived from the Ainu language. For instance, *poro (horo)* means "large," and *betsu* means "a river of steady course." Furthermore, there are places named after the hometowns of immigrants and the number of settlers, for example, Kitahiroshima city in Ishikari Sub-prefecture (the first immigrants, who came from Hiroshima Prefecture) and Nijûyonken in Sapporo city (the first settlers comprised 24 families). In the early Meiji period, American advisors worked for the Development Commission of Hokkaidô. The former Horonai Line connecting Otaru in Shiribeshi, Sapporo in Ishikari, and Horonai in Sorachi was the third railroad built in the country, in which American locomotives equipped with cowcatchers ran a coal transportation line.

Population and Traffic

Hokkaidô has a population of 5,506,000. The main cities are Sapporo (population: 1,914,000), Asahikawa (347,000), Hakodate (279,000), Kushiro (181,000), Tomakomai (173,000), Obihiro (168,000), Otaru (132,000), Kitami (126,000), and Ebetsu (124,000). About one third of the population resides in Sapporo. The area of Hokkaidô is divided into the Dô-ô region in the center of the prefecture, comprising the Ishikari, Shiribeshi, Sorachi, Iburi, and Hidaka subprefectures; the Dônan region in the Oshima Peninsula, comprising the Oshima and Hiyama subprefectures; the Dôhoku region in the north, comprising the Kamikawa, Rumoi, and Sôya subprefectures; and the Dôtô region in the east of Kitami Mountains and Hidaka mountain range, comprising the Okhotsk, Tokachi, Kushiro, and Nemuro subprefectures.

The area measures 83,450 km², and, including the Northern Territories, is almost the same as the total of the Kyûshû, Shikoku, and Chûgoku regions. The distances between the large cities are great. For instance, it is 330 km from Sapporo to Kushiro by land. The areas between the cities are sparsely populated. The main railroads are the Hakodate Main Line, the Muroran Main Line, the Nemuro Main Line, and the Sekishô Line. The view of Tokachi Plain from Karikachi Pass on the Nemuro Main Line was considered by the former Japan National Railways to be one of the three best views from a train window in Japan. Mori Station on the Hakodate Main Line is known for its train box lunches of squid rice *(ika-meshi)*.

Urban areas in the city of Sapporo are designed as grid streets. The base lines are Ôdôri Park for the north and south division, and the Sôsei River for the east and west division. A subway and expressways were opened just before the 1972 Winter Olympics. Residential areas increased on the peatlands in the east of the city during the economic boom from the late 1980s to the early 1990s. Moves to re-concentrate the population to the urban center were undertaken from the 2000s onward.

Primary Sector of Industry

The main agricultural commodities in terms of gross production are raw milk, vegetables, rice, potatoes, legumes, and industrial crops (mainly sugar beet). Dairy farming using the grasslands prospers primarily in the Dôtô and Dôhoku regions. Dairy pilot farms were established in the Konsen Plateau in the Dôtô region between the 1950s and the 1960s. The raw milk produced in the region is mainly for processing, and is shipped to the Tokyo metropolitan area by milk ships between the ports of Kushiro and Hitachi (now the Port of Ibaraki). In terms of vegetable produce, not only did trade in storable root vegetables such as radishes, onions, and carrots increase, but also in fresh vegetables such as asparagus and broccoli after the development of transportation systems, including the opening of the Seikan Tunnel in 1988. The paddy rice cultivation methods for a cold climate were devised in the 1890s (the late Meiji period). Shortly afterward, paddy fields spread into the interior Kamikawa Basin, Kitami Basin, and to the Sea of Okhotsk side, to which ice floes reach in winter. In recent years, tasty and branded rice varieties, such as *Nanatsuboshi* and *Yumepirika*, have been cultivated and distributed within and outside of the prefecture.

In the fishery industry, shoals of herring were caught up in the Sea of Japan side until the early twentieth century. The herring was processed into fertilizer *(nishin-kasu)* in the prefecture, and shipped to the east of the country for the cultivation of cotton and indigo. Although fishing in the North Pacific Ocean flourished after World War II, it was reduced in the 1990s in the wake of the establishment of Exclusive Economic Zones. At present, the main catches are cold-current fish (salmon, Alaska pollock, and

Okhotsk atka mackerel), squid, edible kelp *(konbu)*, and cultured scallops.

Other Industries

The main industrial products in terms of gross production are gasoline, diesel oil, and automobile parts. In terms of number of establishments, the main categories are seafood processing, salt-preserved products, and Western-style fresh cakes. Tomakomai in Iburi is known as a city with paper mills. The main oil refinery was founded by Idemitsu Kôsan Co. in the Tomakomai Western Industrial Zone in the 1970s. In addition, Toyota Motor Corporation and Isuzu Motors have factories producing automobile parts in the city. Muroran in Iburi is also known as an industrial city with steel and refinery industries. In Sapporo, the areas at the north exit of Sapporo Station to Hokkaidô University became known as Sapporo Valley in the 2000s due to the rise of computer-related venture businesses.

In terms of tourism, in addition to Sapporo, there are international tourist sites at Otaru and Niseko in Shiribeshi, Tomamu and Furano in Kamikawa, and Hakodate in Oshima. The ski resorts are famed for their powdery snow. At Niseko ski resort, condominiums have been developed with foreign fund investment from Australia and Hong Kong. At New Chitose Airport in Chitose city, which is a gateway to Hokkaidô Prefecture, an international terminal was built in 2010.

2. Aomori

Aomori is located in the north of the Tôhoku region, facing the Pacific Ocean, the Tsugaru Strait, and the Sea of Japan (Figure 2).

Nature

The summit of the terrain is Mt. Iwaki (1,625 m). It is a symmetrically shaped stratovolcano that formed the body of mountain worship in the Tsugaru region. Mt. Hakkôda (1,584 m) divides the Tsugaru region in the west and the Nanbu region in the east. It is a volcanic complex in the northern tip of the Ôu mountain range. The Tsuta and Sukayu hot springs are located around Lake Towada, which is a caldera lake that was designated as a national park in 1936. Mt. Osore in the Shimokita Peninsula is also a volcanic caldera. It is known for its posthumous spirits

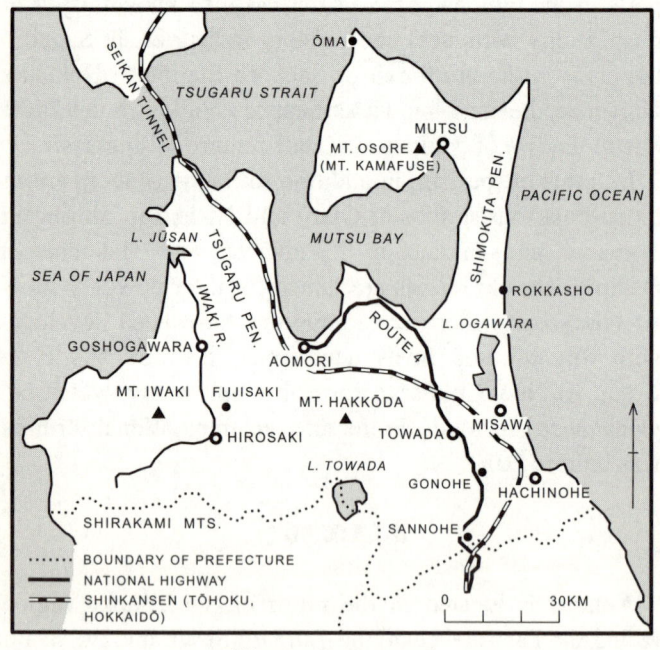

Figure 2 Aomori

being summoned by *itako* (spiritual mediums). The Sarugamori Sand Dunes on the peninsula are the largest sand dune system in the country, although tourists cannot step into the area as it has been designated a ballistic test area by the Ministry of Defense.

According to the Köppen climate classification system, most of the area to the south of the prefecture is categorized as a Cfa climate (temperate climate-warm temperatures). According to the domestic climate classification, the eastern area across Mt. Hakkôda has "a Pacific Ocean-northern Japan climate" (cool in summer, very cold in winter, obscure rainy season, and less snowfall in winter), and the west has a "Sea of Japan-northern Japan climate" (cool in summer, very cold in winter, obscure rainy season, and much snowfall in winter). The whole area has been designated as a heavy snowfall zone, and the mountainous areas have also been designated as a "special heavy snowfall zone." The areas along the Pacific Ocean coast get relatively low snowfalls in winter, while *yamase* (the chill wind in summer) blows from the Chishima Current occasionally.

A primeval forest of beech in the Shirakami Mountains stretches from the southwest of the prefecture to the northwest of Akita Prefecture. It is one of the first World Heritage Sites in the country, after being listed in 1993. According to a viewpoint of the Japanese "beech-forest zone culture" *(bunatai bunka)*, the deciduous broad-leaved trees symbolize the fundamental culture of eastern Japan. Sannai-Maruyama in the city of Aomori was a large settlement site in the mid-Jômon period (from 3,000 BC to 2,000 BC), which the beech-forest zone covers. Although beechwood had been considered as an unsuitable construction material because of its tendency to warp, it has been reevaluated as being suitable for Western-style furniture for its suppleness and fine grain patterns since the early twentieth century (the late Meiji period). The picturesque forests of *hiba (Thujopsis dolabrata)* spread through Shimokita and Tsugaru peninsulas. Since the boards of hiba have good water-resistance, they are used for bath tubs and chopping boards as well as building materials.

History and Culture

Under the ancient Ritsuryô code, the areas of the current Aomori, Iwate, Miyagi, and Fukushima prefectures were included in the Mutsu (Ôshû) Province in the Tôsandô region. In the early Meiji period, the Hirosaki (Tsugaru) domain and the north of the Morioka (Nanbu) domain became part of Aomori Prefecture. The Port of Aomori that had been a small fishing port facing Mutsu Bay became the prefectural capital, because a government military base was based there during the Battle of Hakodate, the last phase of the Boshin War in the late 1860s. In linguistic culture, there remain variations in the dialects between the Tsugaru and Nanbu regions.

In the Tsugaru region, the Nebuta and Tachi-Neputa festivals are held in early August, during the star-festival *(tanabata)* period in the lunar calendar. The festivals consist of dancers *(haneto)* and large floats imitating warriors and folding fans. Nebuta festival has spread outside the prefecture and has been adopted by local and campus festivals. The cherry festival in Hirosaki castle is held in early May, during the Golden Week holidays. The oldest cherry tree, *somei-yoshino (Prunus × yedoensis)*, grows at the castle site. In the Nanbu region, including the northeast part of Iwate Prefecture, there remain numeric place names varying from one to nine, such as the town of Ichinohe and the village of Kunohe. The numbers signified the address of pastures for grazing horses in the Morioka domain, which had an advanced horse grazing system. For instance, they imported Mongolian *(dattan)* horses for crossbreed. The traditional Nanbu horse breed went extinct after the introduction of Stallion Control Raw in the 1930s (the early Shôwa period).

Population and Traffic

The area has a population of 1,373,000. The main cities are Aomori (300,000), Hachinohe (238,000), Hirosaki (183,000), Towada (66,000), Mutsu (61,000), Goshogawara (58,000), and Misawa (41,000). The city of Aomori is the northernmost location of land traffic on Honshû Island. National Route 4, Aoimori Railway Line (the former Tôhoku Main Line), and the Tôhoku Express-way end in the city. The Tôhoku Main Line was connected to Ueno and Aomori stations in the early 1890s. In the high economic growth period (from the mid-1960s to the early 1970s), night trains were full of young people bound for Ueno Station in Tokyo on their way to employment as groups. Seikan Ferries carried trains between Aomori and Hakodate cities until the open of the Seikan Tunnel. Car ferries continue to operate on the routes between Aomori and Hakodate (Seikan), Ôma and Hakodate (Taikan), and Hachinohe and Tomakomai.

Primary Sector of Industry

The main agricultural commodities in terms of gross production are fruit (mainly apples), vegetables, rice, and swine. The cultivated apple area amounts to 21,000 ha, which accounts for 54 percent of the country. Apples are primarily cultivated in the middle reaches of the Iwaki

River on the Tsugaru Plain. Apple cultivation began in 1875 (Meiji 8), when three seedlings of a Western variety were sent to the prefectural government from the Industrial Bureau of the Home Ministry. The incipient apple production was developed based on the natural environment and the discovery of new varieties. One of the main varieties is *Fuji*, which was bred in the town of Fujisaki in the 1950s. Aomori apples are shipped not only to the whole country but also to countries such as China, Taiwan, Thailand, and the United States. Sanbongihara is a plateau extending into the city of Towada. The first reclamation of the uplands was conducted by the Morioka domain at the end of the nineteenth century. After World War II, paddy rice cultivation and swine raising were increased through large-scale reclamation projects. Garlic, yams, and burdock also increased in production after the implementation of the policy of reducing rice production in the 1970s.

Hachinohe is one of the leading fishing ports in the country, whose main catches are squid, mackerel, sardine, flounder, horse crab, and abalone. Fish markets, ice factories, and processing companies are situated around the port. The tuna caught in Tsugaru Strait and landed in the town of Ōma, the northernmost point of Honshū Island, are sold as prime tuna. In terms of inland fishing, the catches of freshwater Asian clam *(yamato shijimi)* are the largest in the country. The clam's main habitat is brackish lakes such as Jūsan and Ogawara.

Other Industries

The main industrial products in terms of gross production are machinery parts, compound feed, and alloy iron. The main machinery parts are optical components produced in the city of Hirosaki and connectors produced in the city of Aomori. General trading companies (sôgô shôsha) and agricultural cooperatives have constructed elevators at the Port of Hachinohe, and supply feed to the northern Tôhoku region. Alloy iron is produced mainly by Pacific Metals Co. at the Hachinohe Coastal Industrial Zone. Regarding the energy industry, the amount of wind power generation is the largest in the country since windmills harnessing westerly winds installed on the Shimokita Peninsula in the 2000s. The Rokkasho Nuclear Fuel Reprocessing Facility has been under construction on the peninsula since the 1990s.

3. Iwate

Iwate is located in the northeast of the Tôhoku region, and is the second-largest prefecture after Hokkaidô (Figure 3).

Nature

The highest peak is Mt. Iwate (2,038 m). It is a polygenetic volcano and the origin of the prefecture's name. Mt. Iwate is the highest peak in the Ôu mountain range, the longest chain of mountains in the country. Mt. Hayachine (1,917 m) is the highest peak in the Kitakami Mountains, which comprise an uplifted peneplain with gentle slopes. Limestone caves, including Akkadô and Ryûsendô, are located in the north of the mountains. Ironworks that used iron sand and iron pebbles *(mochi-tetsu)* were started in the south of the mountains in the eighth century. Nippon Steel & Sumitomo Metal Corporation, which mainly produces wire rods, is located in the city of Kamaishi. It originated as a government-managed steelworks that opened in 1880 (Meiji 13).

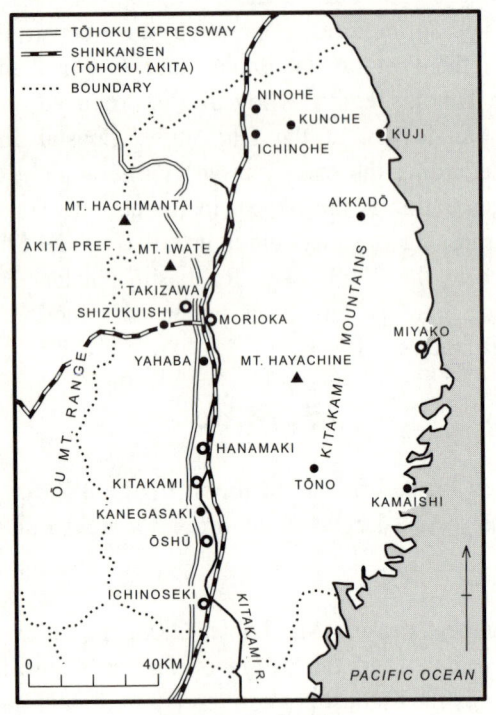

Figure 3   Iwate

The Kitakami River, the longest river in the Tôhoku region, runs north to south in the center of the prefecture. The gradient of the riverbed is gentle, so ship transportation prospered until the opening of the Tôhoku Main Line. The Sanriku coast extends about 600 km from the southeast of Aomori Prefecture to the Oshika Peninsula in Miyagi Prefecture. On the coast, a ria coastline extends from the city of Miyako (formerly the town of Tarô) to the north of Miyagi Prefecture. The coast suffered from the tidal wave damage caused by the 1896 Sanriku earthquake, the 1960 Chile earthquake, and the 2011 Tôhoku earth-quake.

The climate is categorized as a Pacific Ocean-northern Japan one, and the whole area has been designated as a heavy snowfall zone. In the Ôu mountain range, large-scale ski resorts have been developed, such as Appi Kôgen at the foot of Mt. Hachimantai and Shizukuishi in Shizukuishi town. In the Pacific coastal areas, low temperatures occasionally continue into summer due to the cold *yamase* winds that emanate from the Okhotsk air mass.

History and Culture

In the Edo period, the river port *(kashi)* of Kurosawajiri (now the city of Kitakami) on the middle reaches of the Kitakami River, was a distribution center that divided the Morioka domain in the north and the Sendai domain in the south. The Nanbu clan established Morioka (Kozukata) Castle and ruled the Morioka domain. Iron castings for daily necessities *(Nanbu tekki)* are the traditional handicrafts that were pursued in the Morioka domain and the Esashi region (now Ôshû city) in the Sendai domain.

Chûsonji Temple in the city of Ichinoseki in the south is known for its gold hall *(konjikidô)*. It is a Buddhist temple that has links with the Fujiwara clan that ruled Ôshû between the eleventh and the twelfth centuries. Geibikei and Genbikei gorges near the temple have been designated as national scenic sites. A prefectural image of "nostalgia for hometowns" was created in the Ihatov (Utopia) stories of Kenji Miyazawa, the Tôno stories by Kunio Yanagida, and the tanka poems by Takuboku Ishikawa. In food culture, *wanko*-soba (continuous helpings of buckwheat noodles) in Morioka and Hanamaki, Maesawa beef in Maesawa town (now Ôshû city), and cold buckwheat noodle *(reimen)* in Morioka have gained in popularity among tourists.

Population and Traffic

Iwate has a population of 1,330,000. The main municipalities are the cities of Morioka (298,000), Ôshû (125,000), Ichinoseki (119,000), Hanamaki (101,000), Kitakami (93,000), Miyako (59,000), and Takizawa (54,000). The suburbs of Morioka have spread north and south along the Kitakami basin, extending to the town of Yahaba and Takizawa. Once Morioka was an end destination in the north Tôhoku region. The number of hotels and inns, however, decreased after the open of the Tôhoku Shinkansen in the 1980s and Akita Shinkansen in the 1990s. Branches of large companies moved to Sendai, and the population of the prefectural capital declined.

Primary Sector of Industry

The main agricultural commodities in terms of gross production are rice, broilers, and vegetables. The monocultural paddy rice cultivation areas, in which paddy rice accounts for more than 90 percent of all the arable land, extend to the Kitakami basin. The temperature of the region rises in the summer, although the area occasionally suffers from crop failures caused by cool summers. Broiler production there is the largest of all the prefectures. Broilers are raised in the city of Ninohe, in which two major companies have initiated an integrated production system through production, processing, and selling. The production of hops, gentians, and cereals there is the largest of all the prefectures. The moderate and stable temperatures in summer are apposite for specific crops. For instance, hops are cultivated in the city of Tôno. Northern areas such as Iwate and Kunohe counties, and the Esashi region, including the cities of Ôshû and Kitakami. Gentian is cultivated at the foot of Mt. Hachimantai in the city of Hachimantai. Cereals are cultivated in the cities of Hanamaki and Ninohe as substitution crops for paddy rice. Not only traditional cereals, such as foxtail millet *(awa)*, proso millet *(kibi)*, and Japanese barnyard millet *(hie)*, but also new ones such as amaranth were introduced as part of the recent boom in natural food.

The sea off the Sanriku coast is one of the leading fishing grounds in the world because the cold Chishima Current (Oyashio or Kuril Current) meets the warm Japan Current (Kuroshio). The major catches of the fishing grounds are squid and migratory fish such as sardine, bonito, Pacific saury, mackerel, and cod. In the coastal farming fishery, brown seaweed *(wakame)*, abalone, and sea urchin are the main products.

Other Industries

The main industrial products in terms of gross production are cars and electronic circuits. The town of Kanegasaki in the Tankô region has a population of about 16,000 and is known for the production of automobiles and semiconductor devices. In an industrial park adjacent to the Kanegasaki interchange on the Tôhoku Expressway, a Toyota Motor Corporation assembly factory was founded in the 1990s, replacing the one in the city of Yokosuka that closed in 2000. In the same industrial park, a Fujitsu factory was built in the 1980s to produce semiconductor devices to meet consumer demand for word processors. Denso Corporation acquired the factory building in the 2010s and began to produce semiconductor devices for automobiles. As for tourism, Koiwai farm is a general dairy company that owns 3,000 ha of the homestead at the foot of Mt. Iwate. It was founded in the 1890s, began to sell butter and cheese in the early twentieth century, and became a pioneer of agritourism in the 1960s.

4. Miyagi

Miyagi is located in the center of the Tôhoku region, facing the Pacific Ocean (Figure 4).

Nature

The crest of the terrain is the Byôbudake (1,825 m) peak on Mt. Zaô. The mountain is a volcano included in the Nasu volcanic belt. At the foot of the mountain, the Tôgatta, Aone, and Kamasaki hot springs are to be found. The Senpoku Plain in the north of the Sendai Plain is an alluvial plain created by the Naruse and Eai rivers, and it forms an extensive rice-producing center. The Sennan Plain in the south of the Sendai Plain is also an alluvial plain created by the Abukuma and Natori rivers. Paddy rice and horticultural crops are mainly cultivated on the plain. The climate ranges from a Pacific Ocean-northern Japan one to a "Pacific Ocean-central Japan climate" (warm in summer, cold in winter, much rainfall in the rainy season and autumn, and less snowfall in winter).

The Kitakami River formerly flowed into Sendai Bay. Since floods repeatedly doused the lower reaches in the city of Ishinomaki, the river mouth was moved to Oppa Bay, a ria coastline along the Pacific Ocean, through the watercourse constructions conducted from the 1910s to the 1930s. The Teizan Canal is one of the longest canals in Japan. It continues about 60 km from the mouth of the old Kitakami River to the mouth of the Abukuma River via Sendai Bay.

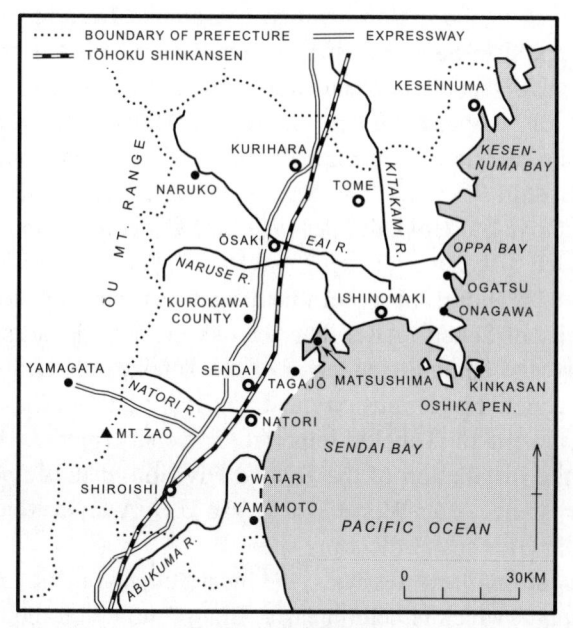

Figure 4 Miyagi

The Matsushima Islands look like they are floating in Sendai Bay. The islands are regarded as one of the three most scenic sites in the country. Kinkasan Island at the head of the Oshika Peninsula is counted as one of the major three sacred grounds in the Ôshû region besides Mt. Osore and the Dewa Three Mountains. Offshore of Sendai Bay, where the Pacific Plate collides with the North American Plate, large earthquakes have occurred, such as the 1978 Miyagiken-oki, the 1998 Miyagiken-nanbu, the 2003 Sanriku-minami, and the 2011 Tôhoku earthquake.

History and Culture

The prefectural name is derived from Miyagi county, in which Taga Castle was designated as the capital of Mutsu

25

Province in the eighth century. Masamune Date relocated the capital to Sendai Castle, which was constructed on the Aoba Hills in the seventeenth century. Its castle town is built on the terraces of the Hirose River. The Sendai domain assisted the former Tokugawa Shogunate army in the Boshin War in 1868. After a defeat, many of the Date clan moved to Hokkaidô, engaged in land reclamation, and founded Tôbetsu in Ishikari and Date in Iburi. In the Meiji period, branches of government agencies were opened in the city of Sendai. After that, the city grew as the administrative and commercial center of the Tôhoku region. It was also denoted a campus city and a military city with the establishment of Tôhoku Imperial University in the 1900s and the installation of the Second Division of the Imperial Army there. After World War II, the U.S. Army settled the Sendai Garrison at the army site.

Regarding local festivals, the most famous one is Sendai *tanabata*, which is held in early August (July 7 on the lunar calendar). During the festival, large streamers are slung from a tall shopping arcade in Aoba Ward in Sendai. The ornaments were flourished as attractions for clientele in the mid-twentieth century. In terms of food culture, Sendai is known for its grilled beef tongue and bamboo leaf-shaped fish paste *(sasa-kamaboko)*. The origin of the beef tongue specialty was the leftovers of the beef sold to the U.S. Army during the occupation. The fish paste grew in popularity as a souvenir of Sendai Station on the Tôhoku Main Line.

Population and Traffic

Miyagi has a population of 2,348,000. The main cities are Sendai (1,046,000: 45 percent of the population), Ishinomaki (161,000), Ôsaki (135,000), Tome (84,000),

Kurihara (75,000), Kesennuma (73,000), and Natori (73,000). Sendai was designated an ordinance city in 1989 after the population exceeded 0.9 million with the municipal merger of the towns of Miyagi and Akiu. The city area then extended to the boundary with the city of Yamagata. Mountainous areas that included the Sakunami and Akiu hot springs were also incorporated into the city. Sendai Airport, astride Natori and Iwanuma cities, is one of the government-run airports. It was founded as Natori Airport, having been built by the former army in 1940. It was returned by the U.S. Army to Japan in 1956, and regular flights to Haneda Airport started the following year. Because it is a mere five meters above sea level, the airport was inundated by the tidal wave that followed the earthquake in 2011.

Primary Sector of Industry

The main agricultural commodities in terms of gross production are rice, vegetables, and beef cattle. Previously, large quantities of the rice produced in the Ôsaki district in the north of the Sendai Plain were shipped to Edo, so it was regarded as standard rice in the Edo period (Illustration 4). Furukawa Agricultural Experiment Station in Ôsaki city has cultivated famous rice varieties, such as *Sasanishiki* and *Hitomebore*. In the towns of Watari and Yamamoto in the south of the Sendai Plain, extensive cropland was immersed in seawater as a result of the earthquake in 2011. To recover strawberry cultivation in the plain, information and communications technology was applied to greenhouse horticulture.

Ishinomaki fishing port at the mouth of the old Kitakami River records the second-largest catches in the Tôhoku region after Hachinohe fishing port. Besides the aforementioned migratory fish caught in the sea off the Sanriku coast, Kinka mackerel and Kinka bonito are caught in the seas around Kinkasan Island. In Sendai Bay, besides the aquafarming of oysters and seed oysters, recreational fishing for red sea bream and flounder is popular.

Other Industries

The main industrial products in terms of gross production are gasoline, cars, and electronic circuits. A JX Nippon Oil & Energy Co. oil refinery has been established in the Port of Sendai. In Kurokawa county, cars and electronic circuits are produced respectively by Toyota Motor Corporation and Tokyo Electron at an industrial park adjacent to the Ôhira interchange on the Tôhoku Expressway. As for traditional crafts, *kokeshi* dolls in Naruko town (now Ôsaki city) and Ogatsu inkstands in Ogatsu town (now Ishinomaki city) are to be found.

The city of Sendai is the center of commerce in the Tôhoku region. Its sales in retail and wholesale goods amount to 7.2 trillion yen according to 2012 Economic Census data. This is about seven times larger than the city of Kôriyama, the second-largest commercial center in the Tôhoku region. Banks and insurance companies are concentrated at Aoba Street in front of the west exit of Sendai Station. Ichiban-chô adjacent to the business street is a shopping area with brand-name shops. However, Sendai city is at the center of branch offices. The percentage of major companies headquartered outside the city stands at 33 percent, the highest proportion of any city whose population exceeds 300,000.

5. Akita

Akita is located in the northwest of the Tôhoku region, facing the Sea of Japan (Figure 5).

Nature

The highest peak in the region is Mt. Akita Komagatake (1,637 m), in the Ôu mountain range, although the apex of the terrain reaches 1,775 m on the slopes of Mt. Chôkai at the boundary with Yamagata Prefecture. Akita Komagatake is a volcano, whose activity is continuously monitored by the Japan Meteorological Agency. There are more than 40 mountains in the country that have the Komagatake (horse mountain) name, and the highest is Kai Komagatake (2,967 m) in Akaishi mountain range. Akita Komgatake means lingering snow *(yuki-gata)* that looks like a horse lying down. The Nyûtô hot springs at the north foot of the mountain are a series of secluded hot springs. Lake Tazawa at the west foot of Mt. Akita Komagatake is the deepest lake, at a depth of 423 m. An endemic species of the caldera lake is *kuni-masu* (black kokanee: *Oncorhynchus kawamurae*), which was believed since the 1940s to have become extinct. However, it was rediscovered in Lake Sai in Yamanashi Prefecture in 2010, because the eggs were sent to some prefectures for artificial hatching during the 1930s.

The Omono River courses from the southernmost part of the prefecture, running through the Yokote Basin, and flowing into the Sea of Japan from the Akita Plain. The river's name is derived from "tribute rice" *(omono)*, since rice was shipped on the river. River ports flourished along the river prior to the opening of the Ôu Main Line. The spring water of Rokugô alluvial fan in Misato town was

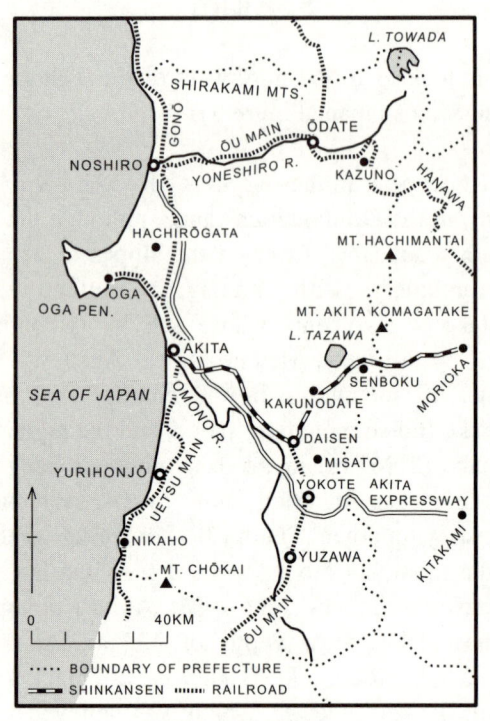

Figure 5 Akita

selected as one of the One Hundred Exquisite Water by the Environment Agency (now the Ministry of the Environment) in 1985. The Oga Peninsula is a land-linked island formed by the sediment left by the Omono and Yoneshiro rivers. Volcanic landforms are to be found on the west section of the peninsula, such as Ichinomegata Lake (a maar) and Toga Bay (a crater bay).

The climate is categorized as a Sea of Japan-northern Japan one. The whole area as a designated as a heavy snowfall zone. The Tamagawa hot spring at the west foot of Mt. Hachimantai, which is known as a radon hot-water spring, was hit by an avalanche in the 2010s. With heavy snowfalls in winter and much rainfall in the rainy season (from mid-June to mid-July), the average number of daylight hours in Akita is the shortest of all the prefectural capitals.

History and Culture

Most of the prefectural area corresponds to the north of Dewa Province during the era of the ancient Ritsuryô code, except for the northeastern part that pertains to Mutsu Province. The Satake clan was moved to Dewa from Hitach (now Ibaraki Prefecture) in the early seventeenth century. It built the Kubota domain and the castle town in Kubota (now the city of Akita). In the beginning of the Meiji period, the domain's name was changed to Akita, referring to an old county that includes Kubota. Subsequently, Akita Prefecture was established. A samurai residence site in the former town of Kakunodate (now Senboku city) was designated as a Preservation District for Groups of Traditional Buildings.

The name of *komachi* has been used as a symbol of the prefecture. For instance, it has been used as a nickname for the Akita Shinkansen *Komachi* and for a rice variety *Akitakomachi*. It is based on a legend of Ono no Komachi, who was a beautiful poet born in Dewa Province in the ninth century. *Matagi* was the traditional hunting group that hunted game in winter, such as hibernating Asian black bears *(Ursus thibetanus)*. The Akita dog, which has been designated as a national monument, was bred from the hunting dogs trained by the hunters.

The Akita Kantô festival is held in mid-August (the *bon* in the lunar calendar). During the festival, people pray for a good harvest of paddy rice by raising the linked lanterns that emulate ears of rice. Folklore demons *(namahage)* in the Oga region and snow huts *(kamakura)* in the Yokote Basin were the new-year events of the lunar calendar (the first full moon festivals). There are various products that form part of the food culture, such as Inaniwa udon (Japanese-style noodles) in the city of Yuzawa, *kiritanpo* (rice bars made of non-glutinous rice), Hinai-*jidori* (a breed of chicken from the basin of the Yoneshiro River), *shottsuru-nabe* (a casserole dish made with fish sauce), and Ôdate *mage-wappa* (oval wooden lunch boxes made from Akita cedar).

Population and Traffic

Akita Prefecture has a population of 1,086,000. The main cities are Akita (324,000), Yokote (98,000), Daisen (88,000), Yurihonjô (85,000), Ôdate (79,000), Noshiro (59,000), and Yuzawa (51,000). The Akita Expressway, which begins at Kitakami and the Akita Shinkansen, which runs from Morioka were opened in the 1990s. Both of them cross the Yokote Basin and run to the Akita Plain. The former Akita Airport was opened on a coastal dune at the mouth of the Omono in 1961. It was moved to an inland hill in Akita city between the Omono and Iwami rivers in 1981 so it could accommodate jetliners. The Port of Akita was initiated as the Port of Tsuchizaki by the Kubota domain. After the port was designated as a major port in 1951, the Akita Coastal Industrial Zone was re-claimed, and oil, metal, chemicals, paper, and wood-working plants were established.

Primary Sector of Industry

The main agricultural commodity in terms of gross pro-duction is rice. Its production is the third largest of all the prefectures after Hokkaidô and Niigata. The leading paddy rice-producing regions are the Yokote Basin, and the Akita and Noshiro plains. The main seed variety of non-glutinous rice was changed from *Kiyonishiki* to *Akitakomachi* in the early 1990s; both of them were bred in the prefecture. Hachirôgata is located at the base of the Oga Peninsula. It used to be the second-largest lake in the country, and freshwater clams were caught in the brackish water. To enhance food production after the war, a large-scale reclamation project started in the 1950s, and Hachirôgata was drained and became agricultural land, where the new settlers began to produce paddy rice.

The fishing ports along the Sea of Japan are small compared with the ones along the Pacific Ocean in the Tôhoku region. *Hatahata* (Japanese sandfish) is designated as the fish of the prefecture. It is also called thunder fish since it approaches the coast from the deep sea during the thunder season from November to December. Although the catches of *hatahata* were plentiful until the 1970s, when they were even processed as fish sauce *(shottsuru)*, the quantities plummeted in the 1980s. The *hatahata* fishery had strict controls imposed on it in the 1990s, and the catches revived in the 2000s.

Other Industries

The main industrial products in terms of gross production are electronic components, medicines, and medical equipment. In terms of number of establishments, the main category is Japanese-style noodles. With regard to electronic component production, TDK Corporation's factories are located in Yurihonjô and at Kisakata district in Nikaho. The former Yuri county was the hometown of the company's founder. Medicines and medical equipment are produced in Yokote and Akita cities, which are traffic hubs and have substantial populations.

The mining industry was initiated by the Kubota domain. Formerly, there were large mines in the mountainous areas, for instance, the Furôkura Mine (copper) in Kazuno, the Innai Silver Mine in the town of Innai (now the city of Yuzawa), and the Hanaoka Mine (lead and zinc) in Ôdate. Akita University, a national university corporation in the city of Akita, had a department of mining until the 1990s. Crude oil is still extracted in the flat areas of the Sarukawa oilfields in Oga and the Yabase oilfields in Akita.

6. Yamagata

Yamagata is located in the southwest of the Tôhoku region, and faces the Sea of Japan (Figure 6).

Nature

The highest peak is Mt. Chôkai (2,236 m) near the boundary with Akita Prefecture. It is a stratovolcano that comprises a part of the Chôkai volcanic belt. Mt. Zaô, on the southeast of the urban areas in the city of Yamagata, forms a boundary with Miyagi Prefecture. It is famous for the caldera lake of Okama and its snow-coated trees *(juhyô)*. A local tourism industry was developed at the foot of the mountain, where there are hot spring resorts, scenic routes, and ski grounds. The three mountains (Mt. Gassan, Mt. Yudono, and Mt. Haguro) of Dewa, between the Shônai and the Murayama regions, are regarded as sacred places of mountain worship by the monks of *Shugendô* (an old syncretic religion).

The Mogami River flows from Mt. Azuma at the boundary of Fukushima Prefecture. It runs through the

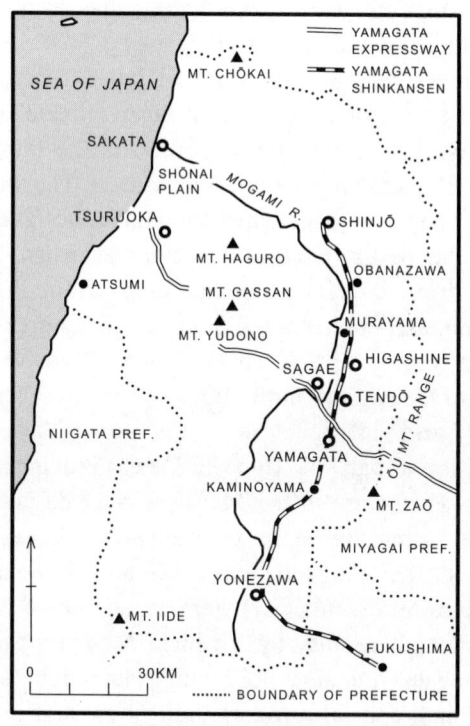

Figure 6 Yamagata

Yonezawa, the Yamagata, and the Shinjô basins, and flows into the Sea of Japan from the Shônai Plain. The area is divided into four regions by the three basins and one plain, namely, the Okitama region in the south, the Murayama region around the Yamagata basin, the Mogami region around the Shinjô basin, and the Shônai region along the Sea of Japan. The seaside region has a cultural contrast to the basins. The Mogami River forms the rapids of the Tôhoku region. Bashô Matsuo, a tanka poet in the Edo period, noted the following: "*Samidare wo atsumete hayashi Mogami gawa*" (Gathering the rain of early summer, the Mogami River swiftly runs).

The climate ranges from a Sea of Japan-northern Japan climate to a "Sea of Japan-central Japan climate" (warm in summer, cold in winter, much rainfall in the rainy season and autumn, and much snowfall in winter). The whole area has been designated as a heavy snowfall zone. The temperature of the basins rises in the summer when the wind descends from the Ôu mountain range from the Pacific Ocean side, and creates a foehn effect. The temperature in Yamagata rose to 40.8 °C in 1933, which was the highest recorded in the country until 2007.

History and Culture

Uzen and a part of Ugo in Dewa Province became Yamagata Prefecture in the Meiji period. The latter corresponds to a northwestern coastal part. Three insecure currents in the Mogami River (Goten, Minokase, and Hayabuse in Murayama city) were ground down in the end of the sixteenth century by Yoshiaki Mogami, the lord of the Yamagata domain. Following that, rice, soybeans, tobacco, and special products, such as safflowers and ramies *(aoso)*, were sold and transported by ship. Sakata at the mouth of the Mogami was once a port for westbound cargo ships *(kitamae-bune)*. Since transportation agents and kimono merchants prospered, Sakata was described as "Sakai in the East."

As part of Yamagata food culture, *imoni* parties are held at the riverside in autumn. *Imoni* means a pot dish cooked with taro, shôyu (or miso), beef (or pork), and vegetables. Yamagata city's *imoni* festival is so large in scale that power shovels are applied for cooking. Atsumi-turnip cultivation in slash-and-burn fields continues in the town of

Atsumi (now the city of Tsuruoka) at the boundary with Niigata Prefecture. Traditional crafts in the prefecture include Japanese lime (linden) weaving *(shina-ori)* in Tsuruoka. It is one of three ancient weaving types in the country, along with Japanese arrowroot weaving *(kuzu-fu)* on the Ôi River and wisteria weaving *(fuji-nuno)* in the Tango region. Of the traditional products available, Japanese chess pieces *(shôgi)* are produced in the city of Tendô and goldfish cultivation takes place in the Shônai region. Among other festivals, the Hanagasa festival, held in mid-August in Yamagata city, has gained in popularity since the 1960s.

Population and Traffic

The population of Yamagata Prefecture is 1,169,000. The main cities are Yamagata (254,000), Tsuruoka (137,000), Sakata (111,000), Yonezawa (89,000), Tendô (62,000), Higashine (46,000), and Sagae (42,000). Following the opening of the Yamagata Expressway in the 1980s, the urban centers of Yamagata and Sendai cities were connected by car within one hour. The city of Yamagata was connected to Tokyo within two-and-a-half hours after the Yamagata Shinkansen opened in the 1990s. There are two airports in the prefecture: Yamagata Airport in the Yamagata Basin and Shônai Airport in the Shônai Plain. The customers of Yamagata Airport have decreased because of the competition with the Shinkansen. Shônai Airport is preferred by employees of the companies that operate in the regional industrial park. Seiko Epson Corporation's company planes connect Shônai and Matsumoto airports.

Primary Sector of Industry

The main agricultural commodities in terms of gross

production are fruit (mainly cherries and apples), rice, and vegetables. The cultivated area for cherries is the largest of all the prefectures, accounting for 3,200 ha, about 65 percent of the country. Cherries are largely cultivated in the cities of Higashine, Tendô, and Sagae in the Yamagata Basin. The origin of cherry cultivation goes back to the early Meiji period when seedlings of the western cherry *(seiyô-mizakura)* were distributed to prefectural offices in 1875, and the ones cultivated in Yamagata showed a good result. The current major variety of cherry grown is *Satônishiki*, which was developed by Mr. Sato in the city of Higashine in the 1910s (the Taishô period). The management of cherry farming has recently diversified into early-ripening cultivation in greenhouses, pick-your-own orchards, and direct-selling to customers by home delivery service.

The Shônai Plain is the center of rice production. The main rice varieties are *Haenuki* and *Tsuyahime*, both of which were bred in the prefecture. The former is consumed as rice balls sold by convenience stores since that particular rice variety maintains a good flavor even after being chilled. Among other agricultural specialties, there are La France pears (a Western variety) in the Yamagata and Yonezawa basins, Yonezawa beef, Obanazawa watermelons, and *dadacha-mame* (a soybean variety developed for harvesting before maturation) in the Shônai Plain.

Other Industries

The main industrial products in terms of gross production are personal computers, medicines, and electronic circuits. Personal computers, integrated circuits, digital cameras, and loudspeakers are produced in the Yonezawa and Yamagata basins. The city of Yonezawa formerly had a prosperous textile industry with the Imperial Artificial Silk Company (now Teijin), which was established in the 1910s. The skills to maintain textile machinery and the entrepreneurial networks in the city have been linked to the establishment of the electronic equipment factories there. In the Shônai region, the Port of Sakata was designated as a major port for the unloading of cargo from foreign ships. The Seiko Epson Corporation factory was established in Sakata in the late 1980s, and opened a semiconductor section in the 1990s. The office of the local media and finance industries are located in the city of Tsuruoka, which used to be a castle town of the Shônai domain.

7. Fukushima

Fukushima is located in the south of the Tôhoku region. It is the third-largest prefecture in the country after Hokkaidô and Iwate (Figure 7).

Nature

Mt. Hiuchigatake (2,356 m) at the boundary with Niigata and Gunma prefectures is the highest peak in the Tôhoku region. It is a volcano that is a piece of the Chôkai volcanic belt, and was designated as Oze National Park along with the Ozegahara Marsh. The Tadami River comes from Oze Lake, becomes the Aga River meeting with the Nippashi River in the Aizu Basin, and flows into the Sea of Japan from the Echigo Plain (the river is called the Agano River in Niigata Prefecture). The Aizu Basin is a graben basin that extends north to south and is surrounded by the Ôu and Echigo mountain ranges and the Iide Mountains. Lake Inawashiro is located to the east of the basin. It is the fourth largest lake in the country, dividing the Aizu and

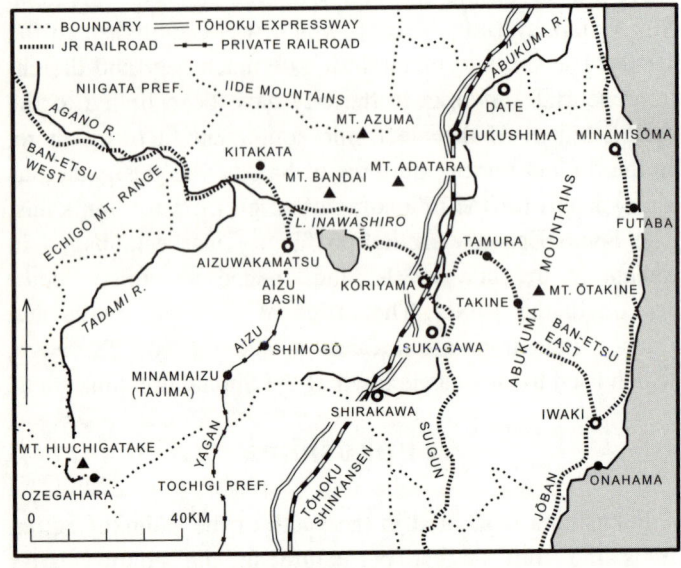

Figure 7 Fukushima

Nakadôri regions.

The Abukuma River begins at Mt. Nasudake on the boundary with Tochigi Prefecture, runs northward through the Kôriyama and the Fukushima basins, and flows into the Pacific Ocean from the Sendai Plain. The Fukushima Basin in the north is surrounded by the Abukuma Mountains and the Ôu mountain range. On the west slope of the basin, there are hot springs, including Iizaka, Takayu, and Tsuchiyu. Mt. Shinobu (275 m), in the Fukushima Basin, is a symbol of Buddhist faith, and is also the northernmost limit of *yuzu (Citrus ichangensis × C. reticulata)* cultivation. The gentle slopes of the Abukuma Mountains extend to the east. The summit of the mountains is Mt. Ôtakine (1,200 m), which divides the river systems between the

Abukuma River and the other short rivers that directly run into the Pacific Ocean. It also separates the Hamadôri region to the east and the Nakadôri region to the west. It is an uplifted landform that includes the cretaceous stratums from which *Futabasaurus* was excavated in the city of Iwaki. Abukuma Cave was discovered in a limestone mine in the town of Takine (now the city of Tamura).

The climate ranges from a Pacific Ocean-central Japan one in the Hamadôri and the Nakadôri regions to a Sea of Japan-central Japan one in the Aizu region. The annual precipitation levels in Fukushima city amount to 1,170 mm (the average from 1981 to 2010). It is seventh smallest value among the prefectural capitals after Nagano, Takamatsu, Okayama, Sapporo, Kôfu, and Yamagata. Ski resorts have been developed around Mt. Bandai and the south of the Aizu region, while the city of Iwaki in the Hamadôri region is the northernmost limit of the natural Japanese cypress forest.

History and Culture

The prefectural name is derived from Fukushima castle, and the castle's name denotes Mt. Shinobu in the Fukushima Basin. Silk farming, or sericulture, flourished until the mid-twentieth century in the basin. The town of Yanagawa (now the city of Date) was given the title of the sericultural capital *(santo)* of Japan owing to the developed economy based on the production of silkworm-egg cards and silkworm cocoons. Even a kabuki theater was opened in the town center. After flood damage, the building is pre-served in Fukushima city.

In the Aizu region, historical sites such as Tsuruga Castle (Wakamatsu Castle) in Aizuwakamatsu city and the Ôuchi-*juku* (a post town on the old Aizu West Road) in

Shimogô town are popular among tourists. The production of Aizu lacquer ware was initiated when the Gamô clan of the Aizu domain invited woodcarving experts *(kiji-shi)* and lacquer experts *(nuri-shi)* from Ômi Province in the late sixteenth century. In the Aizu Mountains until the early twentieth century, there were communities of *kiji-shi* who made non-lacquered wooden material from Japanese *tochi* (horse chestnuts), maples, and beeches. In terms of food culture, the city of Kitakata at the north of the basin is one of the pioneers of the local râmen boom.

Population and Traffic

The population of Fukushima Prefecture is 2,029,000. The main cities are Iwaki (342,000), Kôriyama (339,000), Fukushima (293,000), Aizuwakamatsu (126,000), Sukagawa (79,000), Minamisôma (71,000), Date (66,000), and Shirakawa (65,000). In the Nakadôri region, the Tôhoku Expressway and the Tôhoku Shinkansen were opened in the 1970s and 1980s respectively. Fukushima Airport was opened at the south of the Kôriyama Basin in the 1990s. Kôriyama is a traffic hub that leads to the city of Niigata (formerly Niitsu) by the Ban-etsu West Line, to the city of Iwaki by the Ban-etsu East Line, and to Mito by the Suigun Line. The Aizu Railway runs in parallel with the Aizu West Road. It leads to Asakusa in Tokyo via the Yagan and Tôbu railways.

Primary Sector of Industry

The main agricultural commodities in terms of gross production are rice, vegetables (mainly cucumber), and fruit. The main rice-producing center is the Kôriyama Basin. Although common grasslands occupied a large area in the basin, a change was made to paddy fields after the installation of the trans-divide Asaka Canal in 1883 (Meiji

16), which was undertook as part of the job-creating policy of ex-samurai. The canal supplied irrigation water on 9,000 ha of land. Tasty Aizu rice, whose seed variety is *Koshihikari*, is cultivated in the Aizu Basin because of the abundant water supplied from surrounding mountains and the significant differences in the diurnal temperature. Regarding horticulture, summer-autumn harvested cucumbers are chiefly produced in Sukagawa. In the Fukushima Basin, peaches, apples, and Japanese pears are produced mainly on alluvial fans. Kayaba-*nashi* is the brand name of Japanese pears that have been cultivated at Sasakino district in the basin since the Meiji period.

Other Industries

The main industrial products in terms of gross production are machinery parts, cigarettes, and medicines. With regard to the machinery parts, factories were invited to set up on an industrial park in the city of Aizuwakamatsu, such as the semiconductor factories of Fujitsu and Texas Instruments, and an endoscope factory of Olympus Corporation. In cigarette production, tobacco has been cultivated in the Abukuma Mountains, and processed at Japan Tobacco's factories in the cities of Sukagawa and Kôriyama (currently, most of cigarettes are made with imported tobacco leaves). The water and electric power supply produced by the Asaka Canal had significant implications for silk and spinning industries evolved in Kôriyama during the Meiji and the early Shôwa periods. The city was designated as a "new industry city" in 1962, and machinery factories were moved from the Keihin Industrial Zone. Inland-type industries, such as electrical devices, glasses, resins, and rechargeable batteries were also developed after the city was designated as a "technopolis" in 1986.

In the Hamadôri region, Iwaki previously flourished as a result of Jôban Coalfield and coal-related industries. The coal field spread to the north of Ibaraki. The mining city turned into an industrial city in the 1970s after incorporating heavy and chemical industries along the coast of Onahama. In Futaba county, nuclear power plants were constructed by Tokyo Electric Power Company in the 1960s and the 1970s. The tidal waves caused by the 2011 Tôhoku earthquake wrecked these plants.

8. Ibaraki

Ibaraki is located in the northeast of the Kantô region, and faces the Pacific Ocean (Figure 8).

Nature

The highest peak is Mt. Yamizo (1,022 m) on the boundary with Fukushima Prefecture. The Kuji River runs from the north slope of the mountain. The limpid stream is known for the fishing of sweetfish *(ayu)*. The Fukuroda Falls in Daigo town, on a tributary of the Kuji, forms icefalls in winter. It is counted as one of the famed three falls in the country, along with Kegon Falls and Nachi Falls. The Yamizo Mountains run from the south of Fukushima Prefecture, marking a boundary between Ibaraki and Tochigi prefectures, and lead to Mt. Tsukuba. In the mountains, granite *(mikage-ishi)* for buildings and tombstones was mined plentifully at the town of Makabe (now the city of Sakuragawa) and at Inada district in the city of Kasama.

Mt. Tsukuba is referred to in the phrase, "Mt. Fuji in the west and Mt. Tsukuba in the east," because the two peaks

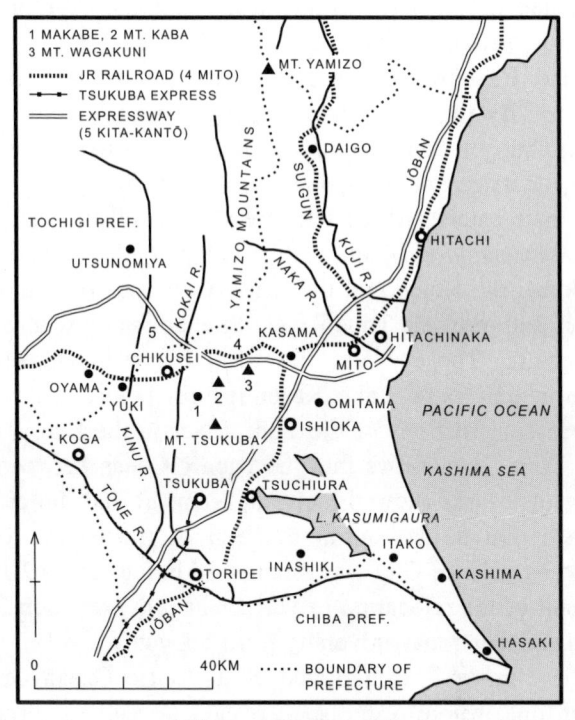

Figure 8　Ibaraki

of Mt. Tsukuba protrude from the Kantô Plain despite the elevation being a mere 877 m. It has been a mountain of faith and tourism since ancient times. Scenic roads including the Tsukuba Skylines have been constructed since the 1960s, and air sports such as hang gliding and paragliding have gained in popularity in the vicinity of the mountain. The Jôsô Plateau and Lake Kasumigaura are situated in the east of Mt. Tsukuba. The plateau forming the east part of the Kantô Plain is covered with a layer of Kantô loam that is accumulated volcanic ash from volcanos to the west of the Kantô region. Agricultural fields and flatland forests extend along the plateau.

Lake Kasumigaura is the second-largest lake in the country. By the sluice gates constructed in the 1960s, the water changes from brackish to fresh. The water is used not only for irrigation and industrial use but also as tap water. The main catches of the lake are smelt, icefish, freshwater prawns *(tenaga-ebi)*, and cultured carp. To the west of Mt. Tsukuba, the Kokai and the Kinu rivers run from north to south, and meet the Tone River at the boundary with Chiba Prefecture. Those rivers flowed into the inland sea of Katorinoumi (now Lake Kasumigaura) before the water-course constructions of the Tone River in the Edo period. The Tone River flows into the Pacific Ocean between the town of Hasaki (now the city of Kamisu) and the city of Chôshi. On a plateau on the east of the Kokai River, Tsukuba Science City was established in the early 1970s as a result of the relocation of various national research institutes and a national university from Tokyo.

The climate is categorized as a Pacific Ocean-central Japan one, where a dry spell occurs in winter. Tornados occur sporadically in the west in summer. Regarding the vegetation, about the area is the northernmost limit of natural evergreen broad-leaved trees such as *sakaki (Cleyera japonica)* and *hiiragi (Osmanthus heterophyllus)*, and the southernmost limit of rugosa rose *(hama-nasu)* along the Pacific Ocean coast. Natural beech trees have been left intact near atop Tsukuba, Kaba, and Wagakuni mountains.

History and Culture

Under the Ritsuryô code, Hitachi Province and a part of Shimôsa Province became part of Ibaraki Prefecture during

46

the Meiji period. The name is derived from a county that included Ishioka, and which was the capital *(koku-fu)* of Hitachi Province from the late seventh to the eleventh century. The Satake clan that had ruled Hitachi Province since the end of Heian period (the late twelfth century) was sent to the north of Dewa Province after the Battle of Sekigahara. Then, one of the three Tokugawa clans, whose place of origin was Mikawa Province (now Aichi Prefecture), laid claim to the Mito domain in the early seventeenth century. Kairakuen in the city of Mito, known for the famous blossoms of 3,000 Japanese apricot (ume) trees, used to be the domain's garden. The Mito School, which is based on Neo-Confucianism *(Shushi-gaku)*, was taught in the domain's academy, Kôdôkan. Mitsukuni Tokugawa is known by the name of Mito Kômon in television plays. He was the second lord of the Mito domain who edited *Dai Nihon-shi (Great history of Japan)*.

In terms of religious culture, Kashmia Jingû held the highest rank in the prefecture according to the former ranking system of the Shintô shrines. Kasama Inari Shrine is counted as one of the grand three *inari* (gods of the harvest) besides Fushimi in Kyôto, Yûtoku in Saga, and Toyakawa in Aichi. The town associated with Tsukubasan Shrine was known for a performance to sell ointments having the trade name Gama (toad). In terms of food culture, the production of *natto* is the largest of all the prefectures. The *natto*, surrounded by rice straws, was sold at Mito Station and drive inns along national routes. Angler fish on the northern coast and Okukuji-*shamo* (gamecock) in the town of Daigo are local foodstuffs presented in earthen casserole dishes. Among the traditional crafts, Yûki pongee *(tsumugi)* in Yûki, Kasama ware in Kasama, and sake (rice wine) breweries in Ishioka cater to local tourism.

Population and Traffic

The population of Ibaraki is 2,970,000. The main cities are Mito (269,000: nine percent of the population), Tsukuba (215,000), Hitachi (193,000), Hitachinaka (157,000), Tsuchiura (144,000), Koga (143,000), Toride (110,000), and Chikusei (109,000). The area is divided into the Kenpoku region in the north, the Ken-ô region in the center, the Rokkô region in the southeast, the Kennan region in the south, and the Kensei region in the west. The main road traffic runs on the Jôban Line and the Jôban Expressway, which extend southwest to northeast along the old Mito Road. The Mito Line and the North Kantô Expressway cross west to east in the Ken-ô and Kensei regions (their starting points are Oyama and Takasaki respectively). In the Kennan region, the Tsukuba Express, which runs from Akihabara, opened in 2005, and new towns were developed on the train stations along this route in the prefecture. Ibaraki Airport, which opened in Omitama city of the Ken-ô region in 2010, is managed in conjunction with Hyakuri air base.

Primary Sector of Industry

The gross agricultural production of the region is the second largest of all the prefectures after Hokkaidô. The main commodities produced are vegetables, rice, swine, and sweet potatoes. Among the vegetables, Ibaraki produces the greatest amounts of Chinese cabbages, green peppers, melons, Japanese honeworts *(mitsu-ba)*, green pak choy *(chingen-sai),* and lotus roots of all the prefectures in Japan. Vegetables are mainly produced in the Kensei region close to consumption centers, and in the Rokkô region, they are cultivated on extensive flat land. Regarding rice production, the main rice variety is *Koshihikari*. Hôjô-*mai*, produced at the foot of Mt. Tsukuba, is the brand for the rice whose variety is *Koshihikari*. Local sushi bars used the rice prior to the tasty-rice boom. Early-ripening rice is cultivated on the lower reaches of the Tone. Its harvest season starts in mid-August in the cities of Inashiki and Itako. The upland paddy fields *(riku-den)* were constructed by bulldozing plateaus in the 1960s.

The other local products are chestnuts in Kasama, turf in Tsukuba, and brand-names of meat, such as Rose pork and Hitachi beef. *Unshû* mandarins are also produced on the western hillside of Mt. Tsukuba, where growers take advantage of the temperate zone at the foot of the mountain. The city of Hitachinaka is the production center of sweet potatoes in the north. These are processed into dried sweet potatoes *(hoshi-imo)*. As for tea production, Okukuji tea in the town of Daigo and Sashima tea in the Kensei region are the northern tea-producing centers along the Pacific Ocean.

Other Industries

The main industrial products in terms of gross production are shovel excavators, nuclear reactor components, and beer. Hitachi, Ltd. was founded as a copper mining company in the Meiji period, and created a company town in the Kenpoku region. The company manufactures construction machinery, rail rolling stock, information equipment, and nuclear reactors. During the 1960s, the first nuclear power generation began in the village of Tôkai in the Kenpoku region, and an extensive excavated wharf constructed for heavy industry was opened on the Kashima Sea in the Rokkô region. The beer production is the largest of all the prefectures of Japan. The major beer company factories are located along the Tone River, from where beer is supplied to the Tokyo metropolitan area.

9. Tochigi

Tochigi is an inland prefecture in the north of the Kantô region (Figure 9).

Nature

Mt. Shirane (Nikkô Shirane: 2,578 m) in the west is the highest peak in Tochigi and Gunma prefectures. It is a stratovolcano whose summit is a lava dome. It was designated as Nikkô National Park in 1934 along with Mt. Nantai, Mt. Nyohô, Lake Chûzenji, and Senjôgahara moor. Mt. Nantai is also a stratovolcano, and is a prominent feature in the north of the Kantô Plain when it is covered with snow. Lake Chûzenji is a dammed lake at an altitude of 1,270 m, and Kegon Falls cascades down 97 m from the lake. The falls were created by an eruption of Mt. Nantai about 20,000 years ago. In the Meiji period, char *(iwana)* and kokanee *(hime-masu)* were stocked in the lake. Senjôgahara, at an altitude of 1,400 m, is a high moor at the headwaters of the lake. Strawberry seedlings and foliage plants are cultivated on the moor and on Mt. Keichô. This method is called *yama-age saibai* (cultivation in high mountains before transplanting to lowlands).

The Kinu River comes off Kinu Pond to the north of the Nikkô Mountains, and runs north and south in the center of the prefecture. Hot spring resorts, forming a section of the Nasu volcanic belt, are to be found on the upper reaches, for instance, Nikkô Yumoto, Kawamata, Kawaji, and Kinugawa. The Naka River courses from the Nasu Mountains, running through the Yamizo Mountains in the east

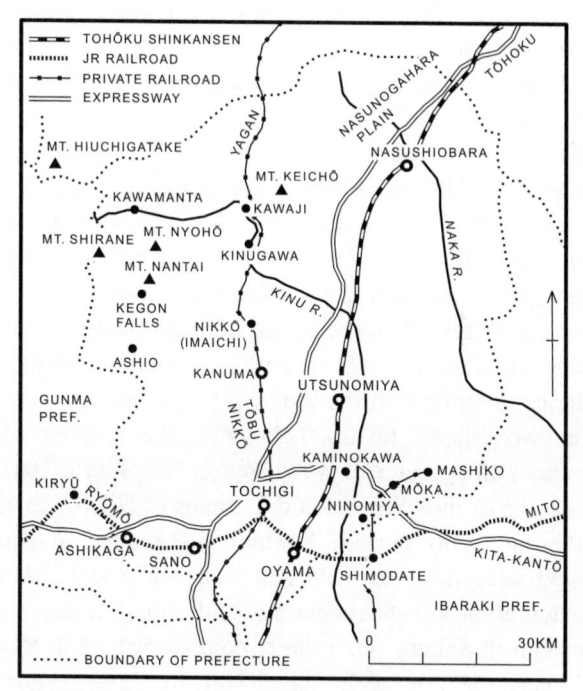

Figure 9 Tochigi

and entering Ibaraki Prefecture. Along the river and tributaries, there are 16 fish-trap sites *(yana)* for tourists to catch the sweetfish running up to the upper streams.

With respect to the climate, most of the prefecture has a Pacific Ocean-central Japan one, although the mountainous areas, which get heavy snowfalls, are categorized as having a Sea of Japan-central Japan climate. Thunder is common during the afternoons of mid-summer in the north of the Kantô Plain, as cumulonimbus clouds form as a result of the cool air descending from the high mountains. Thunder occurs on 25 days per year in the city of

Utsunomiya, a higher frequency than other prefectural capitals in the Kantô region. Thunder Shrines *(Raiden Jinja)* for fending off thunderbolts are to be seen in the north of the Kantô Plain.

History and Culture

Shimotsuke Province under the Ritsuryô code became Tochigi and Utsunomiya prefectures, and they were merged in the early Meiji period. The former Ashikaga School, which opened in the Muromachi period, is known as the oldest school in the country. Traditionally, it offered studies in Confucianism, divinity, military strategy, and medicine. Tôshôgu Shrine in the city of Nikkô is dedicated to the worship of Ieyasu Tokugawa, the founder of the Tokugawa Shogunate. It was listed on the World Heritage Site as one of the "Shrines and Temples of Nikkô" in 1999. In the late Edo period, Sontoku (Takanori) Ninomiya assisted with rural development based on *hôtôku* thought (reconciliation of the economy and morals). He was a statesman in Sakura (now the Ninomiya district in the city of Môka), who is well known for its stone statues of Kinjirô Ninomiya in public schools.

In terms of food culture, potstickers *(gyôza)* in the city of Utsunomiya are popular. They were introduced by retirees of the 14th Division of the Imperial Army in Utsunomiya, after they had been stationed in Manchuria. Small shops that sell only potstickers at low prices are spread around the residential areas in the city. The potstickers became familiar among tourists in the 1990s, and some shops branched out into shopping streets. *Shimotsukare* is a winter food cooked by simmering soybeans, sake lees, and a head of salmon. A geographical study on dialects revealed that the food was distributed from the

Aizu West Road.

Population and Traffic

The population of Tochigi Prefecture is 2,008,000. The main cities are Utsunomiya (512,000), Oyama (164,000), Ashikaga (155,000), Tochigi (139,000), Sano (121,000), Nasushiobara (118,000), and Kanuma (102,000). The prefectural capital is the city of Utsunomiya, 100 km north of the center of Tokyo metropolitan area. It was designated as a core city *(chûkaku shi)* along with the cities of Maebashi and Takasaki in the north Kantô region. In parallel with the old Ôshû and Nikkô roads, the Tôhoku Main Line (the Utsunomiya Line), and National Route 4 run north and south in the center of the prefecture. Along the Aizu West Road, the Yagan Railway runs north and south through the valleys between the Nasu and the Nikkô Mountains. The cities of Oyama, Tochigi, and Sano are junctions in the south, where the east-west directed traffic (the Mito and the Ryômô lines, and the Kita-Kantô Expressway) crosses the north-south directed traffic (the Tôbu Nikkô Line and the Tôhoku Expressway, as well as the Tôhoku Main Line and National Route 4).

Primary Sector of Industry

The main agricultural commodities in terms of gross production are vegetables (mainly strawberries), rice, and raw milk. Strawberries are chiefly cultivated in the town of Ninomiya (now Môka city). They are cultivated in plastic greenhouses constructed in paddy fields, and treated with artificial lighting in winter. The Agricultural Experiment Station of Tochigi Prefecture has bred the main strawberry varieties, for instance, *Nhohô* in the 1980s and *Tochiotome* in the 1990s. The cultivated area of leeks *(nira)*, which is one of the ingredients of *gyôza*, is the largest of all the prefectures. Leeks are cultivated in the city of Kanuma by means of greenhouse horticulture and harvested throughout the year. The volume of barley grown is also the largest of all the prefectures. In the south, barley is cultivated as a secondary crop *(urasaku)* in paddy fields. The area is also the last remaining production center of gourds *(kanpyô)*. The Nasunogahara Plain in the north is a compounded alluvial fan extending from the confluence of the Hôki and the Naka rivers. Although it was a wasteland because the rivers are subterranean, after reclamation projects, including the construction of the Nasu Canal, farms for the nobility and an Imperial villa were constructed in the Meiji period. At present, the main farm types in the region are dairy, paddy rice, garden plants, and agritourism.

Other Industries

The main industrial products in terms of gross production are cigarettes, medicines, and cars. Japan Tobacco is based in the North Kantô Factory in the city of Utsunomia and the Leaf Tobacco Research Institute is based in the city of Oyama. As part of the pharmaceutical industry, there are factories managed by foreign and domestic pharmaceutical companies in the cities of Utsunomiya and Nikkô. In car production, one of Nissan Motor Co.'s main factories is in the town of Kaminokawa. Supporting this, auto parts, electronics, machinery, and food are produced at an industrial park in the city of Môka.

As for mining, Ôya stone comes from the city of Utsunomiya (formerly the town of Ôya). It is a kind of pumice tuff, which has been used as a material in traditional warehouses and fences because of the ease with which it can be cut and transported. The Kanuma soil of Kanuma city is fine pumice, and it has been used for cuttings and seedbeds. The pottery industry flourished in the town of Mashiko since the end of the Edo period based on the plentiful kaolin supply. The Ashio Mine in the city of Nikkô (formerly the town of Ashio) was formerly the largest copper producer in the country. The Watarase retarding basin was constructed on the lower reaches of the Watarase to rectify the Ashio mining pollution incident in the early Meiji period.

10. Gunma

Gunma is an inland prefecture in the northwest of the Kantô region (Figure 10).

Nature

Mt. Akagi, Mt. Haruna, and Mt. Myôgi are the three mountains that make up Jômô. They are apparent features in the landscape when viewed from urban areas and the main roads in the prefecture. Mt. Akagi and Mt. Haruna are volcanos that formed the caldera lakes of Ônuma and Haruna on their upper slopes. Tourists enjoy ice fishing for smelt and skating on the lakes in winter. Mt. Myôgi, with its rugged peaks, includes unique-shaped rocks such as the Candle and Cannon rocks. Mt. Asama is located at the boundary with Nagano Prefecture. On the north slope of the mountain, the village of Kanbara was destroyed by the eruption of 1783. The temple of Kannon *(kannon-dô)* on the hillside was a refuge from the debris flow during that eruption.

Kusatsu hot spring, at the fold of Mt. Motoshirane in the west, is famous for the abundant outflow of hot water. Sulfur is collected at a hot spring field *(yu-batake)* in the center of the resort as souvenirs (Illustration 5). A German

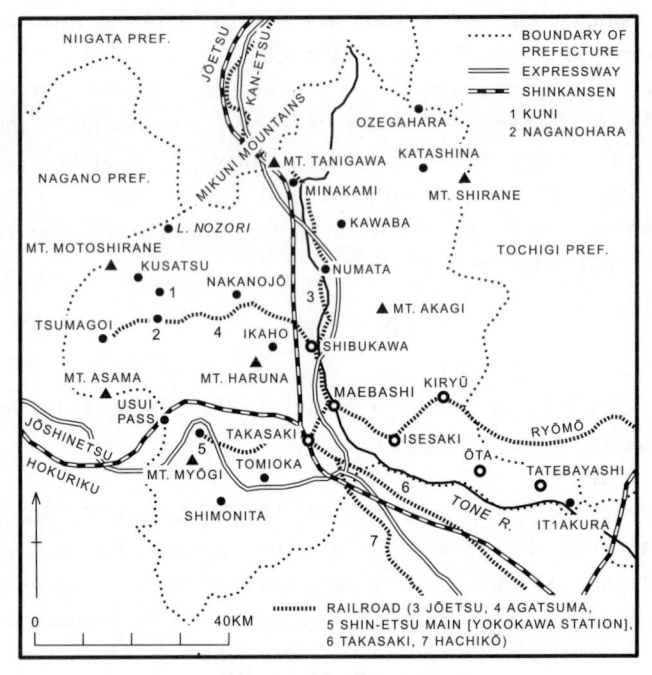

Figure 10 Gunma

doctor, Erwin Von Bälz, a foreign advisor hired by the Meiji government, studied the hot spring cure in Kusatsu. There used to be a custom of "winter living" *(fuyu-zumi)* up to the early Meiji period. That is, the people living in Kusatsu went down to Kosame district in Kuni village in winter since the hot spring is located in a highland area (1,200 m), which gets heavy snowfalls. Besides Kusatsu town, there are famous hot spring resorts in the mountainous areas of Ikaho in Shibukawa, Kawarayu in Naganohara, Manza in Tsumagoi, Minakami, Tanigawa in Minakami, Shima in Nakanojô, and Oigami in Numata.

The area is consistent with the middle and the upper

reaches of the Tone, whose catchment area is the largest in the country. The river runs from the Mikuni Mountains at the boundary with Niigata Prefecture (the range forms a border for the three provinces, Kôzuke, Echigo, and Shinano). Fluvial terraces extend along the Numata Basin at the foot of the range. The catchment areas of some rivers are included adjacent to the Sea of Japan, namely, Ozegahara Marsh lying at the boundary with Fukushima and Niigata prefectures, and Lake Nozori, at the boundary with Nagano Prefecture. Lake Nozori is an artificial reservoir, whose elevation (1,517 m) is the second highest after the Minamiaiki Dam in Nagano Prefecture.

Most of the prefecture has a Pacific Ocean-central Japan climate. The air in winter is dried by a monsoon wind called the *karakkaze*, which blows from the northwest. Local farm houses are protected from the monsoon by high hedges *(kashi-gune)* of evergreen oak *(Quercus myrsinifolia)*. The climate in the mountainous areas is categorized as a Sea of Japan-central Japan one. The areas have also been designated as a heavy snowfall zone. The prefecture has the greatest number of ski resorts in the Kantô region. Among these are Oze Iwakura, Oze Tokura, Marunuma Kôgen, Katashina Kôgen, in Katashina village, Minakami Kôgen, Kawaba, Kusatsu Kokusai, and Manza Hot Springs. They attract skiers from the Tokyo metropolitan area.

History and Culture

Kôzuke Province under the Ritsuryô code became Gunma Prefecture in the Meiji period. The name is derived from a county that included the capital of the province. The prefecture is also called Jôshû or Jômô, which means an ancient province prior to Kôzuke. In the Meiji period, the city of Maebashi, which flourished as a result of raw silk production, became the prefectural capital. The relocating of the capital to the city of Takasaki, adjacent to the city of Maebashi, continued until the Taishô period.

Wheat is cultivated as a secondary crop at paddy fields in the north of the Kantô Plain, and the prefectural residents consume much udon. Tatebayashi, Kiryû, and Mizusawa in Ikaho are the three centers of Jôshû udon production. Yokokawa Station on the Shin-etsu Main Line was famous for *Tôge no kama-meshi* (a small lunch-pot of seasoning rice sold in the pass). Although the railroad from the station to the Usui Pass was abolished when the Nagano Shinkansen opened in 1997, the main stands for selling the lunch pot changed to roadside drive-ins and service areas on the expressway. The city of Takasaki is famed for its daruma doll production, and the daruma lunch box is a specialty of Takasaki Station.

Population and Traffic

The population of Gunma is 2,008,000. The main cities are Takasaki (371,000), Maebashi (340,000), Ôta (216,000), Isesaki (207,000), Kiryû (122,000), Shibukawa (83,000), and Tatebayashi (79,000). The area is divided into the Hokumô region in the north, including the city of Numata, the Chûmô region in the center, including the cities of Maebashi and Isesaki, the Seimô region in the west, including the city of Takasaki, and the Tômô region in the east, which includes the cities of Ôta and Kiryû. The population of Takasaki exceeded the prefectural capital by the great merger of municipalities in the Heisei period in the 2000s. Takasaki Station is a railroad junction in the north of the Kantô region, at which several lines intersect, namely, the Hokuriku Shinkansen (the former Nagano

Shinkansen), the Jôetsu Shinkansen, and the local lines of Takasaki, Jôetsu, and Hachikô. National Routes 18 and 17 were established along the ancient Tôsandô Road (the Nakasendô Road in the Edo period). The culture of Kyôto was once spread to the eastern provinces via the road.

Primary Sector of Industry

The main agricultural commodities in terms of gross production are vegetables, swine, raw milk, and rice. The cultivated cucumber area is the largest of all the prefectures. Cucumber is cultivated mainly in the town of Itakura in the Tômô region in greenhouses distributed in paddy fields. The cultivated cabbage area is the second largest of all the prefectures after Aichi. Cabbages are cultivated around the village of Tsumagoi at the north foot of Mt. Asama. The snowfalls reduce the cabbage damage from continuous cropping. Regarding local specialties, the cultivated *kon-nyaku (Amorphophallus konjac)* area accounts for more than 80 percent of the country's production of the plant. It is produced in Agatsuma county and the city of Shibukawa in the Hokumô region. Shimonita *negi* is a local seed variety of scallion in the town of Shimonita in the Seimô region. The growing period for *kon-nyaku* is two to three years, and fifteen months for the scallion. The cultivated mulberry area represents more than 50 percent of the country's production, even though it has decreased in recent decades. The traditional farm buildings in the *segai-zukuri* and Akagi-styles, with their large second stories, are the vestiges of the sericulture in the area.

Other Industries

The main industrial products in terms of gross production are automobiles and automobile parts. Fuji Heavy Industries (now Subaru Corporation), which sells Subaru-brand cars, operates the main factory in the city of Ôta. The company was founded as Nakajima Aircraft Co. Its founder was from the former town of Ojima (now Ôta). In the town of Ôizumi, adjacent to Ôta, factories of the automobile company and Sanyo Electric Co. are to be found. Second and third-generation Japanese Latin Americans have worked in the town since the 1990s.

Tomioka Silk Mill was opened in 1872, but it closed in 1987. After production ended, the semi-European buildings, including a reeling plant and a cocoon warehouse, were preserved, and were listed as a World Heritage Site in 2014. The city of Kiryû was a leading producer of silk cloth until the spread of Western-style clothes and silk products began to be imported. The techniques for maintaining machinery such as power looms became the basis for automobile parts and *pachinko* machine (Japanese-style pinball) assembly plants. In Jômô-*karuta*, which is a card game used as part of the school education in the prefecture, there is an expression, "*Kakâ tenka to karakkaze*" (Wives wear the pants and a strong dry wind) since women earned a good income from sericulture and the textile industry.

11. Saitama

Saitama is an inland prefecture in the center of the Kantô region (Figure 11).

Nature

The highest peak in the prefecture is Mt. Sanpô (2,483 m) in the Kantô Mountains. The mountains divide the Kantô and the Chûbu regions, and provide the source of the Arakawa River that flows into Tokyo Bay. In the

Chichibu Mountains, a section of the Kantô Mountains, the Mitsumine Shrine is to be found. Its object of worship is the Japanese wolf *(yama-inu)*. Its confraternities *(kô)* are distributed in the Kantô region. At Mt. Bukô in the mountains, limestone is extracted by Chichibu Taiheiyô Cement Corporation. The Nagatoro gorge on the upper reaches of the Arakawa is a tourist destination known for its boat cruises. It has been a landmark of Japanese geology since a German geologist, Heinrich Edmund Naumann, conducted fieldwork there in the Meiji period.

To the east of the prefecture is the low-lying Kantô Plain, where Class A rivers *(ikkyû-kasen)* run, such as the Arakawa, the Moto-arakawa, the Nakagawa, the Tone, and the Ôotoshi-furutone. The lowland was flooded every so often and thus, traditional farmhouses were built on old natural levees, and bamboos were planted at a site facing the upstream to curtail rushing water. The Tone Weir was constructed in Gyôda city in the 1960s to provide tap water

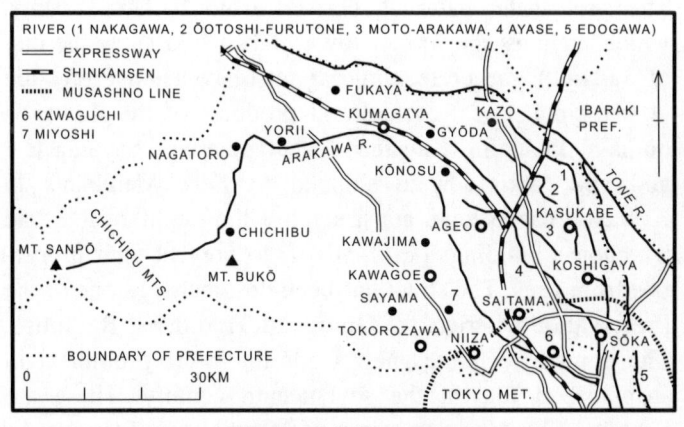

Figure 11 Saitama

61

to the Tokyo metropolitan area and to purify the Sumida River in the downtown area of Tokyo. An underground reservoir (the Metropolitan Area Outer Underground Discharge Channel) was opened in the 2000s to reduce flood damage from the Nakagawa and Ayase rivers.

The climate is categorized as a Pacific Ocean-central Japan one. The temperature of the city of Kumagaya rises in summer from the heat carried from the Tokyo metropolitan area by sea breezes, and also the foehn winds that blow down from the Kantô Mountains. A high of 40.9 °C marked in Kumagaya in 2007 was the highest temperature recorded in the country until 2013. In the Sayama Hills, which covered with a mixed forest of broad-leaf and coniferous trees, the "forest of Totoro," founded by the National Trust is to be seen.

History and Culture

The north of Musashi Province under the Ritsuryô code was once part of the Kawagoe, Iwatsuki, and Oshi prefectures, but it was merged with Saitama in the Meiji period. The prefectural name is derived from Saitama county, which includes the former town of Iwatsuki (now the city of Saitama), the prefectural capital of Iwatsuki Prefecture at that time. Local agricultural products of the Kawagoe domain, including Kawagoe sweet potatoes, Sayama tea, and silk fabrics, were shipped to Edo. Merchants in Kawagoe castle town constructed a thoroughfare that had warehouse buildings *(kura-zukuri)* to prevent their properties from fires. The street has been designated as one of the Preservation Districts for Groups of Traditional Buildings. The domain reclaimed new lands that were prominent in strip-shaped lots in the seventeenth century. These are Santome Shinden in the town of Miyoshi and Tokorozawa city, and Nobidome Shinden in the city of Niiza. The forest of Heirinji Temple in Nobidome Shinden was designated as a natural monument, known as the "Copses of Musashino." The Minuma Canal (Minuma *dai-yôsui*) and Minuma lock gates (Minuma *tsûsen-bori*) were constructed in the eighteenth century by the Tokugawa Shogunate to reclaim agricultural lands. A section of the reclaimed land was conserved as "Minuma paddy fields" in the city of Saitama, providing an open space and a rural landscape to urban residents.

Population and Traffic

The population of the prefecture is 7,195,000, the fifth largest of all of Japan's prefectures. The main cities are Saitama (1,222,000), Kawaguchi (501,000), Kawagoe (343,000), Tokorozawa (342,000), Koshigaya (326,000), Sôka (244,000), Kasukabe (237,000), Ageo (224,000), and Kumagaya (203,000). Urawa, Omiya, and Yono cities were consolidated into Saitama in 2001, which was assigned as an ordinance-designated city in 2003. According to 2010 Population Census data, 853,000 people (24 percent of all of the commuters) attend companies or schools in Tokyo. Migration from Tokyo to the south of the prefecture has taken place as a result of events such as the 1923 Great Kantô earthquake, World War II, and the economic growth periods.

JR East (East Japan Railway Company) railroads run north and south through the prefecture, namely, the Keihin Tôhoku, the Takasaki, and the Utsunomya lines. Not only commerce but also administrative functions are concentrated in the city of Saitama. For instance, branch offices of ministries have been established at the Saitama New Urban Center in Chûô Ward. On the west of the Arakawa River, housing complexes were constructed adjacent to the railroads of Seibu Ikebukuro, Seibu Shinjuku, and Tôbu Tôjô. On the east of the Ayase River, housing complexes were also constructed along the Tôbu Isesaki Line, including the Matsubara-danchi, which opened in 1962. The Musashino Line and the Tokyo Gaikan Expressway are a circular traffic system that connects those densely populated areas in the south.

Primary Sector of Industry

The main agricultural commodities in terms of gross production are vegetables, eggs, and rice. Vegetable production has developed as a form of suburban agriculture. The main vegetables grown are scallions, Japanese mustard spinach *(komatsu-na)*, cucumbers, turnips, broccoli, spinach, and arrowheads *(kuwai)*. Fukaya *negi* is an autumn-winter harvested scallion whose harvest peaks between November and March. It is cultivated in the fields of the natural levees of the Tone River in the city of Fukaya. In the city of Sayama and the town of Miyoshi in the Musashino Plateau, agribusiness companies conduct the integrated management of vegetables that encompasses cultivation, processing, and the packing of salad cups. Floriculture is thriving in the city of Kônosu in the north of the Ômiya Plateau.

Other Industries

The main industrial products in terms of gross production are automobiles, automobile parts, and medicines. The main category of manufacturing is metal products in terms of number of establishments producing these. In the automobile industry, Honda Motor Co. passenger car assembly factories are located in the cities of Yorii and Ageo, and UD Trucks Corporation truck assembly factory is based in the city of Ageo. Of all the prefectures, Saitama produces the largest amounts of medicine production. The main pharmaceutical factories are based in Saitama, Kazo, and Kawagoe cities, and the town of Kawajima. As for metal products, Kawaguchi was famous as a foundry city. It was a location for the movie "Foundry Town" *(Kyûpora no Aru Machi)*, although, ultimately, the number of foundries decreased as urbanization advanced from the south.

Among the traditional crafts, chests and clogs made of paulownia *(kiri-tansu and kiri-geta)* are produced in the city of Kasukabe, and dolls for girls' and boys' festivals are produced in the cities of Iwatsuki and Kônosu. Craftsmen made use of the planks and sawdust of the paulownias planted on plateaus. They were originally developed by craftsmen who stayed at post towns along the old Nikkô and Nakasendô roads, and then their techniques spread to the neighboring farms as off-season agricultural activities. Rice cracker is a specialty in the city of Sôka, which used to be a production center for rice and soy sauce on the Ôshû Road.

12. Chiba

Chiba is located in the southeast of the Kantô region, facing the Pacific Ocean and Tokyo Bay (Figure 12).

Nature

The area consists of plains, uplands, and low mountains. The highest peak is Mt. Atago (408 m) in the Bôsô Hills of the Bôsô Peninsula. The Yôrô and Obitsu rivers flow from the hills and into Tokyo Bay. Yôrô Valley, on the upper reaches of the Yôrô, is a scenic area known for its red and yellow leaves in late autumn, and fresh green leaves in late spring. The Shimôsa Plateau is a flat upland extending to the north of the prefecture. Valleys were created at the edges of the plateau as a result of erosion. They were used as valley-bottom paddies (*yatsu-da*). Owing to a scarcity of water, grazing pastures for horses, such as Kogane-*maki* and Sakura-*maki*, were created on the plateau by the Tokugawa Shogunate in the Edo period. The farmland area increased after the Meiji period as a result of the invention of the Kazusa method for well digging. Long afterward, new housing areas were constructed after the high economic growth period. The water quality of Tega and

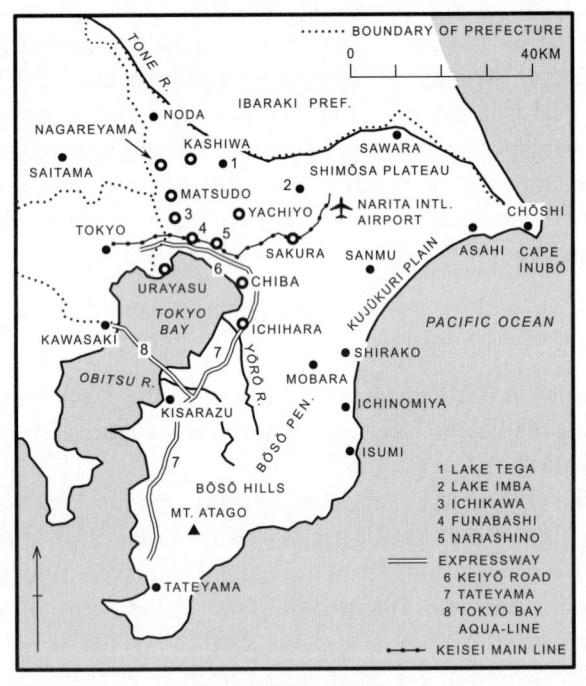

Figure 12 Chiba

66

Inba lakes in the plateau deteriorated in the 1970s from the inflow of domestic sewage. The eutrophication levels in the lakes were the highest of all lakes in Japan at one point.

The coastal Kujûkuri Plain stretches to a length of 60 km. Sand dunes in parallel with the coastline crease the surface of the plain. The sand comes from the sea cliffs —Byôbugaura in Iioka (now Asahi) and Chôshi in the north and Taitômisaki in Isumi in the south. After the construction of jetties, the sandy beaches on the coastline began to be eroded. The Ôtone and the Ryôsô canals, and artificial ponds in the Bôsô Hills, supply irrigation water to the paddy fields in the plain. Those canals take water from the Tone River over the Shimôsa Plateau. Along the tidal flats of Tokyo Bay, laver cultivation and clam fishing continue at Sanban-*ze* and Banzu-*higata*. Yatsu-*higata* is a square tidal flat surrounded by the built-up suburbs of the city of Narashino. It was listed in the Ramsar Convention as a nesting place of waterfowl.

The climate is categorized as a Pacific Ocean-central Japan one. In the south of the Bôsô Hills, there are evergreen broadleaved forests that consist of *shii* (*Castanopsis* spp.) and *tabu* (*Machilus* spp.). The northern limit of coral is located at the tip of the Bôsô Peninsula, whose seawater is warm due to the influence of the Japan Current.

History and Culture

Under the Ritsuryô code, Kazusa and Awa provinces, and a part of Shimôsa Province, were made into Chiba Prefecture in the Meiji period. Chiba town in Chiba county was declared to be the capital. The county name is derived from a manor (*shô-en*) in the Heian period. Dairy farming began at Mineoka ranch at the foot of Mt. Atago in the Bôsô Hills when Indian cattle were imported in the eighteenth century to make *haku-gyû raku* (a dairy drink made from the milk of white cattle) for medical use. The former city of Sawara (now Katori), along the Tone River, has been developed as a river port. The old business street was designated as one of the Preservation Districts for Groups of Traditional Buildings. It was the hometown of Tadataka Inô, who made the first surveyed map of the country *(Dai-nihon enkai-yochi zen-zu)* in the early nineteenth century.

Population and Traffic

Chiba Prefecture's population is 6,216,000. The main cities are Chiba (962,000), Funabashi (609,000), Matsudo (484,000), Ichikawa (474,000), Kashiwa (404,000), Ichihara (280,000), Yachiyo (190,000), Sakura (172,000), Urayasu (165,000), Narashino (165,000), and Nagareyama (164,000). Chiba was designated as an ordinance-designated city in 1992. According to 2010 Population Census data, 719,000 people (25 percent of all the commuters) attend companies or schools in the Tokyo. Dormitory towns were constructed in the north of the prefecture in the 1970s. They include, for instance, Narita New Town along the Narita and the Keisei Main lines, Kaihin New Town along the Keiyô Line, Chiba Ichihara New Town along the Sotobô and Chihara lines, and Chiba New Town along the Hokusô Line. Narita International Airport (formerly New Tokyo International Airport), which handles the largest number of international passengers of any airport in Japan, was opened on the Shimôsa Plateau in 1978. Expressways in the south of the Bôsô Peninsula opened in the late 1990s, such as the Tateyama Expressway and the Tokyo Bay Aqua-Line.

Primary Sector of Industry

The gross agricultural production of the region is the third largest of all the prefectures after Hokkaidô and Ibaraki. The main commodities are vegetables, rice, and swine. Vegetables such as edible crown daisies *(shungiku)*, spinach, turnips, watermelons, and taros, and beans such as groundnuts and fava beans are produced in the Shimôsa Plateau. Swine is reared in the Katori, the Kaisô, and the Sanbu regions in the east (around Katori, Asahi, and Sanmu cities). The production of Japanese pears is the largest of all the prefectures. They are cultivated mainly in suburban areas in the cities of Matsudo and Ichikawa. The main pear varieties are *Hôsui* and *Kôsui*. They are earlier ripening varieties than the *Nijisseiki* that was bred in the city of Matsudo in the beginning of the twentieth century.

Farmers in coastal areas take advantage of the mild climate. Winter-spring harvested cabbages and radishes are cultivated around Cape Inubô, and floriculture thrives in the south of the Bôsô Peninsula. In greenhouse horticulture, winter harvested cucumbers are cultivated in the city of Asahi in the northernmost part of the Kujûkuri Plain, and winter-harvested tomatoes are cultivated in the town of Ichinomiya in the southernmost part of the plain. In the fishing industry, the catches at Chôshi fishing port are the largest in the country. The main catches are sardine, mackerel, saury, horse mackerel, and tuna.

Other Industries

The gross output of the secondary sector of industry is the sixth largest of all the prefectures. The main products are gasoline, light oils, and sheet steel. The prefecture's industrial center is Keiyô Industrial Zone alongside Tokyo Bay, where the principal categories of activity are metal refining, steel manufacturing, shipbuilding, and chemical products. The South Kantô gas fields are distributed in the central portion of the Bôsô Peninsula, around the city of Mobara. Iodine is also extracted from the gas fields and exported to foreign countries. As for the food industry, soy sauce production is the largest of all the prefectures. In the northwest and the northeast of the prefecture, there are major soy sauce factories, namely, Kikkôman Corporation and Kinoene Soy Sauce Co. in Noda city, and Yamasa Corporation and Higeta Shôyu Co. in the city of Chôshi.

With regard to tourism, Tokyo Disneyland is based at Maihama district in the city of Urayasu, and the Makuhari New Urban Center at the mouth of the Hanamigawa in Chiba city was constructed on reclaimed lands alongside Tokyo Bay in the 1980s. Aeon Co., the largest retailer in the country, is headquartered in the Makuhari New Urban Center, Chiba city. On the Kujûkuri Plain, although the use of seine nets to catch sardines thrived until the early twentieth century, the area is now popular for its beach resorts, surfing areas, and sports lodgings for tennis clubs.

13. Tokyo

Tokyo is located in the south of the Kantô region, facing Tokyo Bay (Figure 13).

Nature

The highest peak in the area is Mt. Kumotori (2,017 m) at the boundary with Saitama and Yamanashi prefectures. It forms a piece of the Chichibu Tama Kai National Park. At the foot of the mountain, Nippara Cave and the Hikawa Limestone Mine in Okutama town are to be found. Mt. Takao, at the south of the Kantô Mountains, attracts tourists from the Tokyo metropolitan area. Its vegetation has been preserved as a temple's forest, and also designated as the Meiji no Mori Takao Quasi-National Park in the 1960s.

The source of the Tama River is Mt. Kasatori at the boundary between Saitama and Yamanashi prefectures. The river courses through Lake Okutama, an artificial dam-lake for tap water supply to the capital, runs to the west of the prefecture, and flows into Tokyo Bay at the boundary with Kanagawa Prefecture. The middle reaches of the river are the boundary between the Musashino Plateau in the north and the Tama Hills in the south. The east of the special wards is the alluvial plain called Shita-machi (lower town). The land consists of coastal reclaimed lands and the deltas created by the rivers Sumida, Arakawa, Edogawa, and Nakagawa. The west of the special wards is a part of the Musashino Plateau, and is

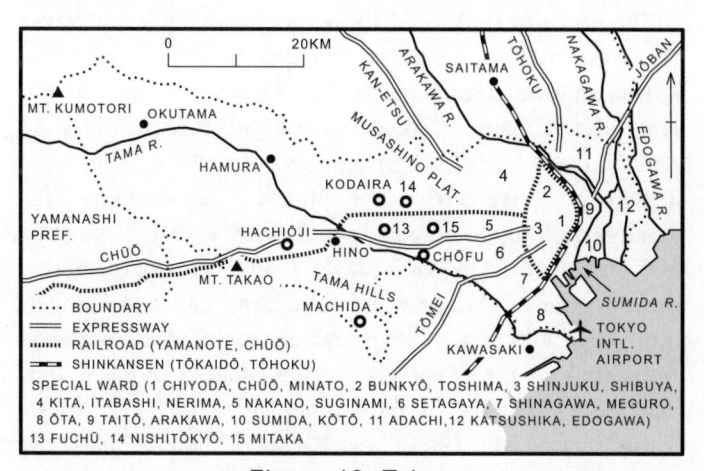

Figure 13 Tokyo

71

called Yamanote (upper town). It forms tongue-shaped, dissected uplands, whose terrain feature a considerable of slopes.

The climate is categorized as a Pacific Ocean-central Japan one. In winter, the "winter days" *(fuyu-bi)* whose minimum temperatures fall below 0 °C decreased, while in summer, the "tropical nights" *(nettai-ya)* whose minimum temperatures do not fall below 25 °C increased, and there are a lot of localized rain showers. The prefectural area embraces remote islands. Ogasawara Islands, known for their eco-tourism, are located at 1,000 km south of the capital. They were designated as a national park in 1972, and listed on the World Heritage Site in 2011. The Okinotori Islands, at 1,850 km from the capital (the southernmost point of the country) and Minamitori Island, which is 1,750 km from the capital (the easternmost point of the country) belong to Tokyo.

History and Culture

The east part of Musashi Province from the Tama River, the west part of Shimôsa Province from the Edogawa River, and the islands in Izu Province under the Ritsuryô code became part of Tokyo-*fu* (Tokyo Prefecture) in 1868, and Tokyo-*to* (Tokyo Metropolis) in 1943. The name Tokyo is derived from the phrase "east capital." The Tokugawa Shogunate was launched by Ieyasu Tokugawa, and continued from 1603 to 1867. Edo was the capital of the Shogunate, and grew to be a large city consisting of more than 800 towns. It occasionally suffered from large fires, such as the Great Fire of the Meireki reign in 1657 and the Great Fire of the Meiwa reign in 1772. In the Taishô period, the 1923 Great Kantô earthquake hit Tokyo and Kanagawa prefectures and killed more than 100,000 people.

The language of the upper town pervaded through the country by means of textbooks and NHK (Nippon Hôsô Kyôkai) radio broadcasting, and became standard Japanese. A specific food culture was created in the lower town. Specialties include *edomae-zushi* (sushi), cooked with the seafood caught in Edo Bay (now Tokyo Bay), *yanagawa,* cooked as a mixed bowl, with loaches, burdocks, and eggs, and pan-fried batter *(monja-yaki)*, sold at candy shops in Tsukishima in Chûô Ward since the 1920s (the Taishô period). Cultural and sports facilities are concentrated in the downtown areas, including Nippon Budôkan, Ryôgoku Kokugikan, the Tokyo Dome, the Suntory Hall, and Ginza Kabukiza.

Population and Traffic

Tokyo's population 13,159,000 and the population density, at 6,016 people per km², is the largest of all the prefectures. The main municipalities are the 23 special wards (8,946,000: 68 percent of the prefecture) and the cities of Hachiôji (580,000), Machida (427,000), Fuchû (256,000), Chôfu (224,000), Nishitôkyô (197,000), Kodaira (187,000), and Mitaka (186,000). Chiyoda, Chûô, and Minato wards are the center of Tokyo *(toshin)*, and Shinjuku, Shibuya, and Ikebukuro wards are the more sub-central areas *(fuku-toshin)*. The Tokyo Metropolitan Government at Marunouchi district in Chiyoda Ward moved to a redevelopment area at the Yodobashi water purification plant in Shinjuku Ward in the 1990s. Tama New Town was established in the 1970s along the Keio and the Odakyû lines in the Tama Hills. It is one of the largest new towns constructed during the economic boom period.

The first railroad was opened in the 1870s, providing 30

km of railroad between Shinbashi and Yokohama stations, and using English-made trains. More transportation facilities were subsequently inaugurated, and include, the subway Ginza Line in the 1920s, Tokyo International Airport in the 1930s, and the Shuto Expressway in the early 1960s. The Tôkaidô Shinkansen and Tokyo Monorail were opened just before the 1964 Summer Olympics. Afterward, the expressways extending from downtown were constructed, including the Tômei and the Chûô expressways in the late 1960s, the Tôhoku and Kan-etsu expressways in the 1970s, the Jôban Expressway in the 1980s, and the Daiba Route of the Shuto Expressway in the 1990s.

Primary Sector of Industry

The main agricultural commodities in terms of gross production are vegetables, flowers, and fruit. Among them, spinach, broccoli, Japanese pears, and sprigs of *udo (Aralia cordata)* are produced on the Musashino Plateau, and Japanese mustard spinach is cultivated in Edogawa Ward. In Nerima Ward, cabbage production arose instead of Nerima radishes, the former branded crop, after large-scale producing centers sprang up in suburbs and truck-farming areas. In floriculture, the main products are cyclamens in Nishitama county in the west, and freesias and ornamental plants on Hachijô Island in the Izu Islands. Although the prefecture's gross agricultural production is the lowest of all the prefectures, the country's agricultural and marine products are sold at central wholesale markets such as Ôta and Tsukiji. In the fisheries industry, Amberstripe scad *(muro-aji)*, flying fish, marlin, and *ten-gusa (Gelidiaceae)* are unloaded on the islands. Freshwater clams are caught in the Arakawa, Kyû-edogawa, and Tama rivers.

Other Industries

The main industrial products in terms of gross production are printed materials, and bus and truck manufacturing. In terms of number of establishments, the main categories are printed materials and pressed machinery parts. In the printing industry, the major book and journal publishers, and the headquarters of the national newspapers are concentrated in special wards, and printing factories are distributed within and outside of them. The main automobile factories are those of Hino Motors, which produces trucks and buses and is located in Hino and Hamura cities. Factories producing pressed machinery parts are concentrated in the Jônan area of Ôta Ward, the Jôtô area of Katsushika Ward, and the Jôhoku area of Itabashi Ward. Smaller industries are based in the wholesale districts in the lower town. For instance, Buddhist altars are made in Asakusa, cooking utensils, in Kappabashi (Illustration 6), and toys, along the Sumida River. Among the specialties on the islands are *ki-hachijô* (checkered yellow silks), camellia oil, *kusaya* (horse mackerel dipped in salt water), and *imo*-shôchû (a liquor distilled from sweet potatoes).

Nagatachô in Chiyoda Ward is the center of politics, and this is where the Diet building stands. Kasumigaseki in Chiyoda Ward, the government quarter, includes the various ministries and the National Diet Library. The foreign embassies are distributed in the Roppongi, Akasaka, and Azabu districts in Minato Ward. Nihonbashi, Kabutochô, Ôtemachi, and Marunouchi in Chûô and Chiyoda wards encompass the financial district, which includes the Tokyo Stock Exchange and the headquarters of major banks and insurance companies. Roppongi Hills is an office complex that was constructed in a redevelopment project of high-density residential areas. It houses information technology companies, investment funds, and TV Asahi Corporation.

14. Kanagawa

Kanagawa is located in the southwest of the Kantô region, facing Tokyo and Sagami bays (Figure 14).

Nature

The highest peak is Mt. Hirugatake (1,673 m) in the Tanzawa Mountains to the west. Mt. Ôyama, to the east of the Tanzawa Mountains, is prominent from the Sagami Plain. It has attracted climbers since ancient times as a sacred place to pray for rain. It was designated as Tanzawa-Ôyama Quasi-National Park in the 1960s. Mt. Hakone in the southwest is a volcano, and at the foot is a dammed caldera, called Lake Ashinoko, which is known for its fishing and boat tours. They were designated as Fuji-Hakone-Izu National Park in 1936. Among the Hakone hot springs, Fujiya Hotel in Miyanoshita was one of the first summer resorts in the country, admitted by foreigners in the Meiji period. Hakone hot-spring resorts were subsequently developed with the opening of the Hakone Tozan Railway and the Odakyu's Odawara Line.

The Sagami River streams from Lake Yamanaka in Yamanashi Prefecture to the northwest of the prefecture, and feeds into Sagami Bay. River terraces were formed on the middle reaches of the Sagami Plain. The climate is categorized as a Pacific Ocean-central Japan one. Beach resorts such as Ôiso, Shônan, and Miura are spread along the sandy coast from Sagami Bay to the Miura Peninsula. Enoshima is a land-tied island that is known as a scenic

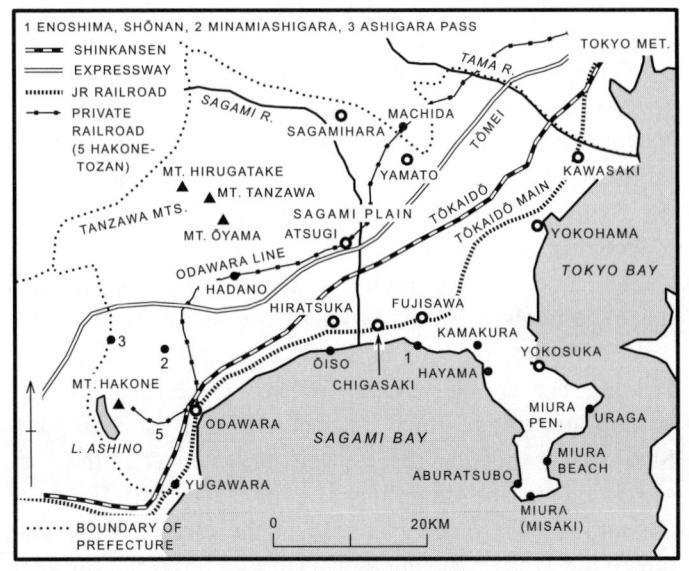

Figure 14 Kanagawa

site on the Shônan coast. The marine leisure industry is thriving at the Pacific Ocean. For instance, there are marinas in Yokohama, Yokosuka, Misaki, Aburatsubo, Hayama, Zushi, and Enoshima.

History and Culture

Sagami Province and a part of Musashi Province in the era of the Ritsuryô code became part of Kanagawa Prefecture in the Meiji period. The name is derived from the Kanagawa-*shuku*, a post town on the old Tôkaidô Road, in which the governor of the Tokugawa Shogunate was settled when the Port of Yokohama opened. In Kamakura, the first samurai regime started in the late twelfth century. The great statue of Buddha at Kôtokuin Temple in Kamakura city is in the open air since the building was de-

77

stroyed by an earthquake and tidal waves in the Muromachi period. In the late Edo period, the Convention of Kanagawa was ratified after Matthew C. Perry, a U.S. Navy Commodore, came to Uraga. After that, the Port of Yokohama was opened, and a foreign settlement was established in the village of Yokohama. One of the mercantile houses in the settlement eventually evolved into Yokohama's Chinatown.

The food culture includes *kamaboko* (steamed fish paste), processed from coastal fish in Odawara along the Tôkaidô Road, and sold at the Odawara post town and the Hakone hot spring resorts. *Shûmai* (steamed pork and scallop dumplings) box lunches are sold at Yokohama Station. The popular dishes were invented after the war, suggested by the dumplings served as appetizers at the Chinatown. Navy curry is sold in the city of Yokosuka, where the Japan Maritime Self-Defense Force and the U.S. Navy bases are situated. The dish is associated with the Royal Navy's curry introduced in the Meiji period.

Population and Traffic

The population of Kanagawa is 9,048,000, making it the second largest of all the prefectures after Tokyo. The main cities are Yokohama (3,689,000), Kawasaki (1,426,000), Sagamihara (718,000), Yokosuka (418,000), Fujisawa (410,000), Hiratsuka (261,000), Chigasaki (235,000), Yamato (228,000), and Atsugi (224,000). Yokohama, Kawasaki, and Sagamihara were assigned as ordinance-designated cities in the 1950s, the 1970s, and the 2010s respectively. According to 2010 Population Census data, 896,000 people (15 percent of all the commuters) attend companies and schools in Tokyo. Kôhoku New Town was one of the largest housing developments in the 1980s. With the emergence of the new town, Tsuzuki Ward was established in Yokohama, and two subway lines to the city center opened.

Railroads and national roads run east and west, including the Tôkaidô Main Line, which opened in the 1870s, National Route 1, originally planned in the 1880s, the Tôkaidô Shinkansen, which opened in 1964, and the Tômei Expressway, which opened in 1968. Private railroads extend from Tokyo, for instance, the Keihin Electric Express Railway from Minato Ward to Miura city, the Tôkyû Den-en-toshi Line from Shibuya Ward to Yamato city, the Odawara Line from Shinjuku Ward to Odawara city, and the Keio Sagamihara Line from Chôfu city to Sagamihara city. The Sagami Line of JR East and the Ken-ô Expressway (Metropolitan Inter-City Expressway) run north and south along the Sagami River. With regard to maritime transportation, the Port of Yokohama is one of the major three trading ports in the country, along with Nagoya and Chiba. The Yokohama International Passenger Terminal and the Japanese Overseas Migration Museum of the Japan International Cooperation Agency (JICA) are located at the new quay of the port. Additionally, the Port of Kawasaki is an industrial port, and the Port of Yokosuka is an industrial and naval port.

Primary Sector of Industry

The main agricultural commodities in terms of gross production are vegetables. Radishes, cabbages, and watermelons are cultivated in the Miura Peninsula. In this mild climate, radishes and cabbages are harvested from winter to spring in the peninsula. Although a seed variety of the Miura Radish used to be cultivated as a branded crop, the main variety was changed to a smaller "blue-neck" as a result of the increase in the number of nuclear families in the suburbs. Various agricultural products are produced in Yokohama, such as vegetables, fruit, flowers, and rice, and livestock is also raised. The number of allotment gardens *(shimin-nôen)* is the second largest of all the prefectures after Tokyo. They are principally distributed in Sagamihara and Hadano cities. Traditional crops are still cultivated in the west, such as Yugawara mandarins and Ashigara tea. Misaki fishing port, at the southern tip of the Miura Peninsula, is a base for the longline tuna fishery.

Other Industries

The gross output of the secondary sector of industry is the second largest of all the prefectures after Aichi. The main products are trucks, automobile parts, and gasoline. Oil refining, steel manufacturing, automobile part production, and shipbuilding are thriving at the Keihin Industrial Zone on Tokyo Bay. As for the automobile industry, factories produce trucks in Fujisawa, cars in Yokosuka city, bulldozers in Sagamihara, and tires in Hiratsuka. Information and communication equipment is also produced in Yokohama, Yokosuka, Hadano, Fujisawa, Odawara, and Minamiashigara. In the food processing industry, the main products are wine, produced in Fujisawa, beer, in Minamiashigara and Kawasaki, and dairy products, in Yokohama. The Sagamihara campus of the Japan Aerospace Exploration Agency has been established in the city of Sagamihara, adjacent to Machida and Hachiôji in Tokyo.

15. Niigata

Niigata is located in the northeast of the Chûbu region

(the Hokuriku region), facing the Sea of Japan (Figure 15).

Nature

The highest peak is Mt. Korenge (2,766 m) in the Hida mountain range at the boundary with Nagano Prefecture. Between Mt. Korenge and Mt. Myôkô, Fossa Magna Itoigawa-Shizuoka tectonic line runs north to south along the Hime River. Mt. Myôkô is a stratovolcano that is called "Echigo Fuji." It was specified as Myôkô Togakushi Renzan National Park, which was separated from Jôshin-etsu Kôgen National Park in 2015. In the westernmost point of the prefecture, there is a precipice named Oyashirazu, which means "so arduous that no passersby could look back at their children." Near Oyashirazu, there are traditional fishing communities, whose buildings consist of hangar houses for fishing boats *(funa-ya)* that are used on the narrow flatlands.

The Echigo mountain range is a boundary between Fukushima and Gunma prefectures. Okutadami Dam, which was built for power generation, was completed in 1960. The artificial Lake Okutadami, created as part of the dam works, has become a tourist site for fishing and boat tours. The range and lake were designated as Echigo Sanzan Tadami Quasi-National Park in the 1970s. Parallel to the range are the Muikamachi Basin, the Uonuma Hills, the Tôkamachi Basin, and the Higashikubiki Hills. The Shinano River is the longest river in the country. It enters the Tôkamachi Basin from Nagano Prefecture and flows into the Sea of Japan from the Echigo Plain. The Sekiya Bunsui and Ôkôzu Bunsui drainage canals were constructed on the plain to deal with river flooding.

The climate is categorized as a Sea of Japan-central Japan one. The whole area has been designated as a heavy

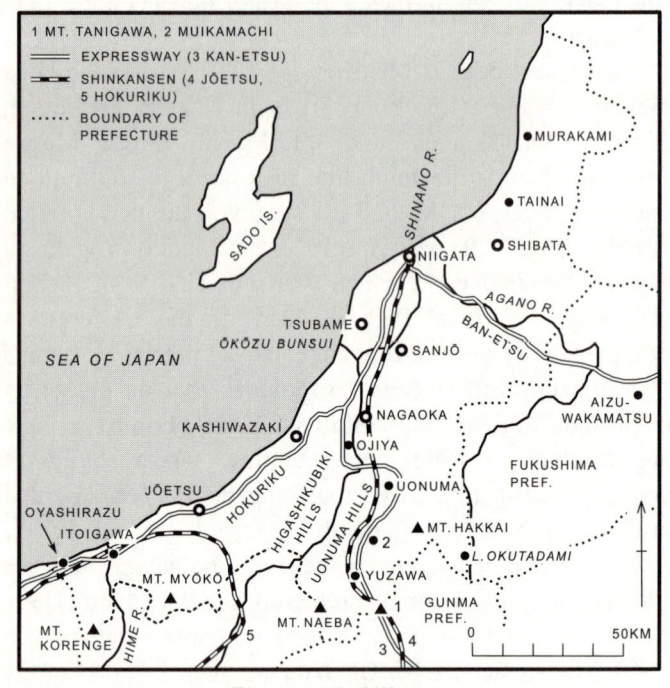

Figure 15 Niigata

snowfall zone. Naeba, Kagura, and Kandatsu are large-scale ski resorts at the Mikuni mountain range that forms the southern section of the Echigo mountain range. Snow-melting pipes, which use running water, are installed under roads at this low latitude. The diurnal temperature of the plains rises in summer as a result of the foehn winds from the Echigo mountain range. Among the natural disasters, earthquakes and serious floods, namely, the 1964 Niigata earthquake, the 2004 Niigata Chûetsu earthquake, the 2007 Niigata Chûetsuoki earthquake, the Niigata torrential downpour in 1998, and the Niigata and Fukushima torren-

82

tial downpours in 2004 and 2011, have severely affected some areas.

History and Culture

Echigo Province in the era of the Ritsuryô code became Niigata and Kashiwazaki prefectures, and they were merged in the early Meiji period. The name is derived from the prefectural capital, whose meaning is derived from "a new tidal flat" *(nii-gata)*, formed at the mouths of the Shinano and the Agano rivers. Immediately after the great prefectural merger in the Meiji period, Niigata was the most populous of all the prefectures. The port of Niigata was established by the Nagaoka domain. It became a jurisdiction of the Tokugawa Shogunate at the end of the Edo period. Shortly afterward, it was designated as one of the five ports designated by the Treaty of Amity and Commerce signed between the United States and Japan. The city of Jôetsu is the birthplace of modern skiing in the country, as Theodore Edler Von Lerch, a major in the Austro-Hungarian army, gave skiing instruction for the 13th Division of the Imperial Army in 1910. Takada district in Jôetsu is famous for its well-preserved *gangi*, which are traditional arcades. The arcades extend from the beams of storehouses, and pedestrians can freely walk along the passages even though they are privately owned.

On Sado Island, the Sado Gold Mine was operated from the early Edo period to the late 1980s. The total gold output amounted to 83 tons, the second largest amount produced in the country after the Hishikari Gold Mine in Kagoshima Prefecture. Shukunegi district on the island was a port for cargo ships in the Edo period. It has been designated as one of the Preservation Districts for Groups of Traditional Buildings. Other distinctive cultural aspects of the island include the cultivation of the *Okesa-gaki* fruit (a persimmon variety), the artificial breeding of crested ibis *(Nipponia nippon)*, and the use of washtub-boats in Ogi port. In the former town of Yamakoshi (now the city of Nagaoka) and the city of Ojiya, bull fighting has been conducted out since the Edo period. It has been designated as an Important Intangible Folk Cultural Property. In those municipalities, the inland aquaculture of varicolored carp is also thriving.

Population and Traffic

The population of Niigata Prefecture is 2,374,000. The main cities are Niigata (812,000), Nagaoka (283,000), Jôetsu (204,000), Sanjô (102,000), Shibata (101,000), Kashiwazaki (91,000), and Tsubame (82,000). The area is divided into the Jôetsu region in the east, including Jôetsu; the Chûetsu region in the center, including Nagaoka; the Kaetsu region in the east, including Niigata; and Sado Island. In terms of road infrastructure, the Jôetsu Shinkansen and the Kan-etsu expressways, which opened in the 1980s, and the Hokuriku and the Ban-etsu expressways, which opened in the 1990s, lead to Niigata. The Kan-etsu Expressway, extending from the Tokyo metropolitan area, goes through Mt. Tanigawa via the Kan-etsu tunnel. At the nearby Yuzawa interchange to the north of the Kan-etsu tunnel, there are condominiums of ski resorts that rise higher than the prefectural government office.

Primary Sector of Industry

The main agricultural commodities in terms of gross production are rice, vegetables, and eggs. There rice cultivation area is 108,000 ha, making it the second-largest area for rice of all the prefectures, after Hokkaidô. The rice is known for its high quality in terms of taste and fragrance.

In particular, Uonuma *Koshihikari* has been rated the highest in the annual tasting rankings of rice. It is a kind of non-glutinous rice cultivated at the foot of Uonuma (Echigo) Three Mountains, made up of Mt. Hakkai, Mt. Echigo Komagatake, and Mt. Nakanodake. The areas devoted to aubergines, green soybeans, lilies, and tulips are the largest of all the prefectures. Aubergines and Le Lectier (pears) are cultivated mainly in the Niigata Sand Dunes at the lower reaches of the Shinano. Green soybeans are cultivated as substitution crops for paddy rice. The city of Murakami in the north has specialized products, for instance, Murakami tea (the northern limit of commercial tea production in the country), the red turnips yielded by slash-and-burn cultivation, and edible mountain plants, such as buds of bracken fern *(warabi)* and Ostrich fern *(kogomi)*.

Other Industries

The main industrial products in terms of gross production are rice crackers, paper printing, and chemical products. In terms of number of establishments, the main categories are metal products and Japanese-style raw cakes. The production of rice crackers such as *senbei* and *arare* is the largest of all the prefectures. The industry evolved in rice-producing regions such as the former town of Kameda (now Kônan Ward in Niigata city), Kita Ward in Niigata, and Nagaoka city. Cutlery, copperware and Buddhist altar production prospered in the Chûetsu region, where Tsubame and Sanjô cities grew as global tableware producing centers. The origin of the metal product manufacturing was the nail production at farms as a winter activity in the Edo period. The oil and natural gas output is the largest of all the prefectures. The main oil and gas fields are located at Minami-nagaoka in Nagaoka, Iwafune (an offshore platform) in Tainai, Higashi-niigata in Niigata, and Katagai in Ojiya. The domestic natural gas is blended with the LNG imported to the Port of Naoetsu in Jôetsu city, and sent to part of the Kantô and the Chûbu regions by pipelines to be consumed as city gas.

16. Toyama

Toyama is located in the north of the Chûbu region (the Hokuriku region), facing the Sea of Japan (Figure 16).

Nature

The highest peak is Mt. Tateyama (Ônanjiyama: 3,015 m) in the Tateyama Mountains to the east. The Ushiro-tateyama Mountains are located to the east of the mountains at the boundary with Nagano Prefecture. Both mountains are found in the Hida mountain range that is regarded as the Northern Alps. The Kurobe gorge, running north and south between the mountains, is a typical V-shaped valley. Yamasaki Kar near the crest of Mt. Tateyama was discovered by a geographer, Naomasa Yamasaki, in the 1900s. Around the peak of Mt. Yakushidake, on the south of the mountain, kars have been designated as natural monuments. Minuscule mountain glaciers remain on the adjoining Mts. Tateyama and Tsurugi.

The rivers of Kurobe, Jôganji, Jinzû, Shôgawa, and Oyabe are categorized as Class A rivers. Because the riverbed gradients are steep, those rivers flow into Toyama Bay a short distance away, making alluvial fans. Power plants have been constructed on the upper reaches of the rivers. Among them, Kurobe Dam, completed in 1963, is

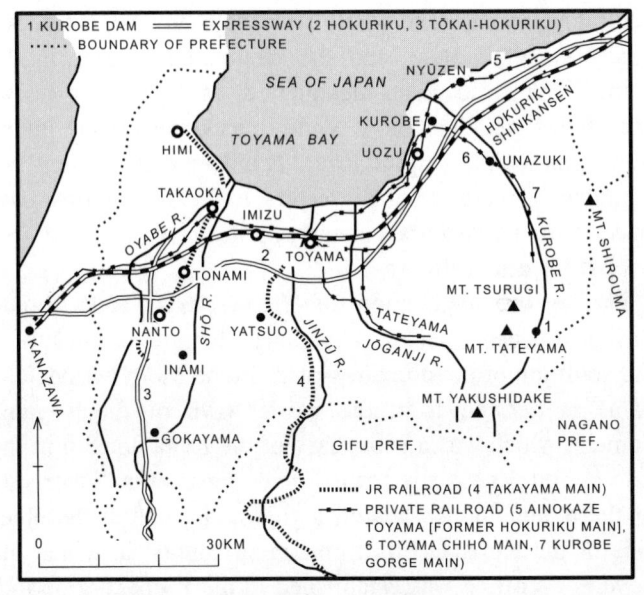

Figure 16 Toyama

the highest (186 m) in the country. The dam and the gorge became popular tourist sites after the Kurobe Gorge Main Line and the Tateyama Kurobe Alpine Route opened in 1971. The railroad extends from the Unazuki hot spring on the lower reaches of the river, and the road extends from the city of Ômachi in Nagano Prefecture and also from the town of Tateyama in Toyama Prefecture. In the basin of the Jinzû River, *itai-itai* disease (mass cadmium poison) continued until the early 1970s as a result of cadmium exuding from the Kamioka Mine in Gifu Prefecture.

The Toyama Bay terrain falls into a deep sea at a 300 to 1,000 m depth. The offshore area from Uozu city to the town of Nyûzen is known for its submerged forest and sea mirages. The climate is categorized as a Sea of Japan-central Japan one. The whole area has been designated as a heavy snowfall zone, and the mountainous areas in the south have also been designated as a special heavy snowfall zone. The Snow Valley (Yuki no Ôtani) in the Tateyama Kurobe Alpine Route is a deep drift of snow accumulating more than 10 meters high. Tour buses pass through the snow murals in early spring.

History and Culture

During the application of the Ritsuryô code, Etchû Province became part of Toyama Prefecture as a result of the abolition of the domain system in the Meiji period. The name is derived from the castle town of the Toyama domain, which was a subsidiary of the Kaga domain in the Edo period. The castle town's name means the "other side of the mountain" *(to-yama)*, as it was located at the other side of the Kureha Hills from Imizu county, in which the governor's office was established in the Kamakura period. Shin Buddhism flourished in the domain. In the Edo period, the believers emigrated to the north of the Kantô region, where the temples of the sect were set up. After the Meiji period, the prefectural residents moved to Hokkaidô to reclaim land, fish, and peddle goods. Toyama peddlers sold patent medicines by offering medicine chests to homes all over the county.

On the upper reaches of the Shôgawa lies the Gokayama community, which is known for its traditional *gasshô-zukuri* (a large house with a steep thatched roof). As it was located in a remote area, gunpowder was covertly produced by the Kaga domain in the Sengoku period. The floor spaces of the houses in the prefecture are generally large, and the proportion of owned houses is also the highest of all the prefectures. In the former town of Inami (now the city of Nanto), the woodcarving industry evolved as a result of the demand for transoms in the houses. In the former town of Yatsuo (now the city of Toyama), the festival of *"Owara kaze no bon"* began in the Edo period. It became famous in the 1980s for a popular song and a novel allusion to the festival. In terms of food culture, there are *masu-zushi* and ornamented *kamaboko*. The former is a kind of sushi made with trout and vinegared rice, with bamboo grass leaves, and pressed in a circular box *(wappa)*. It is sold as train box-lunches at Toyama Station on the Hokuriku Main Line. The latter is the steamed fish paste that takes the shape of a big sea bream. It is frequently given as a present for the guests at a wedding reception. The fish paste rolled in kelp is also a local food. As Toyama was a kelp trading-center, per capita consumption of kelp is the highest here than of all the prefectures.

Population and Traffic

The population of the prefecture is 1,093,000. The main cities are Toyama (422,000), Takaoka (176,000), Imizu (94,000), Nanto (55,000), Himi (52,000), Tonami (49,000), and Uozu (45,000). From the Kureha Hills, the area is divided into the Gotô region in the east and the Gosei region in the west. It has just 15 municipalities, the smallest number of all the prefectures. The city of Toyama area increased six-fold after the great merger of municipalities in the Heisei period. Its area accounts for 29 percent of the prefecture; meanwhile, the neighboring village of Hunahashi is the smallest municipality in the country. As for the road infrastructure, National Route 8, the Hokuriku Main Line, and the Hokuriku Shinkansen cross east to west on the Toyama Plain. The Takayama Main Line and the Toyama Chihô Railway run north to south on the plain. The former connects Toyama and Gifu cities via the city of Takayama, and the latter leads to Unazuki hot spring from Toyama. The Jôhana Line, running north to south on the Tonami Plain, connects the city of Takaoka and the former town of Jôhana (now the city of Nanto).

Primary Sector of Industry

The main agricultural commodity in terms of gross production is rice. Endowed with abundant meltwater, the plains and alluvial fans are given over to paddy rice cultivation. The Tonami Plain has been described by textbooks as a typical landscape of a dispersed rural settlement among paddy fields. It is an alluvial fan created by the Oyabe and the Shôgawa rivers, and the farm houses have high hedges that are used as windbreaks. Tulip bulb cultivation began as a sideline of rice production. The bulbs were exported to the United States in the 1950s and the 1960s. Regarding the fishing industry, yellowtail *(buri)* and firefly squid *(hotaru-ika)* are caught by fixed netting in the Toyama Bay, where the warm Tsushima Current meets the deep cold seawater. Firefly squid glimmer near the surface from Uozu fishing port to the mouth of the Jôganji River. Instead of salmon, a yellowtail is used as a year-end gift in Toyama and Ishikawa prefectures.

Other Industries

The main industrial products in terms of gross production are aluminum sashes, aluminum extrusions, and medicines. Aluminum refining industries were developed based on hydroelectric power, although aluminum ingots have been imported after an energy crisis in the 1970s. In the city of Kurobe, YKK Corporation (former Yoshida Kôgyô

Kabushikigaisha) has its main factory, holding the world's largest share of zippers. Other products being made include medicines produced in Toyama and buses produced by Mitsubishi Fuso Bus Manufacturing Co. in the former town of Fuchû (now Toyama). Baseball bats are produced in the former town of Fukumitsu (now Toyama). They are made not only from imported ash but also from Japanese ash and Manchurian ash brought from Hokkaidô. Regarding traditional crafts, cauldrons were casted in Takaoka, and shipped to Hokkaidô to boil herring.

17. Ishikawa

Ishikawa is located in the north of the Chûbu region (the Hokuriku region). It includes the Noto Peninsula (Figure 17).

Nature

The highest peak is Mt. Hakusan (2,702 m) in the Ryôhaku Mountains that cross Ishikawa, Toyama, Nagano, and Fukui prefectures. This is a stratovolcano, which erupted in 1659. It was designated as Hakusan National Park, and four ski resorts were constructed at the foot of it. The site around a mountain hut, Hakusan *murodô*, is the forest line, at an altitude of 2,450 m, beyond which creeping pines grow. The mountaintop is a sacred place for Hakusan Shrines that are distributed throughout the Chûbu region.

The Kanazawa Plain is an alluvial plain extending north to south, and is occupied by monocultural paddy rice cultivation areas. The Tedori River, which flows through the center of the plain, has rapids, and is designated as a Class A river. It used to be called the Ishikawa (stone river)

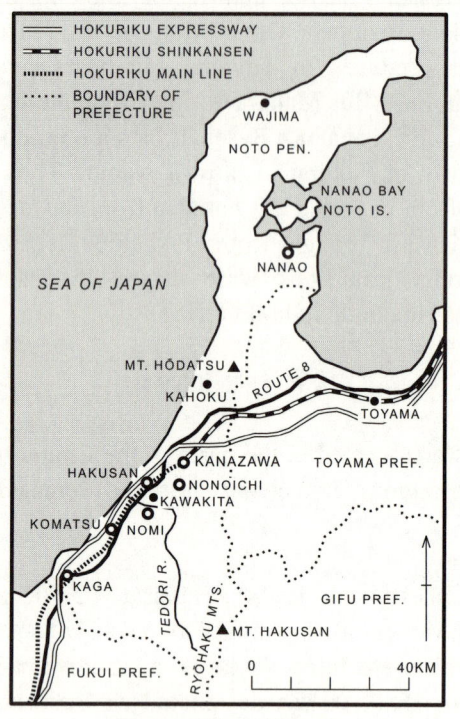

Figure 17 Ishikawa

because of its stony alluvial fans. In the city of Komatsu, a textile industry evolved using the underground water at the end of the alluvial fans. The Sai (Otoko-gawa) and the Asano (Onna-gawa) are Class B rivers *(nikyû-kasen)* that gently run through built-up areas in the city of Kanazawa.

The climate is categorized as a Sea of Japan-central Japan one. The whole area has been designated as a heavy snowfall zone, and mountainous areas have also been designated as a special heavy snowfall zone. The winter monsoon accumulates moisture as it crosses the warm

Tsushima Current, and brings snow clouds by adiabatic expansion when it climbs the Ryôhaku Mountains. The frequency of thunder reaches 42 days a year in Kanazawa, which is the largest of all the prefectural capitals. The thunder in winter is called "yellowtail riser" *(buri-okoshi)* in Ishikawa and Toyama prefectures since it concurs with the high season for fishing. Along the coast of the Noto Peninsula, whitecaps washing up on rocks by the winter monsoon bring about bubbles called the "flowers of the waves" *(nami no hana)*.

History and Culture

Kaga and Noto provinces during the era of the Ritsuryô code became the main tract of the Ishikawa Prefecture in the Meiji period. Shin Buddhism spread and the priests rose in rebellions *(ikkô-ikki)* during the Muromachi period. The Kaga domain, ruled by the Maeda clan, reigned over Kaga, Noto, and Etchû provinces in the early Edo period. Being denominated "Kaga *hyakuman-goku*" (Kaga one-million *koku*: 1 *koku* equals 150 kilograms of rice), it was the largest domain in the country aside from the hereditary domains of Tokugawa Shogunate. The domain's Kanazawa Castle was built on the Kodatsuno Plateau between the Sai and Asano rivers. The domain's garden at the outer ring of the castle is Kenrokuen, whose Kotoji lantern covered with snow is an iconic image. The Kaga-*yashiki*, the largest domain mansion in Edo, was changed into the University of Tokyo in the Meiji period.

With respect to the traditional crafts of the Kaga domain, Kutani ware, Kaga silk dyeing, Buddhist altars, and gold leaves are produced. Kanazawa city still produces the largest amount of gold leaf in the country. In the Noto Peninsula, Wajima lacquerware was established in the Edo period based on techniques of gold inlay *(chin-kin)* and gold lacquer *(maki-e)*. The lacquerware was sold throughout the country via cargo ships and peddlers. Traditional landscapes remain in rural areas in the peninsula, such as rice terraces (Shiroyone Senmaida), while magaki hedges made by Simon bitter bamboos *(me-dake)* to protect from the winter monsoon can be seen.

Population and Traffic

The population of Ishikawa is 1,170,000. The main cities are Kanazawa (462,000), Hakusan (110,000), Komatsu (108,000), Kaga (72,000), Nanao (58,000), Nonoichi (52,000), and Nomi (49,000). The area stretching north to south is divided into the Kaga region, covering Kanazawa city to the south of Mt. Hôdatsu, and the Noto region, including the city of Nanao, to the north of the mountain. In terms of road infrastructure, National Route 8, the Hokuriku Main Line (opened in the 1910s), and the Hokuriku Expressway (opened in the 1980s) run along the old Hokuriku Road. In relation to air transport facilities, Komatsu Airport is found in the city of Komatsu and Noto Airport in the city of Wajima. The former is the main airport shared with Komatsu Air Base.

Narrow streets of crank courses *(kagi-no-te)* and T-shaped junctions *(teiji-ro)* thread through the castle town of Kanzawa. Those streets and old blocks have remained since the city was spared the wartime air raids. Although they were considered as obstacles to traffic flow, they are urban tourism attractions. For instance, Nagamachi district is an area where samurai residents lived surrounded by earthen walls. Kôrinbô district, on the Hokuriku Road, was developed as the largest downtown area in the Hokuriku region.

Primary Sector of Industry

The main agricultural commodity in terms of gross production is rice. It constitutes 70 percent of the total agricultural production. The main seed variety is *Koshihikari*, a kind of non-glutinous paddy rice bred in Fukui Prefecture. Other crops include local vegetables such as *kinji-sô* (*Gynura* spp.) and Kaga *futo-kyûri* (bold cucumbers). The city of Komatsu is the northernmost limit of rush *(igusa)* cultivation in the country. In the forestry, *ate (Thujopsis dolabrata)* is grown in the Noto region and sold under the brand of Noto Hiba. In the fishing industry, the main catch is yellowtail. The yellowtails caught at small fishing ports spread around the Noto Peninsula are auctioned under the brand of Noto Natural Winter Yellowtail. Fish are also the major items in the open-air market of Wajima.

Other Industries

The main industrial products in terms of gross production are shovel excavators, construction machinery, and liquid crystal panels. In terms of number of establishments, the main category is parts for construction machinery. Komatsu is known as a producer of construction machinery, such as hydraulic excavators and bulldozers. The company was founded as an ironworks that performed repairs of machinery at the Yûsenji Copper Mine in Komatsu city. It grew and formed itself as a company town in the city by integrating subcontracting factories. In electronic device production, factories produce image scanners in the city of Kahoku, communication equipment in Hakusan, semiconductors in Nomi, and displays in the town of Kawakita. As for the tourism industry, the Kagaya inn has grown in popularity for foreign tourists. It is located at Wakura hot spring in Nanao city and is a twenty-story modern inn.

18. Fukui

Located in the northwest of the Chûbu region (the Hokuriku region), Fukui faces the Sea of Japan and Wakasa Bay (Figure 18).

Nature

The area is separated from Ishikawa and Gifu prefectures by the Ryôhaku Mountains in the east, and from Shiga and Kyôto prefectures by the Nosaka Mountains in the south. The prefecture's highest peak is Ninomine (1,962 m) in the Ryôhaku Mountains, and the highest spot (2,095 m) is situated on the south slope of Mt. San-nomine, whose the peak, at 2,128 m, is in Ishikawa Prefecture. In the Nosaka Mountains there are a number of old roads, for instance, the Shiotsu Road, connecting Shiotsu (now the city of Nagahama) and Tsuruga, the Nishiômi Road (an off-shoot of the Hokkoku Road), connecting Ôtsu and Tsuruga, and the Wakasa Road, connecting Kyôto and Obama. The Kuzuryû is a Class A river that starts at the Aburasaka Pass in the Ryôhaku Mountains, runs through the Ôno Basin, meets the Hino River in the north of the urban areas of the city of Fukui, and flows into the Sea of Japan from the Echizen (Fukui) Plain. In the Meiji period, power plants were built along the Asuwa River, a tributary of the Kuzuryû, and textile industries of *habutae* (plain weaves of silk) and rayon were developed in the city of Fukui, using the water and power supply.

The Echizen Plain was created by the Kuzuryû, Asuwa, and Hino rivers. As the plain is flat and fertile, paddy rice has been cultivated since ancient times (the Kofun period),

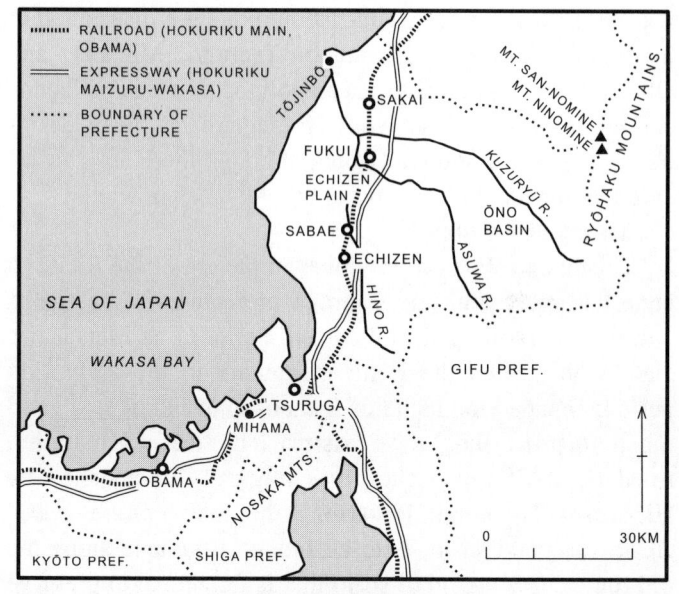

Figure 18 Fukui

even though it has often suffered from floods. The number of paddy fields was increased by river engineering projects in the Meiji period, and also by irrigation works in the Shôwa period. At the mouth of the Kuzuryû is Fukui fishing port (formerly Mikuni port), which sees the largest catches of snow club (Echizen-*gani*). Horticultural crops such as shallots and watermelons are cultivated on the Sanrihama coastal dunes. Tôjinbô cliff is located on the Echizen Coast to the north of the river mouth. The sea cliff, made of basaltic columnar joints, has been designated as a national monument.

A ria coastline extends along Wakasa Bay. The old Wakasa Road was also regarded as a mackerel road (*saba-*

97

kaidô) for merchants carrying marine products including mackerel. Beach resorts and fishing ports are distributed in inlets of Wakasa Bay, namely Tsuruga, Mihama, and Obama bays. The climate is categorized as a Sea of Japan-central Japan one. The whole prefecture has been designated as a heavy snowfall zone, although there are considerable numbers of rainy days at coastal areas in winter.

History and Culture

Echizen and Wakasa provinces in the era of the Ritsuryô code became Fukui and Tsuruga prefectures respectively, and they were merged in the Meiji period. The Matsudaira clan, which ruled the Echizen domain in the early Edo period, changed the name of Kitanoshô to Fukui as a good omen (*fuku-i* meant "luck exists"). The former Kitanoshô, ruled by the Shibata clan, was tragically demolished by Hideyoshi Toyotomi. Regarding the food culture, *saba-zushi* (mackerel sushi) is to be found in the area along the old routes. It is a kind of sushi that is fermented to preserve the fish. Echizen soba is buckwheat noodles with grated radish that is harvested in autumn.

Population and Traffic

The population of Fukui Prefecture is 806,000. The main cities are Fukui (267,000), Sakai (92,000), Echizen (86,000), Tsuruga (68,000), and Sabae (67,000). As for the road infrastructure, National Route 8, the Hokuriku Main Line, and the Hokuriku Expressway extend along the Hokuriku Road in the Echizen region in the northeast. The Obama Line and the Maizuru-Wakasa Expressway run along coastal areas in Wakasa region in the southwest. After the 1948 Fukui earthquake, more than 3,700 people were dead or missing in the city of Fukui. The Kuzuryû River also brought flood damage in the basin, including the urban center of Fukui, for instance, the torrential downpour in 1948, the Isewan Typhoon (Typhoon Vera) in 1959, the Second Muroto Typhoon (Super Typhoon Nancy) in 1961, and the Okuetsu downpour in 1965.

Primary Sector of Industry

The main agricultural commodity in terms of gross production is rice, which accounts for 65 percent of the region's total agricultural production. Other principal crops are taros, scallions, radishes, and six-row barley. Monocultural paddy rice-cultivation areas are to be found on the Echizen Plain. They account for about 50 percent of the prefectural paddy fields. After the implementation of the policy of reducing rice production in the 1970s, the cultivation areas devoted to six-row barley and buckwheat increased on the plain. As it is located in a heavy snowfall zone, double cropping of rice and barley was impossible, so farmers cultivated buckwheat after barley. A representative seed variety of non-glutinous rice is *Koshihikarari*, which was cross-bred in the Agricultural Experiment Station of Fukui Prefecture in the 1940s. It was designated as a recommended variety in Niigata Prefecture in the 1950s. The name *Koshihikarari* means the light of Koshi region (the provinces of Echigo, Etchû, Noto, and Echizen).

Other Industries

The main industrial products in terms of number of establishments are eyeglass frames and eyeglass parts. More than 90 percent of the country's eyeglass frame production occurs in the city of Sabae. It was begun by craftsmen who were invited from Ôsaka and Tokyo, and spread to nearby farmers as a winter occupation. It developed through special procurements in the two world wars, and saw increasing demand in the high economic growth period. Fukui Coastal Industrial Zone was reclaimed from sandbars at the mouth of the Kuzuryû in the 1970s. A Hokuriku Electric Power Company thermal power plant, an oil storage station, and chemical factories were constructed at the industrial zone. Wakasa Bay was not suitable for agricultural and industrial production because of its narrow flatlands. Nuclear power plants were developed along the bay by Kansai Electric Power Co. and by Japan Atomic Power Co. to supply power to the Ôsaka metropolitan area. The first electricity generated by a nuclear plant in the bay area was sent to the Ôsaka Expo in 1970. All of the nuclear power plants have ceased operations since the 2011 Tôhoku earthquake. Among the traditional crafts made in the area, Echizen-*hôsho* is a kind of superior Japanese paper made from *kôzo* (*Broussonetia kazinoki* × *B. papyrifera*, a kind of paper mulberry), and it is used for Japanese paintings.

19. Yamanashi

Yamanashi is an inland prefecture in the east of the Chûbu region (Figure 19). Yamanashi and Nagano prefectures are regarded as Kôshin region.

Nature

The highest peak is Mt. Fuji at the boundary with Shizuoka Prefecture. It is a stratovolcano, whose volcanic ash reached as far as Edo after the eruption in 1707 during the Hôei reign (it occurred quite recently in the geological time scale). There are four trails to the mountain top, namely, Yoshida-*guchi* in Yamanashi Prefecture, and Fujinomiya-*guchi*, Subashiri-*guchi*, and Gotemba-*guchi* in

Shizuoka Prefecture. A total of 235,000 climbers climbed to the top in 2013, and 60 percent of them took the Yoshida-*guchi* trail. On the trail, climbers can access the fifth station at an altitude of 2,300 m by car using the Fuji Subaru Line. Furthermore, there are more than 10 mountain huts along the trail, and is the mountain has been brought closer to the Tokyo metropolitan area through the Chûô Expressway. The Fuji Five Lakes area and the Aoki-gahara Sea of Trees are located at the north foot of Mt. Fuji. The lakes are Motosu, Shôji, Sai, Kawaguchi, and Yamanaka. They were formed by the eruption of Mt. Fuji and have since been dammed. The lakes and the vicinity are known as a resort for the smelt fishing, pleasure craft

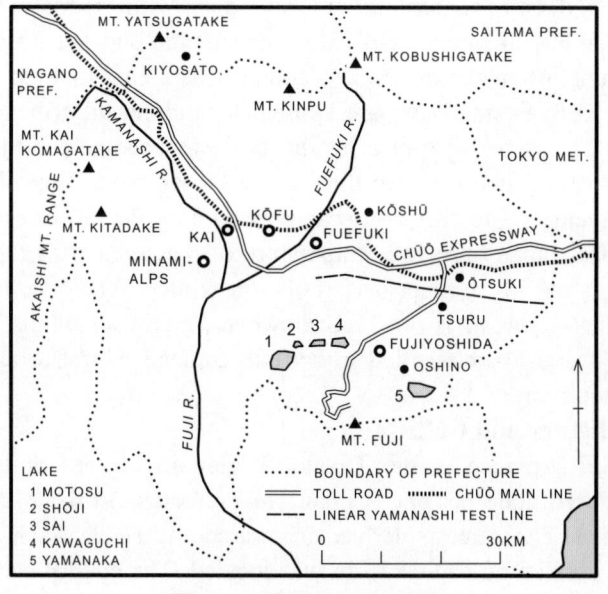

Figure 19 Yamanashi

101

and canoes, hot spring resorts, and villas.

The Akaishi mountain range runs north to south in the west. It includes Mt. Kitadake (3,193 m), the second highest mountain in the country, in the city of Minami-Alps. Mt. Yatsugatake is located at the boundary with Nagano Prefecture in the northwest. The Kiyosato Highland is located at the south foot of the mountain. As being addressed as the "Kiyosato Boom," it became famous for a summer resort in the 1980s. Seisenryô was a Christian training facility founded in 1930 by Paul Rusch, an Anglican Church missionary.

The Kamanashi River flows from the Akaishi mountain range, and runs north to south in the west. Along the river, embankments called Shingen-*zutsumi* were constructed in the sixteenth century in order to deal with floods. The River Fuefuki runs from Mt. Kobushigatake at the Kantô Mountains in the north, and courses from east to west in the Kôfu Basin. There are alluvial fans along the tributaries. The two rivers meet at the basin to become the Fuji River, and it flows into the Pacific Ocean from Shizuoka Prefecture. The climate is categorized as a Pacific Ocean-central Japan one. The temperature of the basin rises considerably in summer and falls in winter. The average annual snowfall is not high; however, heavy snowfalls in 1998 and 2014 resulted in serious damage to traffic and agriculture.

History and Culture

Kai Province in the Tôkaidô region in the era of the Ritsuryô code became Yamanashi Prefecture in the Meiji period. The name is derived from a county name in which the prefectural capital Kôfu was located. The county name signifies "the region abundant with *yama-nashi*" (*Pyrus pyrifolia,* the so-called mountain pear). Shingen Takeda was the lord of the Kôfu domain in the Sengoku period, and he enlarged his fiefdom into Shinano Province. In the Edo period, the Kôfu domain was ruled directly by the Tokugawa Shogunate. The old Kôshû Road was considered one of the Edo Five Roads along with Tôkaidô, Nakasendô, Ôshû, and Nikkô. It connected Nihonbashi and Shimosuwa via Naitô-shinjuku, Hachiôji, and Kôfu.

In terms of the local food culture, a specialty is *hôtô,* thick and flat wheat noodles boiled in miso soup with vegetables, including squash. It originated in the rations supplied by the army of the Takeda clan, and squash was a newly imported crop at that time. It spread to rural areas of the Kôfu domain, whose paddy fields where rice was grown were narrow as it was surrounded by mountains. In the village of Iwai (now the district of Katsunuma in Kôshû city), the Dainihon Wine Company was established in 1877 as the first private winery (a governmental winery was opened in Sapporo in 1876) in the country.

Population and Traffic

The population of Yamanashi is 863,000. The main cities are Kôfu (199,000), Kai (74,000), Minami-Alps (73,000), Fuefuki (71,000), and Fujiyoshida (51,000). Regarding the road infrastructure, National Route 20, the Chûô Main Line, and the Chûô Expressway run east to west in parallel with the Kôshû Road. Following the opening of bypasses in the Kôfu Basin, commercial facilities were constructed in suburbs, and in front of Kôfu Station, privately-run stores closed and "shuttered streets" emerged. The Linear Yamanashi Test Line was introduced in the cities of Ôtsuki and Tsuru in the late 1990s. It was subsequently moved from Miyazaki Prefecture since

Yamanashi had the advantage of being able to run tests on slopes and in tunnels, and the possibility remained of developing a business line.

Primary Sector of Industry

The main agricultural commodities in terms of gross production are fruit. The proportions of land planted with grapes and peaches has reached 4,200 ha and 3,500 ha respectively, both of which are the largest of all prefectures. The orchards near the lower reaches of the Kôfu basin are propitious for peach cultivation because of the long daylight hours and adequate warm temperatures in the growing season. Grape cultivation is prominent on the east side of the basin because of the low precipitation levels. A considerable number of grape orchards were changed over to peach orchards after trellises were destroyed by heavy snowfall in the 1990s. From the Meiji period to a while after World War II, mulberries were cultivated on the sloping alluvial fans. Thereafter, fruit cultivation flourished as cash crops based on their accessibility to the Tokyo metropolitan area.

Other Industries

The main industrial products in terms of gross production are numerical control devices and numerical control robots. In terms of number of establishments producing goods, the main categories are precious metal ornaments and wine. Fanuc Corporation accounts for about 50 percent of industrial robot production in the world. The company moved from Hino city in Tokyo to the village of Oshino at the foot of Mt. Fuji in the 1980s to acquire a large site. The traditional crafts of Kôfu Basin include jewelry, seal making, and *inden* (bags of deer skin with printed patterns by lacquerware). Those goods were based on raw materials available in the mountains. For instance, the jewel craftwork originated in the hand polishing of the crystals found in deposits at the foot of Mt. Kinpu. Other industrial products include bottled water, made in factories that use groundwater from Mt. Fuji and the South Alps. Necktie production in Fujiyoshida city is also the largest in the country.

20. Nagano

Nagano is an inland prefecture in the center of the Chûbu region. It is the fourth largest prefecture after Hokkaidô, Iwate, and Fukushima (Figure 20).

Nature

The prefecture is regarded as "the roof of the country" since high mountains of over 2,000 m extend north to south. Those are the Hida mountain range (the North Alps) in the northwest, at the boundary with Toyama and Gifu prefectures, the Kiso mountain range (the Central Alps) in the southwest, and the Akaishi mountain range (the South Alps) in the south, at the boundary with Yamanashi and Shizuoka prefectures. Mt. Hotaka (Okuhotaka: 3,190 m) in the Hida mountain range is the third highest peak in the country. The Kamikôchi highlands are located at an altitude of 1,500 m on the mountain foot (Illustration 7). It is a scenic site that includes Taishô Pond, created by an eruption of Mt. Yakedake in 1915 (Taishô 4), and the Imperial Hotel, which opened in 1933.

The Chikuma River flows from Mt. Kobushigatake, and runs through the basins of Saku, Ueda, and Nagano. The river becomes the Shinano River in Niigata Prefecture. The Azusa River is a tributary of the Chikuma. It emerges from

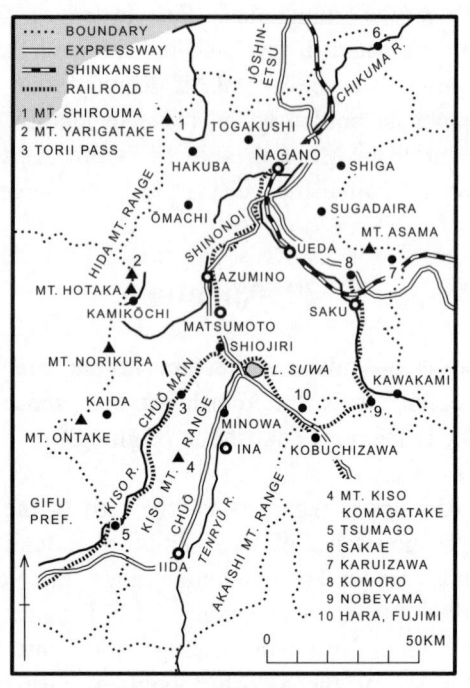

Figure 20 Nagano

Mt. Yarigatake in the Hida mountain range, and becomes the Sai River after meeting with the Narai River in the Matsumoto Basin. Hydroelectric power plants have been constructed along the river, resulting in catches of salmon decreasing in the Meiji period. The Hime River arises from Mt. Shirouma (Shiroumadake) in the Hida mountain range. Its course conforms to the Itoigawa-shizuoka Tectonic Line along the west side of the Fossa Magna.

The Tenryû River originates from the Kamaguchi sluice at Lake Suwa, running from north to south in the Ina Basin, and entering the Enshû Sea. The Kiso River flows

106

from the south of the Hida mountain range, runs into Gifu Prefecture from Kiso Valley, and flows into Ise Bay at the boundary between Aichi and Mie prefectures. The Kiso *hinoki* (Japanese cypress) forest in the basin is regarded as one of three beautiful natural forests, along with the Tsugaru *hiba* and Akita *sugi* (Japanese cedar) forests. Lumber floating flourished in these rivers until dams for power generation were installed in the early twentieth century.

The climate ranges from a Pacific Ocean-central Japan one to a Sea of Japan-central Japan one to an "inland climate" (cold in winter and less rainfall throughout the year). Being surrounded by high mountains, the region's annual precipitation levels are low, for instance, 930 mm in the city of Nagano. The temperature in the highlands of Sugadaira, Karuizawa, Kaida, and Nobeyama fall in winter. Those areas have been classified as a Df climate (humid continental) according to the Köppen climate classification system. The entire prefectural area has been designated as a heavy snowfall zone. In the 1998 Winter Olympics, ski jumping competitions were held in the village of Hakuba and Alpine skiing competitions in the Shiga Highland area.

History and Culture

Shinano Province in the Tôsandô region during the era of the Ritsuryô code, otherwise known as Shinshû, became Nagano Prefecture in the Meiji period. The provincial name is derived from the native tree of *shina-no-ki* (*Tilia japonica*, a kind of linden). The prefectural name is derived from "a long basin," which stands for Zenkôji *daira*, an old name for the Nagano Basin. Arguments over transferring the capital to Matsumoto, or dividing the area into the north and the south were taking place during the Meiji period. Regarding the religious culture of the area, Zenkôji Temple has attracted plentiful worshippers since the Edo period. The temple is known for its saying: "cows lead you to Zenkôji" (alternatively, goslings lead the geese to water). Suwa Taisha in the town of Shimosuwa is the center for the Suwa Shrines that are distributed mainly in the Chûbu region. It is known for the *Onbashira* (honored pillars) festival held every six years.

In terms of food culture, places famed for buckwheat noodles are spread around the prefecture, such as Togakushi, Kaida, and Karasawa. Buckwheat was cultivated in the mountainous areas as it grows well in the cool climate, and its growing period is short, ranging from 60 to 70 days. People began to make buckwheat into noodles on formal days *(hare)* during the Edo period. Buckwheat noodles, red peppers, pickles, the seeds of *nozawa-na* (*Brassica rapa* L. var. *hakabura*, a kind of leaf vegetable), and grilled buns *(oyaki)* filled with *nozawa-na* are sold at souvenir shops in front of temples and shrines. Agar has been produced on the shore of Lake Suwa by virtue of cold temperatures in winter.

Population and Traffic

The population of Nagano Prefecture is 2,152,000. The main cities are Nagano (382,000), Matsumoto (243,000), Ueda (160,000), Iida (105,000), Saku (101,000), Azumino (96,000), and Ina (71,000). The area is divided into the Hokushin region, which comprises the Nagano Basin, the Chûshin region including the Matsumoto Basin and Kiso Valley, the Tôshin region, including the Saku and Ueda basins and the Nobeyama Highland, and the Nanshin region, which includes the Suwa and Ina basins.

Along the old Nakasendô Road, National Route 20 and the Chûô Main Line lead out from Tokyo to Shiojiri. National Route 19 and the Chûô line then go through Kiso Valley. The Torii Pass of National Route 19 (1,197 m: the current New Trii Tunnel) was a divide between the Sea of Japan and the Pacific Ocean. The post towns of Narai near the pass and Tsumago in the southwest have been designated as Preservation Districts for Groups of Traditional Buildings. The old Chikuni Road led to inland Matsumoto from coastal Itoigawa, and the old Sanshû Road led to inland Shiojiri from coastal Okazaki. "Shiojiri" meant a terminal or a junction of salt transportation. There are three Shiojiri in the prefecture, namely, the city of Shiojiri, Shiojiri district in the city of Ueda, and Shiojiri district in the village of Sakae. The Nomugi Pass (1,672 m), whose name relates to bamboo grasses, crosses the south of Mt. Norikura. The yellowtails caught in the Sea of Japan were shipped to Shinano Province through the pass. From the Meiji to the Taishô periods, women workers in Gifu Prefecture walked across the pass for working at silk mills in the Suwa Basin.

The Koumi Line connects Kobuchizawa Station in the city of Hokuto and Komoro Station in the city of Komoro via Kiyosato Station. Nobeyama Station on the line is the highest (1,345 m) one among the JR lines. On the Shinonoi Line, the view looking over the Zenkôji-*daira* from Obasute Station was considered one of the prime three views from train windows by the former Japan National Railways. Matsumoto Electric Railway Co.'s Kamikôchi Line (now Alpico Holdings Co.) connects Matsumoto and Shin-shimashima stations. The former Shimashima Station was a gateway to the highlands of

Norikura and Kamikôchi, but was closed following a landslide caused by a typhoon.

Primary Sector of Industry

The main agricultural commodities in terms of gross production in the region are vegetables, fruit, and rice. The cultivation areas devoted to lettuces and celery are the largest of all the prefectures. The vegetables are cultivated mainly in the high altitude cool-climate regions, including the villages of Kawakami and Hara, and Sugadaira Highland. They are harvested in summer, the pre-harvest season of the plains, and shipped to the metropolitan areas of Tokyo, Nagoya, and Ôsaka. Japanese horseradishes are cultivated at the brooks of the alluvial fans in the Azumino region. The fields are soaked in running water and surrounded by locust trees. The cultivation areas devoted to apples and grapes are the second largest of all the prefectures. They are grown mostly in the basins of Nagano, Matsumoto, and Ina.

Other Industries

The main industrial products in terms of gross production are electronic circuits, communication devices, and automobile parts. A silk industry evolved around Lake Suwa after the Meiji period. Factories were evacuated from the Keihin Industrial Zone during World War II, and a precision machinery industry was developed around the lake after the war. One of the largest companies is Seiko Epson Corporation, whose headquarters is in the city of Suwa. The company's factories extend to the municipalities of Shiojiri, Matsumoto, Azumino, Fujimi, and Minowa.

21. Gifu

Gifu is an inland prefecture to the west of the Chûbu region (Figure 21).

Nature

The highest peak is Mt. Hotaka in the Hida mountain range at the boundary with Nagano Prefecture. The Hida River flows from Mt. Norikura in the mountain range through the Takayama Basin, meeting the Kiso River at the city of Minokamo. The Nagara River flows from Mt. Dainichi in the south of the Ryôhaku Mountains, runs southward over the Nôbi Plain, and meets the Ibi River in Mie Prefecture. The Neo Valley fault, at a tributary of the Ibi in the west, was the epicenter of the 1891 Mino-Owari earthquake, in which more than 7,000 people were killed. Chrysanthemum stones, a basalt with a radial calcite, are mined from the valley. The Kiso's Three Rivers refer to the Kiso, the Nagara, and the Ibi rivers. On the Nôbi Plain in the lower reaches, local communities are enclosed by dikes *(wajû)* that have been developed to avert flood damage. Flood evacuation huts *(mizu-ya)*, paddy boats *(ta-bune)*, and hanging boats under eaves *(age-bune)* are displayed at the Wajû Life Museum in the city of Ôgaki and Kiso Sansen Park Center in Kaizu city.

Regarding the climate, the greater part of the region can be described as an inland one, which is characterized as being hot in summer and cold in winter. The north of the Hida region has a Sea of Japan-central Japan climate. The mountainous area has been designated as a heavy snowfall zone. The village of Shirakawagô, at the basin of the Shôgawa River, is known for having a landscape of *gasshô-zukuri* covered with snow. The village was listed as

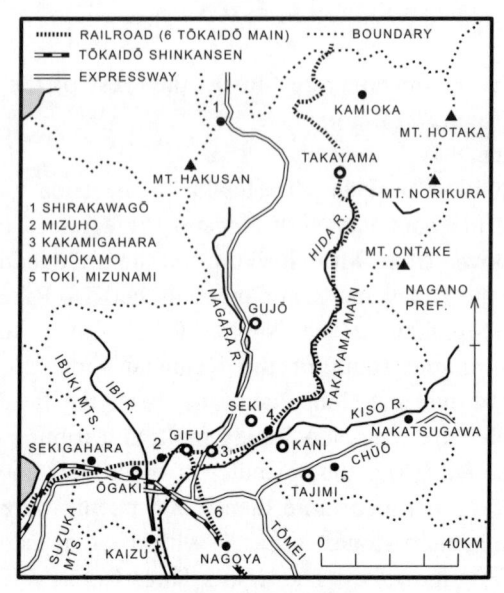

Figure 21   Gifu

a World Heritage Site together with the village of Gokayama in the downstream region of Toyama Prefecture. Even in the Mino region in the south, snow accumulates on a narrow plain between the Ibuki and Suzuka mountains. For instance, the town of Sekigahara, known as a decisive battle site in the Azuchi-Momoyama period, sometimes receives heavy snowfall as it is located on a passage of the winter monsoon (Ibuki-*oroshi*).

History and Culture

During the era of the Ritsuryô code, Mino and Hida provinces became Gifu Prefecture in the Meiji period. When Nobunaga Oda captured Inaba Castle on the top of Mt. Inaba at the end of the Muromachi period, he named the castle town as Gifu, referring to an ancient Chinese legend. The mountain was named Mt. Kinkazan in the Meiji period after the gold colored flowers of *tsubura-jii* (Japanese Chinquapin: *Castanopsis cuspidata*), a kind of native broadleaf evergreen tree.

In terms of the region's food culture, *hôba-yaki (hôba-miso)* is known as a local dish in the city of Takayama. Edible wild plants are roasted with *miso* on a leaf of *hô-no-ki* (Japanese bigleaf magnolia) with a portable Hida stove on the table. Gujô-*odori* is a big dance festival held in the Hachiman-*chô* district of Gujô city. It is held for 32 nights, before and after the *bon* of the lunar calendar (from the middle of July to the beginning of September). In the Nagara River, cormorant fishing *(ukai)* is carried out as a tourist activity. The Japanese cormorants that catch sweet-fish are migratory birds caught on a coastal cliff in the former town of Jûô (now the city of Hitachi) in Ibaraki.

Population and Traffic

The population of Gifu Prefecture is 2,081,000. The main cities are Gifu (413,000), Ôgaki (161,000), Kakamigahara (146,000), Tajimi (113,000), Kani (97,000), Takayama (93,000), and Seki (91,000). Takayama in the Hida region is the largest city in the country. The city's area is 2,178 km^2, identical to Tokyo (2,191 km^2). The village of Yamaguchi in the Kiso county of Nagano Prefecture was incorporated into the city of Nakatsugawa in the Mino region. It was the only cross-prefectural incorporation that took place as a result of the great merger of municipalities in the Heisei period. The center of population in Japan is moving east. According to population census data, it was located in the village of Minami (now Gujô city) in 1980 and 1990, in Mugi town in 2000 (now Seki city), and in Seki city in 2010.

National Route 19 and the Chûô Expressway run in a southeasterly direction along the old Nakasendô Road. In Nakatsugawa city, the old post town of Magome on the road has been restored (e.g., electric poles were removed). The Tôkaidô and the Takayama main lines of JR Central (Central Japan Railway Company), and the Nagoya Main and the Kakamigahara lines of Nagoya Railroad Co. lead to Gifu Station in the prefectural capital. The northern exit of the station was developed as a wholesale district for textiles, where small shops dealing in secondhand clothes and military uniforms formed after World War II.

Primary Sector of Industry

The main agricultural commodities in terms of gross production are vegetables (mainly tomatoes, spinach, and strawberries), rice, and eggs. In the area of vegetable production, summer-autumn harvested tomatoes are cultivated in the highlands of the Hida region, and winter-spring harvested tomatoes are cultivated on the plains in the Mino region. These are then shipped largely to the Nagoya metropolitan area. The main rice variety is *Hatsushimo*, which means "the first frost" as it is a late-ripening variety harvested in October. It has been cultivated in the prefecture only since the 1950s. Farmers tend to plant the late-ripening variety rather than *Koshihikari*, the main variety in the Hokuriku region, since *Koshihikari* ripens earlier by the summer heat, meaning the flavor is dismissed. Persimmons and eggs are produced on the Nôbi Plain, which continues into Aichi Prefecture. The main variety of non-astringent persimmons is *Fuyu*, which was bred in the town of Sunami (now Mizuho city). In forestry, Japanese cypresses have been grown in the southeast since the Edo period. The wood is sold under the Tônô *hinoki* brand.

Other Industries

The main industrial products in terms of gross production are medicines, aircraft parts, and trucks. The most popular activity in relation to the number of establishments is ceramics. The Chûkyô Industrial Zone in the Nôbi Plain extends to the Aichi, Gifu, and Mie prefectures. In the city of Kakamigahara, on the plain, Kawasaki Heavy Industries and Mitsubishi Heavy Industries produce aircraft, and Gifu Auto Body Co. (the Toyota auto body group) assembles trucks. Mino ware is the pottery made in the cities of Toki, Tajimi, and Mizunami. Their production accounts for about half of the ceramics fired in the country. The factories manufacturing cutlery and edged tools are concentrated in the city of Seki. Among them, Kai Corporation, founded in the Meiji period, has developed as a multinational company for razor products. In this area, sword production by swordsmiths thrived from the Kamakura period to the Sengoku period.

22. Shizuoka

Shizuoka, located in the southeast of the Chûbu region, faces the Enshû Sea and Suruga Bay (Figure 22).

Nature

The highest peak is Mt. Fuji, on the boundary with Yamanashi Prefecture. There are three trails to the mountain top in the prefecture. The most popular one is the Fujinomiya-*guchi* mountain trail, which goes up the south slope. Using the Fujisan Skyline road, climbers can access the fifth station of the trial (2,380 m: the highest point reachable by private car). A campaign to nominate the mountain as a World Heritage Site was launched in 1992.

Although it was prolonged due to problems with garbage disposal and opposition movements, the mountain was eventually listed as a World Cultural Heritage site in 2013. Several scenic sites that are away from the mountain, such as Miho Pine Grove in Shimizu (now Shizuoka city) and Shiraito Falls in Fujinomiya, were put on the same listing Incidentally, there are 16 Shiraito falls in the country.

The Ôi River flows from Mt. Ainodake in the Akaishi mountain range, running through the center of the prefecture as a boundary between the Suruga and the Enshû regions, and flowing into Suruga Bay. It was a chokepoint on the old Tôkaidô Road that was used to defend Edo, so no bridges and ferries were used in the Edo period. The Ôigawa Railway Co. was established in the 1920s to construct dams and carry out lumber. It is known as a tourism

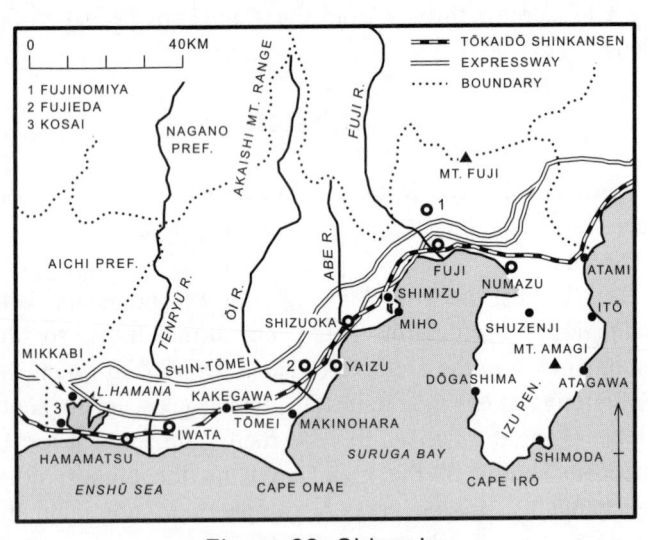

Figure 22 Shizuoka

railroad since the 1970s as a result of the revival of steam locomotives. The course of the Abe River corresponds with the Itoigawa-shizuoka Tectonic Line along the west side of the Fossa Magna. Dams have been constructed on the Ôi River since the Meiji period, whereas no dams were built on the Abe River because of the amount of gravel that is carried in it. At the mouth of the Fuji River, paper mills were established because of the plentiful water. The factories produce recycled paper from the used paper transported from the Tokyo metropolitan area.

The Izu Peninsula is located at the boundary of the Philippine Sea Plate, the North American Plate, and the Eurasia Plate. Mt. Fuji was formed on the Suruga Trough, which extends from the boundary. Hot spring resorts are to be found on the peninsula, such as Atami, Itô, Atagawa, Shimoda, Shuzenji, and Dôgashima. The climate is categorized as a Pacific Ocean-central Japan one. The coastal areas and the Izu Peninsula experience mild temperatures under the effect of the warm Japan Current.

History and Culture

Under the Ritsuryô code, Izu, Suruga, and Tôtoumi provinces became part of Shizuoka Prefecture in the Meiji period. The name is derived from Mt. Shizuhata in the current Shizuoka city. The area stretching east and west had 22 post towns out of 53 along the Tôkaido Road in the Edo period. Abekawa rice cake coated with soybean flour and white sugar is a popular snack that was served at tea houses on the road as it ran adjacent to the bridge of the Abe River. The city of Shizuoka was called Fuchû or Sunpu in the Edo period. The former referred to the capital of Suruga, and the latter was a contraction of Suruga and Fuchû. It was the place in which the first tycoon of the

Tokugawa Shogunate went into retirement, and the last tycoon (Yoshinobu Tokugawa) was confined.

Population and Traffic

The population of Shizuoka Prefecture is 3,765,000. The main cities are Hamamatsu (801,000), Shizuoka (716,000), Fuji (254,000), Numazu (202,000), Iwata (169,000), Yaizu (143,000), Fujieda (142,000), and Fujinomiya (132,000). The area is divided into the Izu region in the east, the Suruga region in the center, and the Enshû (former Tôtoumi) region in the west. Shizuoka and Hamamatsu are ordinance-designated cities, being assigned so in the 2000s. Hamamatsu was merged with the neighboring municipalities in 2005, and became the second largest city in the country. The prefectural capital, Shizuoka, was the largest city in the country when it merged with the city of Shimizu in 2003 (currently, it is the fifth largest city, after Takayama, Hamamatsu, Nikkô, and Kitami). Before the merger, Shizuoka was a core city *(chûkaku-shi)* and Shimizu, a special city *(tokurei-shi)*. With regard to transportation systems, Shizuoka Airport was opened on the Makinohara Plateau in 2009. The Tôkaidô Shinkansen passes under the runway, besides it goes through the tea-growing hills.

Primary Sector of Industry

The main agricultural commodities in terms of gross production are tea, *unshû* mandarins, and rice. The cultivated tea area amounts to 18,300 ha, about 40 percent of the country's total (Illustration 8). Tea leaves are categorized as first, second, and third, according to their harvest periods. Although the third tea is less expensive than the first and the second ones, the value has increased as the demand has risen for bottled teas. The Itô En factories, which manufacture tea products, are located in the city of Makinohara. The Port of Shimizu is an international hub port, which was developed for exporting tea to the United States in the Meiji period.

As well as tea, *unshû* mandarins are cultivated in the warm climate. The citrus producing regions are the town of Mikkabi, on the north shore of Lake Hamana, the south of the city of Shizuoka, and the north of the Izu Peninsula at the city of Numazu. In Shizuoka's Suruga Ward, strawberries are produced according to a stone-wall method on the slopes facing the Pacific Ocean. Pick-your-own farms comprise the agritourism in the area. Japanese horseradish production is the second largest of all the prefectures after Nagano. They are cultivated in fields soaked in running water and surrounded by alders at the foot of Mt. Amagi on the Izu Peninsula. Regarding fisheries, the catches of tuna and bonito are the largest in the country. Yaizu fishing port is a base for the pelagic fishery. Since glass eels were caught in the brackish lake, eels have been farmed around Lake Hamana, although the amount is decreasing.

Other Industries

The gross output of the secondary sector of industry is the third largest of all the prefectures after Aichi and Kanagawa. The main products are automobile parts and small and light cars. Tôkai Industrial Zone comprises Hamamatsu, Kakegawa, Iwata, and Kosai cities in the west. The headquarters and related companies of Yamaha Corporation and Suzuki Motor Corporations are situated in the industrial area. The former produces outboard motors, motorcycles, and musical instruments, and the latter makes light cars and motorcycles. The founder of Yamaha Corporation was Torakusu Yamaha, who worked as a medical device mechanic. He repaired an American organ at elementary school in Hamamatsu in the 1880s, and went on to establish the corporation. Suzuki Motor Corporation began life as Suzuki Loom Works also in Hamamtsu in the 1900s. Honda Motor Co., which manufactures automobiles and motorcycles, was founded in Hamamatsu too. It was founded by Sôichirô Honda, who studied metal engineering in Hamamatsu Higher Technical School (now the Faculty of Engineering, Shizuoka University) as an auditor before the war. He assumed the presidency of Tôkai Seiki Heavy Industry in the 1930s, and launched the Honda Technical Research Institute in 1946.

23. Aichi

Aichi is located in the southwest of the Chûbu region. It faces Ise Bay on the Pacific Ocean (Figure 23).

Nature

The highest peak is Mt. Chausu (1,416 m) in the east of the Minomikawa Highland at the boundary with Nagano Prefecture. The highland is an uplifted peneplain that consists of gentle slopes. Its china clay was supplied to Seto ware in the city of Seto and Mino ware in Gifu Prefecture. The former is synonymous with ceramics in Japanese *(seto-mono)*. The Yahagi and the Kiso rivers created valleys on the Minomikawa Highland. The Yahagi branches into the main stream and the old Yahagi River in Nishio city. The main stream is an artificial waterway constructed in the Edo period to deal with flood damage. With the sand brought by the main stream, land for agriculture was reclaimed around the mouth during this period. The climate ranges from a Pacific Ocean-central Japan one to

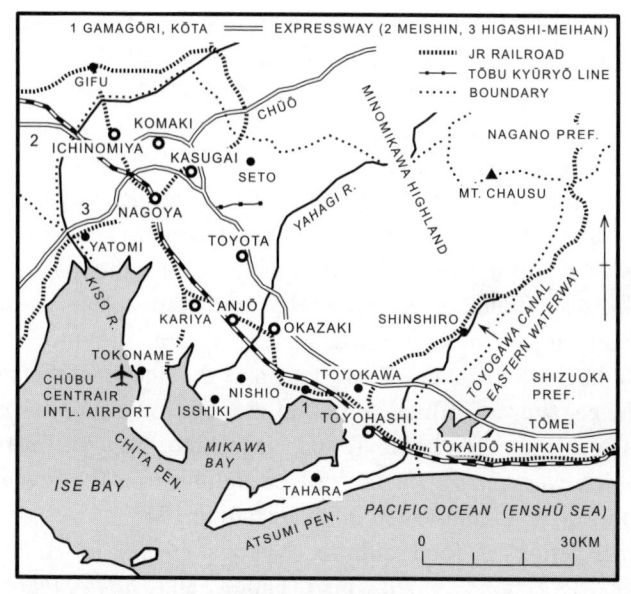

Figure 23 Aichi

an inland one. In the city of Nagoya, it is hot and humid in summer for heat island phenomena; nonetheless, it becomes chilly in winter because of the Ibuki-*oroshi* monsoon.

On the Atsumi Peninsula, the Toyogawa Canal was completed in the late 1960s. Its eastern waterway is derived from the Ure Dam and weirs in the Toyogawa river system, and travels for 76 km until it reaches Hattachi Pond at the tip of the peninsula. The north of the Chita Peninsula is an industrial area that is a continuation of the Port of Nagoya. In the city of Tokoname, in the center of the peninsula, ceramics has been produced based on the abundance of the clay soil output. The headquarters of INAX

121

Corporation (now known as LIXIL Corporation), a multinational company that produces toilets and tiles, is located in the city. Offshore of Ise Bay in the city, Chûbu Centrair International Airport was opened in 2005 before the opening of the Aichi Expo.

History and Culture

Owari and Mikawa provinces under the Ritsuryô code became Aichi Prefecture in the Meiji period. The name is derived from a lagoon (Ayuchi-*gata*) in the south of Nagoya. Being a geopolitically important place in the Sengoku period, major lords appeared in the provinces, including the Oda, the Toyotomi, and the Tokugawa clans. Hence, sites of influential battlefields are to be found, such as Nagakute, Okehazama, and Nagashino. Nagoya Castle, which was known for the golden dolphins on the tower's rooftop, was demolished in an air raid in 1945.

In terms of food culture, Nagoya *côchin* (a chicken breed), Hatchô miso, miso cutlet, and *hitsu-mabushi* (broiled eel in a small rice tub) are specialties. The origin of Nagoya-*côchin* was the poultry cooked by unemployed samurai in the Owari domain after the Meiji Restoration. Hatchô miso was a local specialty in the former village of Hatcho (now Okazaki city). It was processed from Yahagi soybeans purchased on the Yahagi River, and salt produced in the Chita Peninsula. In popular culture, the first *pachinko* shop was opened in the city of Nagoya in 1930. *Pachinko* was a game made from the recycled bearings manufactured in munitions factories.

Population and Traffic

The population of Aichi is 7,411,000, making it the fourth largest of all the prefectures. The main cities are Nagoya (2,264,000), Toyota (421,000), Ichinomiya

(379,000), Toyohashi (377,000), Okazaki (372,000), Kasugai (306,000), Toyokawa (182,000), Anjô (179,000), Komaki (147,000), and Kariya (145,000). The area is divided into the Owari region, including Nagoya, the West Mikawa region, which includes the cities of Okazaki and Toyota, and the East Mikawa region, which includes the city of Toyohashi.

Nagoya is a junction of railroads in the Chûbu region. The Tôkaidô Shinkansen and the Tôkaidô main lines of JR Central, and other railroads of Nagoya Railroad Co. (Meitetsu) lead to Nagoya Station. The Komaki interchange in Komai city is the terminal of the Tômei and the Chûô expressways, and a starting point for the Meishin Expressway. The Tôbu Kyûryô Line, built by Aichi Rapid Transit Co., is the first magnetic levitation railroad in Japan. It was opened in the Meitô Ward of Nagoya in 2005 to connect the Nagoya Municipal Subway and the Aichi Expo grounds. The Port of Nagoya handles the largest quantities of freight in the country. Its main freight are cars for export. Nagoya was assigned as one of the first ordinance-designated cities in 1956, along with Yokohama, Kyôto, Ôsaka, and Kôbe cities. A subway line and an underground shopping center were opened in 1957 in the city. Kôzôji New Town in Kasugai city is one of the earliest new towns, whose occupation commenced in the 1960s. It currently faces the problem of an aging population.

Primary Sector of Industry

The main agricultural commodities produced in the region in terms of gross production are vegetables and flowers. The Atsumi Peninsula in the East Mikawa region is a leading production center of horticultural crops in the country. The production is based on the mild climate and accessibility to large areas of consumption, such as Nagoya, Ôsaka, and Tokyo. The gross agricultural product of Tahara city in the peninsula is the largest of all the municipalities. In particular, the city's cultivated cabbage area amounts to no less than 5,600 ha. Broccoli, Chinese cabbages, and greenhouse crops such as roses and light cultured chrysanthemums are also extensively cultivated. In the city of Toyohashi, adjacent to Tahara, quail egg and perilla *(shiso)* production prospers. The former town of Isshiki (now Nishio city), facing Chita Bay on the mouth of the old Yahagi River, is an eel cultivating center.

Other Industries

The prefecture's gross domestic product is the third largest of all the prefectures after Tokyo and Ôsaka. The gross output of the secondary sector of industry is the largest of all the prefectures. The main industrial products are automobiles and automobile parts. The industrial center is Chûkyô Industrial Zone, extending to the northwest and the west including into the south of Gifu and the north of Mie prefectures. The main products of the industrial zone changed from aircraft and textiles to automobiles, petrochemicals, and steel after the war.

Headquartered in the city of Toyota, Toyota Motor Corporation has the largest sales of all the companies in the country. It originated as Toyoda Automatic Loom Works, which was established in the city of Kariya. The company launched the automotive section in the 1930s by constructing the first factory in the former town of Koromo (now Toyota city). The location was selected because of an invitation from the town, the availability of a tract of inexpensive and extensive land, and accessibility to Kariya via the Mikawa Line of Nagoya Railroad Co. Factories involved producing transportation implements were also established, for instance, trucks in Kariya and Nagoya, tires in Toyota and Shinshiro, car air conditioners in the town of Kôta, and motorcycles, outboard motors, and rail vehicles in Toyokawa. Many Japanese Latin Americans, mainly Japanese Brazilians, also work in these factories.

24. Mie

Mie is located in the southeast of the Kinki region, facing Ise Bay and the Kumano Sea (Figure 24).

Nature

Mountains extend from north to southwest. These comprise the Yôrô Mountains, the Suzuka mountain range, the Nunobiki Mountains, the Takami Mountains, and the Kii Mountains. The highest peak is Mt. Ôdaigahara (1,695 m) in the Kii Mountains, at the boundary with Nara Prefecture. The Suzuka mountain range is a horst that ranges from 900 m to 1,000 m above sea level, extending 50 km north and south. Alluvial fans are located at the east foot of the range. Horizontal wells, named *manbo*, were constructed on the fans because of the scarcity of water.

On the Ise Plain along Ise Bay, large cities are distributed, such as Yokkaichi, Tsu, and Matsusaka. At the mouths of the Kiso's Three Rivers, the communities are surrounded by dikes at the town of Kisosaki and the city of Kuwana. They suffered from extensive flood damage caused by the Isewan Typhoon in 1959. The Shima Peninsula in the south embraces a ria coastline that includes the bays of Ago, Matoya, and Gokasho. The coastal areas have been designated as Ise-Shima National Park. Regarding the climate, a Pacific Ocean-central Japan one prevails in most

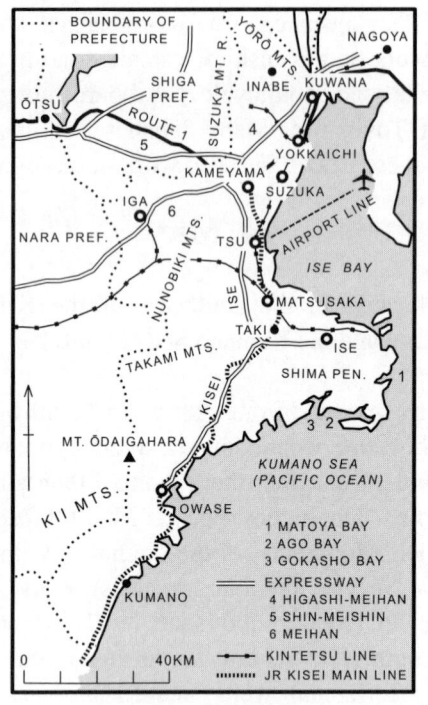

Figure 24 Mie

of the prefectural area, although there are differences by region since the area extends north and south. The annual precipitation levels amount to 1,360 mm in Iga city in the Ueno Basin, whereas they amount to 3,850 mm in Owase city in the south along the Pacific Coast.

History and Culture

Ise, Shima, and Iga provinces, and part of Kii Province in the era of the Ritsuryô code, became eight prefectures with the abolition of the domain system. Subsequently, in the Meiji period, they were merged. The name "Mie" is

126

derived from Mie county, which included the first prefectural capital, Yokkaichi. The county name came from the Ancient Matters Record *(Kojiki)* that was compiled in the eighth century. The place name "Yokkaichi" signifies that local markets were opened on days that had a four in their number in the calendar month, namely, the 4th, 14th, and 24th. The place name of the current prefectural capital, Tsu, denotes a "port." It was developed in the Edo period as a post town for pilgrimages to Ise Shrine. The shrine in Ise city was rebuilt every 20 years. That practice is called *sengû*, and it has continued since the seventh century. The shrine owns a forest of 5,500 ha that consists of natural and artificial cypress woods used for the reconstruction. In the south of the prefecture, Nachi black stones are quarried in the city of Kumano. They are processed into *go* stones, inkstones, and gravel.

Population and Traffic

The population of Mie is 1,855,000. The main cities are Yokkaichi (308,000), Tsu (286,000), Suzuka (199,000), Matsusaka (168,000), Kuwana (140,000), Ise (130,000), and Iga (97,000). The area is divided into the Hokusei region, and includes Yokkaichi, Suzuka and Kuwana cities, the Chûsei region, including Tsu and Matsusaka cities, Iga region, Nansei region, including Ise city, and Higashikishû region, which encompasses Owase city. National Route 1 crosses Yokkaichi as it was the site of an important post town on the old Tôkaidô Road, although the Tôkaidô Main Line and the Tôkaidô Shinkansen detoured around the prefecture on account of the Suzuka mountain range. The number of passengers carried is greater on private railroads than with JR. The major railroads are operated by Kintetsu Corporation, such as the Nagoya Line from Matsusaka to

Nagoya, the Ôsaka Line from Ôsaka to Matsusaka, and the Yamada Line from Matsusaka to Ise. The Ôsaka Line crosses the Nunobiki Mountains and enters the Nara Basin, before going ending at Ôsaka. With regard to maritime traffic, high-speed passenger crafts connect the city of Tsu with Chûbu Centrair International Airport across Ise Bay.

Primary Sector of Industry

The main agricultural commodities in terms of gross production are rice, eggs, and beef cattle. In terms of meat production, Matsusaka beef is known as an expensive brand. The farms grazing the cattle purchase the calves of the Japanese Black breed mainly from Tajima and other regions in Hyôgo Prefecture, and rear them for about three years with mixed feed to achieve a marbled meat effect (even beer was fed to the cattle to stimulate their appetite). Regarding industrial crops, green tea production is the third largest of all the prefectures after Shizuoka and Kagoshima. Although the tea used to be exported, it is currently sold under the brand of Ise-*cha* mainly for domestic markets, including bottled tea factories. The fishing industry is thriving along the coast of the Shima Peninsula. The catches of Japanese spiny lobster (Ise-*ebi*) are still the largest of all the prefectures. Green laver, oysters, and blown algae *(hijiki)* are produced by aquaculture. Ago Bay in the Shima Peninsula is known for its cultured pearl production. A technique for making circled pearls in Akoya pearl oysters was devised in the bay in the early twentieth century.

Other Industries

The main industrial products in terms of gross production are automobiles, trucks, and liquid crystal displays. In Suzuka city, Honda Motor Co. established a factory to assemble passenger cars in 1960, and built Suzuka International Racing Course in 1962. At the invitation of the city, the company was able to avail of the naval airfield and arsenal sites. Trucks are produced by Toyota Auto Body Co. in Inabe city, near the boundary with Gifu and Shiga prefectures. The liquid-crystal display production is the largest of all the prefectures. The Sharp Corporation factories were established in the town of Taki in the 1990s, and in the city of Kameyama in the 2000s. These were constructed near to expressway junctions for ease of transportation and commuting. The north of the prefecture comprises a part of Chûkyô Industrial Zone that continues from Aichi Prefecture. The Yokkaichi Petrochemical Complex was built after the late 1950s at a naval fuel arsenal site on the coast of Yokkaichi. And in the 1960s, the asthma caused by sulfurous acid gas expelled from factories raised concerns about pollution-related diseases.

25. Shiga

Shiga is an inland prefecture in the northeast of the Kinki region (Figure 25).

Nature

The highest peak is Mt. Ibuki (1,377 m) in the Ibuki Mountains at the boundary with Gifu Prefecture. Because the mountains contain limestone, a large cement factory was established during the high economic growth period, and it supplied construction material to the Keihanshin region (Kyôto, Ôsaka, and Kôbe). Various native herbs grow on the mountain. Among them, mugworts *(yomogi)*, angelicas *(tôki)*, and *senkyû (Cnidium officinale* Makino) are counted as the major three herbs of Mt. Ibuki. The moxa for moxibustion, which is made from the mountain's mugwort, is famous as it was invoked in *Hyakunin isshu* (the anthology of *tanka* poems compiled in the early thirteenth century, the Kamakura period).

The Hira Mountains, whose elevations range from 1,000 m to 1,200 m, run in a north-south direction to the west of Lake Biwa. They are counted as one of the eight scenic sites of Ômi for the "*Hira no bosetsu*" (evening snow of Hira) scenery. To the south of the mountains, Enryakuji Temple on Mt. Hieizan was listed as a World

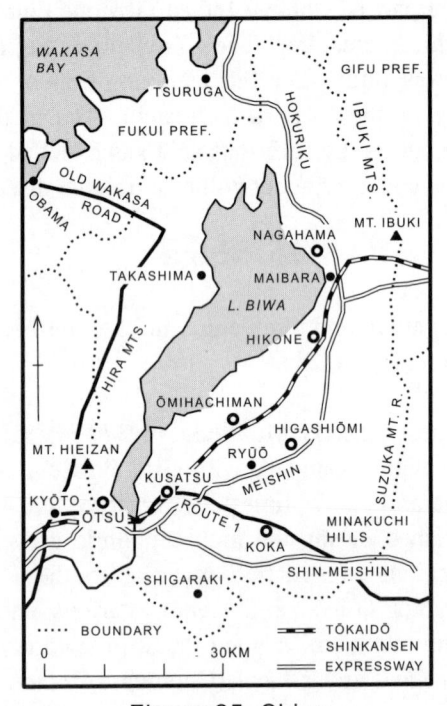

Figure 25 Shiga

Heritage Site in 1994, and is described as one of the "Historic Monuments of Ancient Kyôto." In the southeast of the prefecture, the Minakuchi Hills are located at the west foot of the Suzuka mountain range. In the hills, the Konan and Minakuchi industrial parks were developed along National Route 1 during the high economic growth period.

Lake Biwa in the center of Ômi Basin is the largest lake in the country, extending to 669 km^2 and accounting for about one-sixth of the prefectural area. It was called Chikatsu-awaumi in ancient times. The old name means "the sea of freshwater near the capital." The word relates to the ancient Ômi province. The shape of the lake resembles a *biwa* (a kind of lute), and thus it was named Lake Biwa in the Edo period. The Seta River flows from the lake and into Ôsaka Bay. It is called the Uji River in Kyôto Prefecture and the Yodo River in Ôsaka Prefecture. The climate ranges from an inland one to a "Setouchi climate" (warm in summer, slightly cold in winter, and less rainfall throughout the year) to a Sea of Japan-central Japan climate. The north receives a considerable quantity of snowfall.

History and Culture

Under the Ritsuryô code, Ômi province became Shiga Prefecture in the Meiji period. The name is derived from a county that included the prefectural capital, Ôtsu, and the county name meant a rocky place *(shika)*. In the former town of Azuchi (now Ômihachiman city), on the east bank of Lake Biwa, Nobunaga Oda fortified Azuchi Castle and advanced the unification of the country in the late sixteenth century. On the west foot and the south foot of the Suzuka mountain range, there were schools of ninja (spies or warriors skilled in the Japanese art of Ninjutsu), who engaged in agriculture and trade in between wars.

Although the mountainous Ômi land was unsuitable as extensive arable land, it was a valuable commercial location since the main roads passed through the province, for instance, the Tôkaidô, Nakasendô, Hokkoku (Hokuriku), and Wakasa roads. The Ômi merchants were active between the Kamakura and the Shôwa periods. Some of them became the founders of general trading companies and major department stores. With respect to the area's food culture, there is *funa-zushi*, a kind of sushi made from *nigoro-buna* (*Carassius auratus grandoculis*, a kind of crucian). Salt is put into the fish caught in Lake Biwa in spring, and boiled rice is added after removing the salt in summer. Then, the sushi is fermented for a period ranging from four months to three years.

Population and Traffic

The population of Shiga is 1,411,000. The main cities are Ôtsu (338,000), Kusatsu (131,000), Nagahama (124,000), Higashiômi (115,000), Hikone (112,000), Kôka (93,000), and Ômihachiman (82,000). The area is divided into the Konan region in the south, including the cities of Ôtsu and Kusatsu; the Kotô region in the east, including Higashiômi, Ômihachiman, and Hikone; the Kohoku region in the north, which includes Nagahama; and the Kosei region in the west, which encompasses the city of Takashima. The prefectural capital, Ôtsu, faces Kyôto across the Hira Mountains. The direct distance between the capitals is merely eight kilometers. The old Tôkaidô and Nakasendô roads ran along part of National Route 1 between Kusatsu and Kyôto. On the outskirts of Ôtsu can be seen the Ôsaka-*seki* stone monument, which was a checkpoint between the Ômi and Yamashiro provinces. Maibara Station, to the east of Lake Biwa, forms the junction of the Hokuriku Main and the Tôkaidô Main lines.

Primary Sector of Industry

The main agricultural commodity in terms of gross production is rice. Paddy fields account for more than 90 percent of the total arable land, and more than 90 percent of farmers are part-time ones. The adoption rate of agricultural machinery is also high. For instance, more than 70 percent of the farmers own combine harvesters. The main rice varieties are *Koshihikari* and *Kinuhikari* bred in the Hokuriku region. In Lake Biwa, there were 40 inner lakes prior to the coastal improvement projects carried out in the mid-twentieth century. The largest, Lake Dainaka (now cities of Ômihachiman and Higashiômi), was dried and converted to agricultural land to produce paddy rice, Dainaka watermelons, and Ômi cattle of the Japanese Black breed. In the fishing industry, *nigoro-buna*, sweetfish, Biwa trout *(Oncorhynchus rhodurus)*, and Seta small mussel *(Corbicula sandai)* are caught in Lake Biwa. The fishery resources are maintained by artificial incubation and spat cultivation.

Other Industries

The main industrial products in terms of gross production are medicines, automobiles, and glass. As for the pharmaceutical industry, a Nissin Pharmaceutical Industries Co. factory, which produces lozenges, is located in the city of Kôka. The prefectural medicine production has a tradition since the ninja peddlers of Kôka in the costume of mountain priests *(yama-bushi)* sold medicinal herbs throughout the country (current medicines are produced mostly using the state-of-the-art technology in factories in industrial parks). In terms of automobile production, a Daihatsu Motor Co. assembly factory produces light cars in the town of Ryûô. Meanwhile, the main glass production factories of Nippon Electric Glass Co. are located in Ôtsu, Nagahama, and Kusatsu.

Shigaraki ware is produced in Kôka in one of the six oldest potteries in Japan, along with the centers producing Echizen ware in Fukui, Seto and Tokoname ware in Aichi, Tanba ware in Hyôgo, and Bizen ware in Okayama. Shigaraki ware includes daily necessities, such as water jars, urns, sake bottles, and charcoal heating pots. Today, Shigaraki produces not only daily necessities but also diversified goods, such as umbrella stands, western tiles, figurines of raccoon dogs, and garden pottery, including garden statues, tables, and chairs. A large ceramic figure of a raccoon dog with a sake bottle is displayed in front of potters' workshops producing Kasama and Mashiko ware since they are derived from Shigaraki ware.

26. Kyôto

Kyôto is located in the north of the Kinki region, facing the Sea of Japan (Figure 26).

Nature

The Tanba Highland in the center are an uplifted peneplain, whose elevation reaches 600 m to 800 m. The highest peak is Mt. Minago (972 m) in the southeast of the highland at the boundary with Shiga Prefecture. Mt. Kurama is known for the legend of Kurama Tengu (long-nosed goblins in Kurama) and for being the training ground of Ushiwakamaru (the childhood name of Yoshitsune Minamoto). Both of the mountains are located in Sakyô Ward in the city of Kyôto. Mt. Ôe in the Tango Mountains in the north, at the boundary with Hyôgo Prefecture, is known for the legend of Shuten Dôji (the head of demons that delights in drinking sake).

The Katsura, Kamo, and Uji rivers flow through the Kyôto Basin, the largest basin in the south. On the shores of the Kamo River, flowing southward through the old downtown area of Kyôto, Japanese and Western-style restaurants are to be found, and evening floors *(nôryô-yuka)* are aligned on the shore in summer. The Ôi River streams

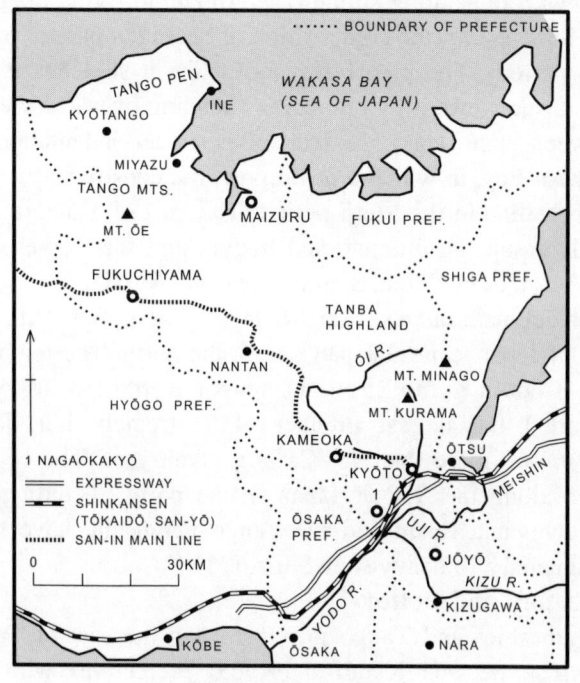

Figure 26 Kyôto

southward in the Kameoka Basin, and its name changes to the Katsura River on entering Arashiyama in Kyôto city. The Katsura River then becomes the Yodo River, meeting with the Uji and the Kizu rivers at the boundary with Ôsaka Prefecture.

The Tango Peninsula protrudes into the Sea of Japan from the western edge of Wakasa Bay. Amanohashidate in Miyazu city, at the end of the peninsula, has one of the three most scenic sites in the country. It is a sand spit at 3.5 km length covered with black pine woods. Depending on the viewpoint, the views are described as *naname-ichimonji* (a slanting straight), *hiryû-kan* (a flying dragon), and Sesshû-*kan* (the composition of Sesshû, a painter in the Edo period). The pine forest looks like it stretches to the sky if one views it by crouching (bending over and view it between your legs). Maizuru Bay is an indentation of Wakasa Bay, in which a naval port was constructed on the ria coastline in the Meiji period. The Port of Maizuru currently equips an international trading port that serves container routes to China, South Korea, and Russia.

The climate ranges from a Setouchi one in the south to a Sea of Japan-central Japan one in the north. The temperature is hot in Kyôto Basin, whereupon Kyôto city has often recorded the largest number of "extremely hot days" (*môsho-bi*, more than 35 °C) in a given year. The coastal areas along the Sea of Japan in the north, including the Fukuchiyama Basin and the Tango Peninsula, have been designated as a heavy snowfall zone.

History and Culture

Yamashiro and Tango provinces and the east of Tanba Province became Kyôto-*fu* (Kyôto Prefecture) with the abolition of the domain system in the Meiji period. *Fu* referred to the districts directly managed by the Tokugawa Shogunate, or the ports opened at the end of the Edo period, namely, Hakodate, Tokyo, Kanagawa, Echigo, Kai, Watarai, Nara, Kyôto, Ôsaka, and Nagasaki. *Kyô* referred to the capital from which the Emperor administered the country. The capital was moved to Heiankyô in the Kyôto Basin at the end of the eighth century from Heijôkyô in the Nara Basin. Afterwards, the Imperial Palace was established in the basin until the end of nineteenth century, the beginning of the Meiji period.

Buildings that are national treasures and gardens of special scenic value have been listed as some of the "Historic Monuments of Ancient Kyôto" that has been designated a World Heritage Site. The buildings are the Shimogamo and Kamigamo shrines, known for the Aoi festival, the Kiyomizu temple, known for its "stage" (a large wooden veranda: Illustration 9), the Daigoji Temple with its five-story pagoda, the Byôdôin Temple, whose phoenix hall was designed with 10 yen coins and 10,000 yen notes, Kôzanji Temple, which has the *Chôjû Jinbutsu Giga* (scrolls of frolicking animals), and Nijô Castle, in which the restoration of imperial rule (the Meiji Restoration) was mediated. Other buildings of note are Ginkaku Temple (Jishôji Temple), Tôji Temple, Ninnaji Temple, and Ujigami Shrine in the city of Uji. The gardens of special scenic value are included in Ryôanji Temple, known for its *kare-sansui* (a dry landscape garden), Saihôji Temple, a so-called moss temple, Tenryûji Temple, Kinkaku Temple (Rokuonji Temple), and Nishihonganji Temple. Although the Katsura Imperial Villa is not included in the heritage site, the buildings and gardens are known to be masterpieces of their kind. Those historic spots attract so many people.

The prefecture's number of Preservation Districts for Groups of Traditional Buildings is also the largest of all the prefectures. In Kyôto city, one can find Gion district, a shrine town in front of Yasaka Shrine in Higashiyama Ward; Sannei-zaka, a sloped stone pavement in front of Kiyomizu Temple in Higashiyama Ward; Kamigamo *shake-mach*, a row of priests' houses in Kita Ward; and Saga *torii-moto*, a shrine town in front of Atago Shrine in Ukyô Ward. Gion is also the old Kyôto downtown area, and is known for its *maiko* (apprentice geisha). Outside the city, the districts are to be found at Kayabuki no Sato (a thatched houses' village) at Kita district in the former town of Miyama (now Nantan city), *funa-ya* (hangar houses containing fishing boats) in Ine town, and *chirimen* (silk crepe) road in Yosano town to the north of Mt. Ôe.

Population and Traffic

The population of Kyôto Prefecture is 2,636,000. The main cities are Kyôto (1,474,000), Uji (190,000), Kameoka (92,000), Maizuru (89,000), Jôyô (80,000), Nagaokakyô (80,000), and Fukuchiyama (80,000). Kyôto is an ordinance-designated city, in which 56 percent of the population is concentrated. The Kyôto Basin is a traffic artery, where National Route 1, the Tôkaidô Main Line, the Meishin Expressway (a section between Rittô and Amagasaki was opened in 1963), and the Tôkaidô Shinkansen converge. The socio-economic conditions in the prefecture were considered typical North-South problems because of the large differences in population and development. Following the opening of the Kyôto Jûkan Expressway along National Route 9 and the San-in Main Line (the old San-in Road) in the 2010s, the Miyazu

Amanohashidate interchange in the Tango Peninsula and the Ôyamazaki junction in the Kyôto Basin are connectable within one and half hours.

Primary Sector of Industry

The main agricultural commodities in terms of gross production are vegetables (aubergines, green onions, spinach, and bamboo shoots), rice, and tea. Traditional seed varieties of vegetables are sold as Kyô-*yasai*, for instance, Kamo-*nasu* (aubergines), Kujô-*negi* (scallions), Kintoki-*ninjin* (carrots), Manganji-*tôgarashi* (green peppers), Fushimi-*tôgarashi* (green peppers), and Shôgoin-*kabu* (turnips). Tea is also sold under the brand of Uji tea. Among the marine products, Tango-*torigai* (cockles) is a specialty along the inner bays of Miyazu, Kunda, and Maizuru.

Other Industries

The main industrial products in terms of gross production are data storage devices for games, and cigarettes. In terms of number of establishments, the main category is silk narrow fabrics. The headquarters of Nintendo Co. is located in Kyôto city. The company does not possess factories since the game hardware is produced overseas, although data storage devices are still produced in assembly shops in the prefecture. In the tobacco industry, Japan Tobacco operates the Kansai Factory in Fushimi Ward in Kyôto city. Besides these companies, the headquarters of such major companies as Kyôcera Corporation, Takara Shuzô Co., Sagawa Express Co., Omron Corporation, Wacoal Holdings Corporation, and Takii & Co. are located in Kyôto city. As for traditional crafts, the area is renowned for the production of silk fabric, such as Nishijin-*ori* and Kyô-*yûzen*.

27. Ôsaka

Ôsaka, facing Ôsaka Bay (Figure 27), is located in the center of the Kinki region.

Nature

The Ikoma and the Kongô mountains, running north to south in the east, form the boundary with the Nara Prefecture. The Izumi Mountains, running east to west in the south, mark the boundary with Wakayama Prefecture. The highest peak is Mt. Katsuragi (959 m) in the Kongô Mountains, although the highest spot, at 1,056 m, is the nearby summit of Mt. Kongô, which lies in Nara prefecture. Mt. Kongô was a sacred mountain, where En no Gyôja (En no Ozuno) practiced religious austerity in the seventh century. A ropeway and walking paths were constructed on the Ôsaka Prefecture side, and it has become a tourist site for nearby large cities.

The Yodo River flows through the Ôsaka Plain, feeding into Ôsaka Bay near the boundary with Hyôgo Prefecture. Following land reclamation and industrial development, few untouched stretches of seafront remain in the bay. Although the prefecture used to be the smallest of all the prefectures, it has been enlarged mainly by land reclamation. The Ôsaka Nankô (10.5 km^2) are large artificial islands, in which residential areas and schools were constructed near the mouth of the Yodo, along with Kansai International Airport (10.6 km^2), which is located five kilometers from the coast of Ôsaka Bay. The climate is categorized as a Setouchi one. Summer nights are hot and sultry, and temperatures hardly fall less than 25 °C *(nettai-ya)*. On summer days, daytime temperatures usually rise

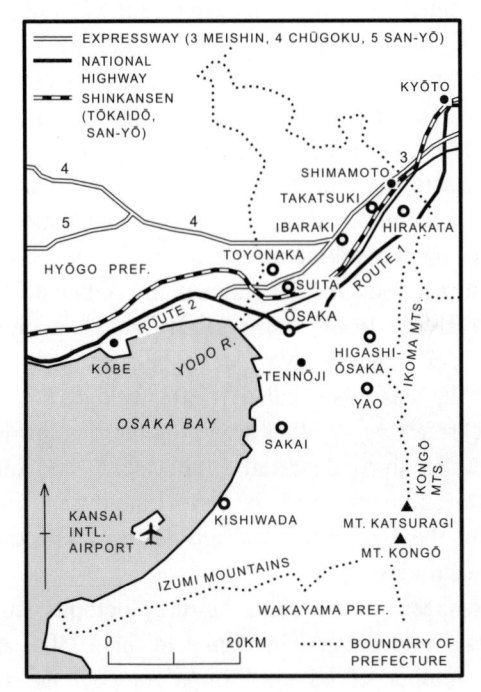

Figure 27 Ôsaka

above 30 °C *(natsu-bi)*. Barely any snow accumulates in winter. In the built-up areas of Ôsaka city, it is estimated that the energy for cooling in summer exceeds the energy for heating in winter.

History and Culture

Under the Ritsuryô code, Kawachi and Izumi provinces, and the east of Settsu Province became part of Ôsaka-*fu* (prefecture) in the Meiji period. The origin of the name is the Ôsakagobô Temple of Shin Buddhism, which became Ishiyama Honganji Temple in the Sengoku period. Naniwa-*tsu* and Suminoe-*tsu* were outer ports of the

141

Imperial Court from the Nara period to the Heian period. In those days, convoys headed to the Suí and the Táng dynasties after prayers for safe navigation were said at Sumiyoshi Taisha Shrine. In the Sengoku period, Sakai was developed as an autonomous city by funds made from gun manufacturing and trade with the Ming dynasty. A tea ceremony also bloomed in the city. Ôsaka Castle was built by Hideyoshi Toyotomi at a site of Ishiyama Honganji Temple surrounded by the moat of the Ôkawa River (the old Yodo River). In the Edo period, Ôsaka's economy was so developed that it was described as the "nation's kitchen." It was also called "808 bridges" *(happyaku yabashi)*, referring to the area's numerous bridges and canals. Cargo ships departed from Ôsaka, and undertook business circumnavigating the Seto Inland Sea, the Sea of Japan, and the Ezo region. *Nishin-kasu* of Hokkaidô was one of their trades.

With respect to the food culture, octopus dumplings *(tako-yaki)* were created in Ôsaka in the 1930s. After the war, the number of takeout shops for cabbage pancakes *(okonomi-yaki)* increased in the lower town of Ôsaka. Suntory Yamazaki Distillery in Shimamoto town is the oldest whiskey brewery that was established in 1923. In linguistic culture, the Ôsaka dialect is well known throughout the country for its large number of speakers and the comic dialogue broadcast on TV shows.

Population and Traffic

The population of Ôsaka Prefecture is 8,865,000, making it the third largest of all the prefectures after Tokyo and Kanagawa. The main cities are Ôsaka (2,665,000), Sakai (842,000), Higashiôsaka (510,000), Hirakata (408,000), Toyonaka (389,000), Takatsuki (357,000),

Suita (356,000), Ibaraki (275,000), and Yao (271,000). Ôsaka and Sakai were assigned as ordinance-designated cities in the 1950s and 2000s respectively. Senba is the central business district of Chûô Ward in Ôsaka city, where the offices of banks, insurance companies, stock exchanges, and the headquarters of large companies are to be found. The skyscrapers to the east of Ôsaka Castle are part of Ôsaka Business Park, which was constructed in a redevelopment project of an artillery arsenal site. Minami (south) is the largest downtown area along the Dôtonbori River, running between Shinsaibashi and Namba, to the south of Senba. Shinsekai (the new world) in Naniwa Ward, to the south of Minami, is another downtown, which is known for Tsûtenkaku Tower (reaching heaven tower) is prominent. To the south of Shinsekai is Airin district, which was once known as a labor camp for day workers *(yose-ba)*. Tnnôji station, to the southeast of Shinsekai, is the terminal of southern downtown.

Senri New Town between Toyonaka and Suita cities is a long-established new town, the occupation of which began in the early 1960s. In the Senri Hills to the northeast of the new town, a world exposition was held in 1970. At the time, it was a first for Asia. At the intersection of Umeda Shindô in front of JR Ôsaka Station is the terminal of National Route 1, and the starting point of National Route 2. Adjacent to the station are Hankyû Umeda and Hanshin Umeda stations, as well as department stores run by the railroad companies.

Primary Sector of Industry

The gross agricultural production is the second lowest after Tokyo. The main agricultural commodities in terms of gross production are vegetables, rice, and fruit. Regarding the vegetables, the main crops are scallions, aubergines, edible crown daisies, and giant butterburs *(fuki)*. As for fruit, the main crops are grapes and *unshû* mandarins. The local brands of Naniwa vegetables were revived, and include, for instance, Tennôji-*kabura* (turnips), Kema-*kyûri* (cucumbers), Tanabe-*daikon* (radishes), and Kotsuma-*nankin* (pumpkins). The commodification of rural space advanced with the direct selling of agricultural products to consumers, and the conservation of woodland near communities *(sato-yama)*.

Other Industries

The gross output of the secondary sector of industry is the fourth largest after Aichi, Kanagawa, and Shizuoka prefectures. The main products are gasoline, medicines, and automobiles. Hanshin Industrial Zone, extending from Ôsaka Prefecture to Hyôgo Prefecture, is one of the major industrial zones in the country. It was developed based on several geographical conditions: the large nearby capitals and markets of Ôsaka, Kyôto, and Hyôgo prefectures, abundant water for industrial use, and the water transportation availability on the Yodo River. Heavy and chemical industries, such as petrochemicals, machinery, and steel, have been developed on the reclaimed land along Ôsaka Bay in the industrial zone. Some major electronics and machinery-based companies are headquartered in this prefecture, for example, Panasonic Corporation, Sharp Corporation, Daihatsu Motor Co., Yanmar Holdings Co., Kubota Corporation, and Keyence Corporation. In the medicine and food sectors, Takeda Pharmaceutical Co., Shionogi & Co., Nissin Foods Holdings Co., and Ôtsuka Foods Co. are based here, and, in fibers and textiles, Teijin, and Mizuno Corporation.

28. Hyôgo

Hyôgo is located in the west of the Kinki region, facing Ôsaka Bay, the Harima Sea, and the Sea of Japan (Figure 28).

Nature

The highest peak is Mt. Hyônosen (1,510 m) at the boundary with Tottori Prefecture. It is the second highest mountain in the Chûgoku region after Mt. Daisen. Three ski resorts have been constructed on the slopes of the mountain and of the neighboring Mt. Hachibuse. The Chûgoku Mountains, the backbone of the Chûgoku region, run east to west in the center of the prefecture. In Asago city in the Tajima region, there is a Takeda Castle site that is known as a mountain castle that floats in the mist. The lords of the castle had developed the Ikuno Silver Mine and the Akenobe Tin Mine, both of which were assigned as the first government-managed mines in the Meiji period. The Rokkô Mountains run east to west in the north of Kôbe city. They were designated as Setonaikai National Park in the 1930s. Arima hot springs at the north foot of the mountains consist of the oldest three hot springs besides the Shirahama hot springs in Wakayama Prefecture and the Dôgo hot springs in Ehime Prefecture. Traverse climbing on the Rokkô Mountains was initiated by an alpinist, Buntarô Kato, in the 1920s.

The Harima five rivers (the Kako, the Ichi, the Ibo, the Chikusa, and the Yumesaki) start at the Chûgoku Mountains, dividing the prefecture into regions, and cease in Harima Sea (the Seto Inland Sea) from Harima Plain. The Maruyama River takes a course in the opposite direction to

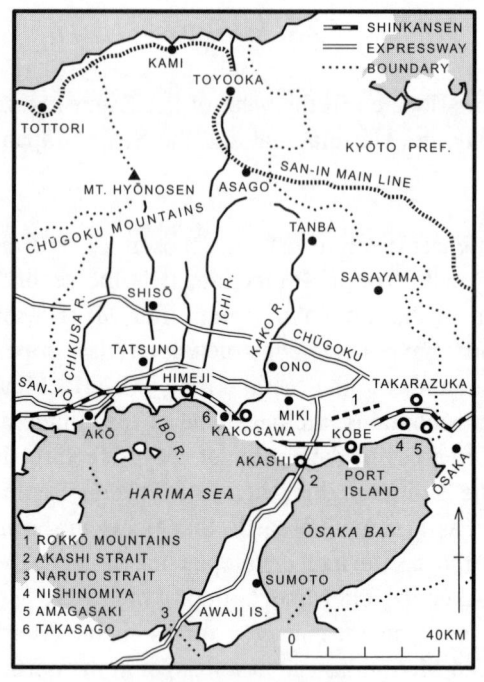

Figure 28 Hyôgo

those rivers, running through the Toyooka Basin and into the Sea of Japan. The former town of Hikami (now the city of Tanba) is located at longitude 135 degrees east, the meridian by which Japan Standard Time is set. In the city can be found the lowest watershed (95 m) between the Pacific Ocean and the Sea of Japan. Wicker trunks *(yanagi-gôri)* used to be produced from native willows *(Salix koriyanagi)* grown in the Toyooka Basin. The craft evolved into a large bag producing center. A stork-preservation center was established to produce artificial breeding storks in the basin. The climate ranges from a Sea

146

of Japan-central Japan one in the north to a Setouchi one in the south. It snows in winter in the north, while precipitation levels are low in summer in the south. The salt-producing regions were widely located along the Seto Inland Sea. Salt production remains in the city of Akô, which is a place remembered in connection with *47 Rônin (Chûshingura)*.

History and Culture

Tajima and Harima provinces, and the west of Settsu and Tanba provinces, became Hyôgo Prefecture in the Meiji period. The name is derived from Hyôgo-*tsu*, in which Kôbe port office was established at the end of the Edo period. The Port of Kôbe was constructed on a site of the Naval Training Center of the Tokugawa Shogunate in the wake of the ending of the isolation policy. It was developed as a trading and passenger's port, in which Kôbe customs, the national silk laboratory, and a foreign settlement were established.

In food culture, Hyôgo's production of sake and Japanese-style thin noodles *(sômen)* is the largest of all the prefectures. Sake production was developed in the Nada area (Kôbe and Nishinomiya cities) because of several pre-existing advantages: the existence of rice polishing mills by means of hydropower, the deftness of the master brewers from the Tanba region (Tanba-*tôji*), and the accessibility to a large port for distribution. The noodles are produced in the cities of Shisô, Tatsuno, and Himeji, and in the town of Taishi. They are located on the lower and middle reaches of the Ibo on the Seto Inland Sea side. The making of noodles has flourished in those areas since the Edo period because of the ready supply of raw materials, such as water, salt, and wheat.

Population and Traffic

The population of Hyôgo is 5,588,000. The main cities are Kôbe (1,544,000), Himeji (536,000), Nishinomiya (483,000), Amagasaki (454,000), Akashi (291,000), Kakogawa (267,000), and Takarazuka (226,000). The area is divided into the Hanshin region, including Kôbe city; the Harima region, including Himeji city; the Tanba region, including Tanba city; the Tajima region, including Toyooka city; and Awaji Island. Kôbe is an ordinance-designated city, whose built-up area and main traffic lines are concentrated in a narrow plain sandwiched between the Rokkô Mountains and Ôsaka Bay. The city, therefore, suffered severe damage from the 1995 Great Hanshin earthquake. Artificial islands have been constructed offshore of the Port of Kôbe such as Port Island (8.3 km^2), Rokkô Island (6.0 km^2), and Kôbe Airport (2.7 km^2). Port Island was the largest artificial island in the world when the occupation of residents started on a 4.4 km^2 area in 1980.

The Port of Kôbe consisted of one of the five ports opened by the Ansei Five-Power Treaties at the end of the Edo period, along with the ports of Hakodate, Yokohama, Niigata, and Nagasaki. The Nankin (Nanjing) street was built by Chinese migrants in the foreign settlement, and developed into Kôbe's Chinatown. The second railroad, connecting Ôsaka and Kôbe stations, was opened in 1874. The Kôbe-Awaji-Naruto Expressway opened in 1998. It runs from Kôbe, passing through Awaji Island across Akashi Kaikyô Bridge, the world's longest suspension bridge (3.9 km), and extends to Naruto city on Shikoku Island after crossing Ônaruto Bridge.

Primary Sector of Industry

The main agricultural commodities in terms of gross production are rice, vegetables, eggs, and beef cattle. Brewer-rice production in Hyôgo is the largest of all the prefectures. The main seed variety of brewer rice is *Yamadanishiki*, and of non-glutinous rice, *Koshihikari*. The former was bred in the prefecture in the 1920s. In Awaji Island, horticultural crop production, such as vegetables, flowers, and fruit, thrive based on the warm climate and accessibility to large cities. The Tajima region is the origin of Japanese Black cattle. The pedigree originated from a bull, *Tajirigô*, which was bred in Kami town in 1939. The calves of Tajima cattle are supplied to the farmers, who fatten them so that they can be branded as Kôbe, Matsusaka, or Ômi beef. Regarding seafood specialties, snow club and firefly squid are caught in the Sea of Japan, and Japanese sand lance, whitebaits, octopus, and laver are caught in the Seto Inland Sea. The local food of the Harima region includes *kugini* (simmered Japanese sand lances), whose etymology is "crooked rusty nails" since this is what the fish resembles when it is boiled down.

Other Industries

The gross output of secondary industry is the fifth largest of all the prefectures. The main products are medicines, shovel excavators, and electronic devices for automobiles. Medicines, vessels, and railroad vehicles are produced in Hanshin Industrial Zone stretching to the coast from Ôsaka to Amagasaki to Kôbe cities. Heavy and chemical industries, including steel, iron, synthetic resins, and chemical fertilizers, are thriving in Harima Coastal Industrial Zone drawing in the coast from Kakogawa to Takasago to Himeji cities. Among the traditional industries are cutlery in Miki city, abacus manufacturing in Ono city, and soy sauce making in Tatsuno city.

29. Nara

Nara is an inland prefecture in the center of the Kinki region (Figure 29).

Nature

The Kii Mountains are to be found in the south of Nara Prefecture. Mt. Hakkyôgatake (1,915 m) in the mountains is the highest peak in the Kinki region. Kimpusen Temple, which is used for mountain worship, was established by En no Gyôja in the late seventh century at Mt. Yoshino in the center of the prefecture. The approach to the temple is a scenic site surrounded by cherry tree groves, which are denominated as the lower thousand, the middle thousand, the upper thousand, and the inner thousand. Tsukigase Bairin in the Kasagi Mountains to the north is an arboretum to behold for Japanese apricot blossoms.

Yoshino River flows from Mt. Ôdaigahara and into the Kii Channel. It runs to the northwest from the source, and does not enter the Nara Basin, but curves to the west along the Median Tectonic Line. The name changes to the Kinokawa River in Wakayama Prefecture. The Totsukawa River flows from Mt. Sanjôgadake (Ômine) and powers into the Kumano Sea. In Wakayama and Mie prefectures, the river is known as the Kumano. The upper reaches of the river receive a lot of rainfall. Following a destructive flood in 1889 (Meiji 22), about 2,500 residents of Totsukawa village moved to Hokkaidô, and then established Shintotsukawa village along the middle reaches of the Ishikari River.

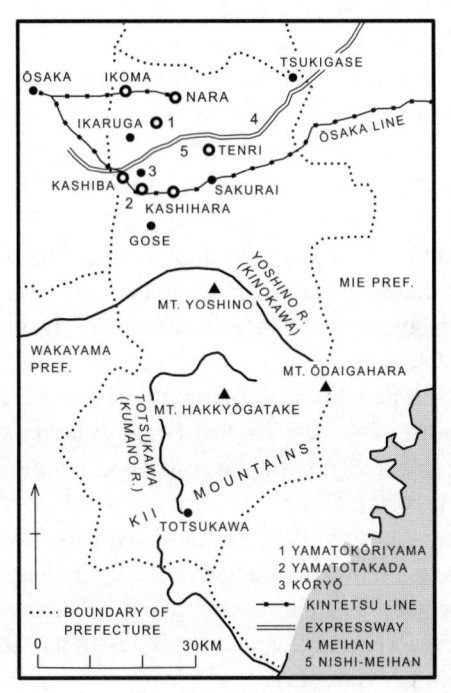

Figure 29 Nara

The climate ranges from an inland one in the north to a Pacific Ocean-central Japan one in the south. Thick mist sometimes hangs over the Nara Basin in early autumn, and makes driving difficult. The vegetation consists of broad-leaved evergreen forests, such as oaks *(kashi)* and chinquapins *(shii)*, and of secondary forests of red pines. At the forestry area on the upper reaches of the Yoshino, dense planted forests of cedars and Japanese cypresses are maintained.

History and Culture

Under the Ritsuryô code, Yamato Province became Nara

Prefecture in the Meiji period. Yamato denotes the east of the Nara Basin, and Nara means a planar surface. From the Asuka to the Nara periods (between the sixth and the eighth centuries), the capital of the country was based in the Nara Basin. Hôryûji Temple in Ikaruga town, constructed by Prince Shôtoku in 607 to spread Buddhism, is the oldest wooden building in the world. The temple carpenters used 1,000-year-old Japanese cypresses to construct the building that would outlast 1,000 years. Under the refurbishment of the temple, conducted from the 1930s to the 1980s, about 35 percent of the cypress timbers were replaced with new ones, and large cypresses were imported from Taiwan. The hall of the Great Buddha in Tôdaiji Temple in Nara city is the largest wooden building in the world. The original hall was established in the eighth century, and is also built of Japanese cypress. It was burned down in wars and reconstructed twice in the Kamakura and the Edo periods. For the reconstructions, cedars, red pines, and zelkovas *(keyaki)* were used due to the shortage of large Japanese cypresses.

Hôryûji, Tôdaiji, and Shôsôin (a Tôdaiji treasure house) have been designated as national treasures, and, collectively, were the first monument in Japan to be listed as a World Heritage Site (cultural site), in 1993, along with Himeji castle. Those historical places have, as well as the ones in Kyôto Prefecture, gained in popularity among foreign tourists and schoolchildren. In terms of the food culture, *Goshogaki* is a variety of sweet persimmon that was bred in Gose city. The fruit was mentioned in a poem by Shiki Masaoka as follows: "*Kaki kueba, kanega narunari, Hôryûji*" (I eat a persimmon, and a bell tolls at Hôryûji). *Kakinoha-zushi* is a box lunch sold at several stations in Nara and Wakayama prefectures. It is vinegared rice topped with vinegared mackerel and simmered shiitake mushrooms, wrapped with astringent-persimmon leaves.

Population and Traffic

The population of Nara Prefecture is 1,401,000. The main cities are Nara (367,000), Kashihara (126,000), Ikoma (118,000), Yamatokôriyama (89,000), Kashiba (75,000), Tenri (69,000), and Yamatotakada (68,000). To the north of the Nara Basin, Kintetsu Corporation's Nara Line connects Ôsaka and Nara. To the south of the basin, the Kintetsu's Ôsaka Line connects Ôsaka, Kashihara, and Matsusaka. Housing lots along the railroads were developed after the high economic growth period. Those are dormitory towns for the commuters to Ôsaka and Kyôto prefectures, so they were nicknamed "Nara-*fumin*" (residents in Nara Prefecture who commute to Ôsaka-*fu* and Kyôto-*fu*).

Primary Sector of Industry

The main agricultural commodities in terms of gross production are vegetables, rice, and fruit (mainly persimmons). Rice cultivation is concentrated in the Nara Basin in the northwest. A considerable number of reservoirs *(tame-ike)* for paddy fields were constructed in the basin. These were used because of the low rainfall in summer. The main rice variety is the *Hinohikari* bred in Miyazaki Prefecture. Strawberry, aubergine, and flower production increased in the basin after the implementation of a policy of reducing rice production. The persimmon producing center is the basin of the Yoshino River, continuing from Wakayama. In terms of inland fish farming, the city of Yamatokôriyama is one of the major goldfish cultivating centers besides Yatomi city in Aichi. The main breed is common goldfish *(wa-kin)* categorized as tiny red *(ko-aka)* for goldfish scooping games. The goldfish culture was initiated as a sideline of the samurai at the end of the Edo period. The water fleas in reservoirs were used for feed.

Other Industries

The main industrial products in terms of gross production are socks, Japanese-style noodles, and lumber. Sock production in Nara is the largest of all the prefectures. Socks are produced in the city of Yamatotakada and the town of Kôryô in the Chûwa region. The origin of the industry is the cotton cultivation and weaving that arose as sidelines of rice farming in the Edo period. Noodles are produced in Sakurai city in the Miwa region, which is the birthplace of Japanese-style thin noodles. The origin of the noodles is the *mugi-nawa* (wheat rope) that was imported from the Táng dynasty in the Nara period. In terms of traditional crafts, bamboo-whisk *(cha-sen)* production at Takayama district in Ikoma city amounts to 90 percent of the country's total. It is a tea ceremony utensil processed from the Henon bamboo *(ha-chiku)* that can be split thinly. It was invented by a renga poet at Takayama in the fifteenth century.

30. Wakayama

Wakayama is located in the southwest of the Kinki region, facing the Kii Channel and the Kumano Sea (Figure 30).

Nature

The highest peak is Mt. Ryûjindake (1,382 m) of the Kii Mountains in the east. Mt. Gomadan was once regarded as the highest peak; however, a 10 m higher peak was found

700 m to the east in 2000. It was named Ryûjindake (dragon god mountain) in a public consultation process, reflecting an image of grandness and mysteriousness. There are three sacred sites in the Kii mountains, namely, Mt. Kôya, on the left bank of the Kinokawa River, the Kumano Three Mountains, on the right bank of the Kumano River, and Mt. Yoshino, on the left bank of the Yoshino River (the upper reaches of the Kinokawa River). Those sites and their pilgrimage routes were listed as a World Heritage Site in 2004. Mt. Kôya is a sacred place for the esoteric form of Shingon Buddhism founded by Kûkai (Kôbô Daishi) in the

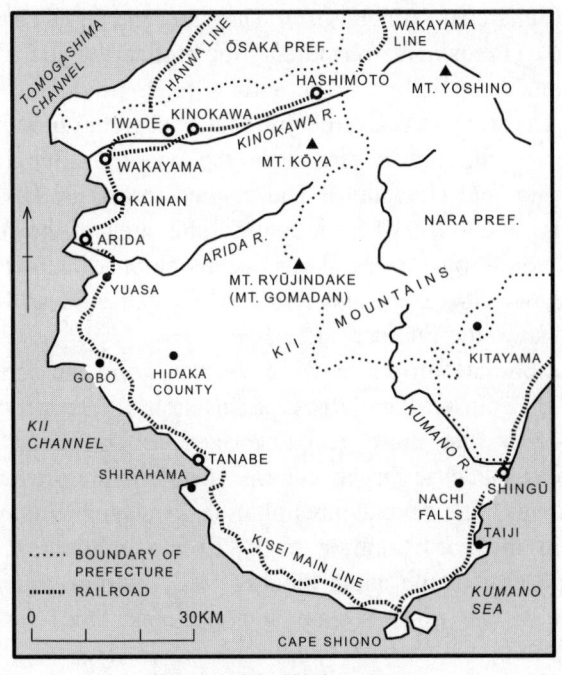

Figure 30 Wakayama

155

early ninth century after he returned from the Táng dynasty. The Kumano Three Mountains were developed in the Heian period for mountain worship by Shugendô devotees. Kumano Nachi Taisha Shrine comprises a shrine forest including 47 falls for religious austerity purposes. Among them, the Nachi Falls plunge 133 m, the highest fall in the country. To the south of the cataract is Cape Shiono, the southernmost point of Honshû Island (Illustration 10).

The vegetation area is categorized as a "broad-leaved evergreen forest zone." Among the trees, *ubame-gashi (Quercus phillyraeoides)* has been used as the material for Kishû charcoal (Binchô-*tan*). The hard and light charcoal is used in expensive restaurants for broiled eel and grilled chicken since it burns for a long time, producing little smoke (parenthetically, the prefectural charcoal production center is the fourth largest in the country after Iwate, Shimane, and Hokkaidô). The planted forests of Japanese cypress and cedar cover a considerable area of the forest. The coniferous trees have been shipped along the Kinokawa, Kumano, and Arida rivers and sold as Kishû wood since the Edo period.

The climate differs between the north and the south in the Kii Peninsula, the largest peninsula in the country. The climate in the north is categorized as an inland one, whereas a Pacific Ocean-central Japan climate prevails in the south. The annual precipitation levels of Wakayama city in the north amount to 1,320 mm, while levels in Shingû city in the south amount to 3,130 mm under the effect of the rainy season and typhoons from June to September.

History and Culture

Under the Ritsuryô code, Kii (Nanki) Province in Nankaidô (south sea circuit), together with Shikoku Island, became Wakayama and a part of the Mie Prefecture in the Meiji period. The name is derived from Wakayama castle built by Hideyoshi Toyotomi in the late sixteenth century, and the castle's name is derived from a scenic site along Wakanoura Bay. In the Edo period, the Kishû domain ruled by one of the three Tokugawa clans encompassed the whole Kii Province and the south of Ise Province.

With regard to food culture, the town of Taiji was known for whale fishing, and the cuisine there includes *tatsuta-age*, or deep fried whale meat. Whales currently are tourism and education resources, being the attraction for whale-watching tours and aquarium displays, even though they were served in school lunches after the war as a low-cost source of protein for pupils. *Mehari-zushi* is a packed lunch sold in the Kinan region, mainly at Shingû Station. It is small rice balls wrapped with pickled leaf mustard *(taka-na)*, whose origin was a huge rice ball that was quick lunch for lumberjacks working in remote mountains. It is derived from "rice ball" *(sushi)*, and "so large as to be astonished" *(me wo miharu)*.

Population and Traffic

The population of Wakayama Prefecture is 1,002,000. The main cities are Wakayama (370,000), Tanabe (79,000), Hashimoto (66,000), Kinokawa (66,000), Kainan (55,000), Iwade (53,000), Shingû (31,000), and Arida (31,000). The area is divided into the Kihoku region in the north and Kinan region in the south. The regions are separated at the boundary between the cities of Gobô and Tanabe. Dormitory towns were constructed in Hashimoto and Iwade cities in the northernmost place of the prefecture, from where Nankai Electric Railway Co.'s Nankai Main Line and JR West's Hanwa Line run from the city of Ôsaka. The Kisei Main Line runs from Kameyama Station in Mie Prefecture along the coast of the Kii Peninsula via Shirahama Station, and leads to Wakayamashi Station. The railroad is managed by JR West from the west of Shingû Station, and by JR Central from the east of the station. Kitayama village in the south of the Kii Mountains between Nara and Mie prefectures is the only exclave municipality. The population (486) is the second smallest of the municipalities, except for the islands (c.f., the lowest is 411 in Ôkawa village, Kôchi Prefecture). Located in the basin of the Kitayama River, a tributary of the Kumano, its economy is connected to Shingu's via lumber floating.

Primary Sector of Industry

The main agricultural commodities in terms of gross production are fruit. The cultivation areas devoted to *unshû* mandarins, persimmons, and Japanese apricots are the largest of all the prefectures; and the cultivated fig area is the second largest one after Aichi. Among the *unshû* mandarins, Arida-*mikan* is grown on the lower reaches of the Arida. Along the west-flowing Kinokawa River, figs are cultivated on the lower reaches, and persimmons are cultivated on the middle reaches. Japanese apricots are cultivated mainly in Hidaka county in the center of the prefecture. The cultivation of fruit was developed based on the warm regional temperature, inclined fields, and variations in precipitation levels. In addition to the fruit, Japanese peppers are produced on the middle reaches of the Arida, while the largehead hairtail *(tachi-uo)* catches in Minoshima fishing port at the mouth of the river are the largest in the country.

Other Industries

The main industrial products in terms of gross production are steel and gasoline. Industrial parks were reclaimed from the surf fringe of the Kii Channel in Wakayama Plain, whereupon factories were constructed by major companies such as Nippon Steel & Sumitomo Metal Corporation and Kaô Corporation (a chemical and cosmetics company). A Tôa Nenryô Kôgyô factory that produced aircraft fuel was constructed in the city of Arida in the early 1940s. It became a refinery that was run by the Tônen General Sekiyu Co. after the war. The main category of production according to numbers of establishments is pickles. Processing plants of salt plums are distributed along the west coast of the Kii Peninsula. They deal in the branded salt plums with a variety of *Nankô*, which was named after a high school where the discoverer taught horticulture. The variety has the advantages of soft pulp, thin skin, and small seeds, however, these features require a high level technique in processing. Among the traditional and light industries, there are soy sauce businesses in the town of Yuasa, *mah-jong* tiles in Gobô, pyrethrums in Arida, and knitted products in Wakayama.

31. Tottori

Tottori is located in the northeast of the Chûgoku region, facing the Sea of Japan (Figure 31).

Nature

The area is divided from Okayama Prefecture by the Chûgoku Mountains running east to west in the south. The highest peak is Mt. Daisen (1,729 m) in the west. Mt.

Daisen is a stratovolcano that belongs to the Hakusan volcanic belt. It was designated as Daisen National Park in 1936 (now Daisen-Oki National Park). Beeches grow on the slopes higher than 800 m above sea level. A pure forest of Japanese yews around the summit has been designated as a special natural monument.

The Sendai River flows from the Chûgoku Mountains in the southeast, and feeds into the Sea of Japan from the Tottori Plain. Among the sand dunes extending around the mouth of the river, the Tottori Sand Dunes on the right bank at Hamasaka district in Tottori city are known as a scenic site in the San-in region. Camel excursions and lift tours are provided for visitors enjoying a unique landscape without vegetative cover. The Tomiura coast of granite sea cliffs in Iwami was designated as San-in Kaigan National Park in the 1955, along with coastline from Hyôgo and Kyôto prefectures. The national park was also certified as San-in Kaigan Global Geopark in 2010.

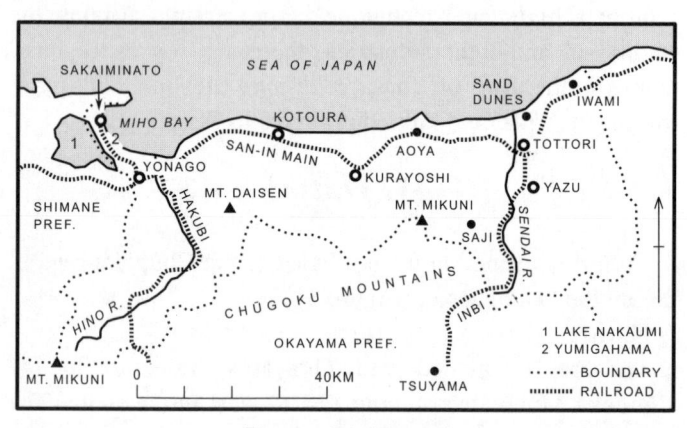

Figure 31 Tottori

160

To the west of the Sendai River, on the left bank near the mouth, boat tours are provided at Koyama Pond around the small islands. It is the largest pond in the country, and was a lagoon of brackish water. The water was desalinated after it damaged surrounding paddy fields; nonetheless, it reverted to being a brackish lake after sluice gates were opened in the 2000s to reduce water pollution. The Hino River originates at Mt. Mikuni in the west of the Chûgoku Mountains at the boundary with the old provinces of Hôki, Izumo, and Bingo. It runs through the Yonago Plain in the west, and feeds into Miho Bay. Yumigahama is known as a scenic site lying at the mouth of the river. As for the climate, the whole area is categorized as a Sea of Japan-central Japan one. It is the westernmost prefecture in Japan, whose whole area has been designated as a heavy snowfall zone. Two ski resorts have been established at the foot of Mt. Daisen.

History and Culture

Under the Ritsuryô code, Inaba and Hôki provinces became Tottori Prefecture in the Meiji period. The name is derived from the prefectural capital. The civic name is derived from *totori-be*, the local hunter groups that pursued waterfowl in ancient times. The Hakuto coast and Hakuto Shrine in Tottori city are the setting of the Japanese myth *Inaba no Shirousagi*. In the tale, the god of opulence (Daikoku) saves a white hare that was skinned of its fur by sharks. The myth was quoted in a song for *Jinjô* elementary schools (the first compulsory education from the 1880s to the 1940s). The city of Sakaiminato in the north of Yumigahama is the birthplace of a manga artist, Shigeru Mizuki. The road with a motif of his *GeGeGe no Kitarô* was completed in the city center, and is a popular attraction for tourists.

Population and Traffic

The population of Tottori Prefecture is 589,000, making it the smallest by number of all the prefectures. The main municipalities are Tottori (197,000), Yonago (148,000), Kurayoshi (51,000), and Sakaiminato (35,000) cities, and Kotoura (19,000), and Yazu (18,000) towns. The prefectural area stretching east to west is divided into the Inaba (Inshû) region to the east of Mt. Mikuni and the Hôki region to the west. In parallel with the old San-in Road, the San-in Main Line and National Route 9 cross the coastal plains facing the Sea of Japan. Among the north-south directed railroads, the Inbi Line, connecting Tottori and Tsuyama in Okayama Prefecture (the old Mimasaka Province), runs along the Sendai River, and crosses the Chûgoku Mountains in the east. In the west, the Hakubi Line connects Kurashiki in Okayama and Hôki-daisen Station in the city of Yonago, and the Sakai Line runs from Yonago Station to Sakaiminato Station. Those four railroads are operated by JR West. In terms of air transport, the prefecture has two airports, Tottori Airport in Tottori city, whose nickname is Tottori Conan Airport (derived from the birthplace of another manga artist), and Yonago Airport in Sakaiminato city, which is known as Yonago Kitarô Airport.

Primary Sector of Industry

The main agricultural commodities in terms of gross production are vegetables, rice, broilers, raw milk, and Japanese pears. In terms of vegetable cultivation, shallots, white scallions, and taros are cultivated widely on the upland fields near the coast. The purple flowers of shallot in autumn are also attractions for tourists in the environs of

162

the Tottori Sand Dunes. Production of *Nijisseiki* (a variety of Japanese pear) is the largest of all the prefectures. They are known as "blue pears" after the pale green exocarp grown in bagging cultivation to protect the fruit from disease. The *Nijisseiki* harvest lags behind as compared with the varieties of "red pears" such as *Kôsui* and *Hôsui*. The Japanese Pear Museum was opened in the city of Kurayoshi, which is the main *Nijisseiki* producing center. Sakaiminato is one of the largest fishing ports in the country. The main catches are sardine, mackerel, horse mackerel, and crab. In particular, the catches of Champagne crab *(matsuba-gani)* are the largest of all the fishing ports. Among the local foods, there are crab miso soup and *ago-no-yaki* (grilled cake of flying fish).

Other Industries

The main industrial products in terms of gross production are liquid crystal displays, printing paper, and wireless devices. In Tottori city, liquid crystal displays are produced by Seiko Epson Corporation and car navigation systems by Sanyo Techno Solutions Tottori Co. In the city of Yonago, Ôji Paper Co. was established because of the plentiful water supply and the hydroelectric power that comes from the Hino River. The paper mill utilizes domestic material produced by chip factories in the Chûgoku Mountains for up to 15 percent of its total raw material. Inshû-*washi* is the traditional Japanese paper produced in the former town of Aoya (now Tottori), and also in the former village of Saji (also now Tottori). It is made from *kôzo* and *mitsumata (Edgeworthia chrysantha)*, and its production accounts for about 60 percent of the total calligraphy paper used in the country.

32. Shimane

Shimane is located in the north of the Chûgoku region, facing the Sea of Japan (Figure 32).

Nature

The highest peak is Mt. Osorakan (1,346 m) in the Kanmuriyama Mountains in the western tip of the Chûgoku Mountains, at the boundary with Hiroshima Prefecture. Mt. Sanbe, in the center of the area, is an active volcano belonging to the Hakusan volcanic belt. It has been designated as Daisen-Oki National Park. Lava domes and a crater lake remain on the summit. The Gônokawa River (the Gôgawa) springs from Mt. Asa, runs through Miyoshi Basin in Hiroshima Prefecture, and feeds into the Sea of Japan from Gôtsu city. It is the longest river and it has the largest catchment area of all the rivers in the Chûgoku region. Towns along the river basin were developed as river ports, such as Misato and Kawamoto.

Lake Nakaumi and Lake Shinji have brackish water. Asian clams and ark bloody clams *(aka-gai)* have been caught in the lakes. The lakes are also wintering sites for tundra swans, and are the southern limit of the habitat for smelts. The Kotogahama coast in the city of Ôda is known for its singing sand, which was selected as one of the 100 Soundscapes by the Environment Agency (now the Ministry of the Environment). In the city, a huge sandglass that counts one year was built as a symbol of the coast.

Most of the area has a Sea of Japan-central Japan climate. Ski resorts were constructed along the Chûgoku Mountains, such as Kotobiki Forest Park at the foot of Mt. Kotobiki and Asahi Tenguston at the foot of Mt. Tenguishi in the former town of Asahi (now Hamada city). The

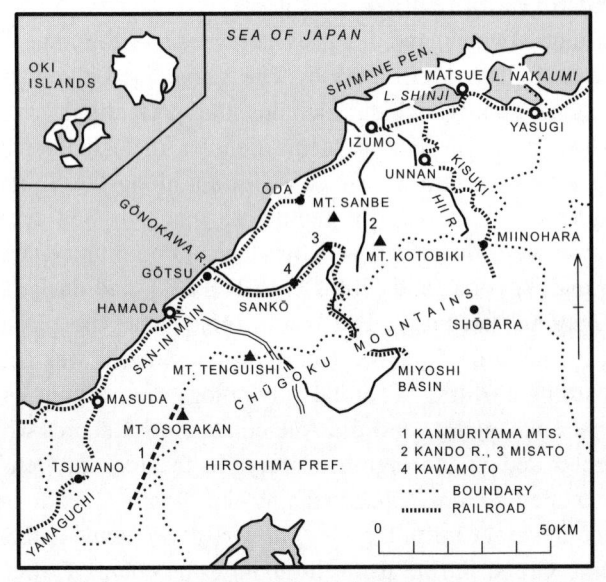

Figure 32 Shimane

Izumo Plain in the east is the largest plain in the San-in region. Paddy fields are found extensively on the plain, and the traditional farms are flanked by *tsuiji-matsu* (high hedges of Japanese black pine) to obstruct the winter monsoon (Illustration 11). In mountainous areas in the Izumo region in the east, iron was produced by means of *tatara* (furnace and bellow iron manufacturing). On the upper reaches of the Hii and the Kando, iron sand was gathered by *kanna-nagashi* (demolishing hills using water flow) in the Edo period. Although the iron manufacturing consumed bulk charcoal for fuel, the number of bare mountains *(hage-yama)* was less in the Chûgoku Mountains compared to the Seto Inland Sea side, since the area receives sufficient precipitation.

165

History and Culture

Izumo, Iwami, and Iki provinces became Shimane Prefecture in the Meiji period. The name is derived from Shimane county, which includes the prefectural capital, Matsue city. The county name denotes the island-shaped ridges that refer to the ria coast terrain along the Shimane Peninsula. In the city of Izumo, as much as 358 bronze swords were unearthed at Kôjindani, a community site of the mid-Yayoi period (200 BC to 100 BC), and designated as national treasures. The Izumo region was the place in which the god of the sea (Susanoo no Mikoto) was active according to the recorded mythology in *Nihon shoki (Japan chronicles)* and the Ancient Matters Record, which were edited in the eighth century. In the region, October was called *kamiari-zuki*, meaning the month of gods exist since the eight million gods *(yaoyorozu no kami)* gather at Izumo Grand Shrine from throughout the country, whereas the month was called *kanna-zuki*, meaning the month of gods absent, in the other regions. The Iwami Silver Mine site in Ôda has been listed as a World Heritage Site. The silver was shipped to Europe by Portuguese and Dutch traders in the Edo period.

Population and Traffic

The population of Shimane is 717,000. The main cities are Matsue (194,000), Izumo (144,000), Hamada (62,000), Masuda (50,000), Unnan (42,000), and Yasugi (42,000). The area is divided into the Izumo region to the east of Mt. Sanbe, the Iwami region to the west, and the Oki Islands. Although the population is the second smallest next to Tottori, two prime ministers have come from the prefecture, namely, Wakatsuki Reijirô (the 25th and the 28th) and Noboru Takeshita (the 74th). Regarding the transport infrastructure, these are several JR West railroads transcending the divide between the Sea of Japan and the Seto Inland Sea, that is to say, the Kisuki Line, connecting Matsue and Shôbara cities, the Yamaguchi Line, connecting Yamaguchi and Masuda cities, and the Sankô Line, connecting Gôtsu and Miyoshi cities. Miinohara Station, on the Kisuki Line, is linked directly to a skiing ground. Steam locomotives provide services between Tsuwano and Yamaguchi stations on the Yamaguchi Line. After the opening of the Hamada Expressway that runs north and south, the Iwami region strengthened ties with Hiroshima Prefecture. In terms of air transport, the prefecture has three airports; Izumo Airport in Izumo city and Oki Airport in the Oki Islands, which were opened in the 1960s, and Iwami Airport in Masuda city opened in the 1990s.

Primary Sector of Industry

The main agricultural commodity in terms of gross production is rice. The main rice varieties are *Koshihikari* and *Kinumusume*. The latter was bred by the National Agricultural Research Center for Kyûshû Okinawa Region. Although the gross agricultural production is decreasing, new activities have been taking place at a designated special agricultural zone in the city of Gôtsu. For instance, non-agricultural companies including a civil engineering contractor have moved into organic rice cultivation, organic mulberry cultivation, and mulberry tea processing. Japanese beef cattle have been reared on the Oki Islands. Farming that combines grazing beef cattle and crop cultivation on the islands is called *maki-hata*, which means rotation fields of grassland and cropland. In the fishing industry, the catches of sardine are the largest of all the prefectures, and the catches of horse mackerel are the second largest after Nagasaki. Those fish are trapped by purse seines with light bulbs, and Hamada is the largest fishing port. The catches of freshwater clam in Lake Shinji used to be the largest in the country, however, the amounts fell due to the increase in phytoplankton in the water.

Other Industries

The main industrial products in terms of gross production are personal computers, capacitors, and tools. Personal computer production is the second largest of all the prefectures after Yamagata. A Fujitsu Group factory in the city of Izumo produces laptops. Tools such as screwdrivers and pliers are produced by the main Vessel Co. factory in Izumo. In terms of traditional crafts, Sekishû roofing tiles have traditionally been used in local houses (Sekishû was another name of Iwami Province). The reddish-brown tiles are one of the three roofing tiles produced in the country, along with Awaji roofing tiles, produced on Awaji Island, and Sanshû roofing tiles produced in the Mikawa region.

33. Okayama

Okayama is located in the east of the Chûgoku region, facing the Seto Inland Sea (Figure 33).

Nature

The highest peak is Mt. Ushiro (Ushiroyama: 1,345 m) in the easternmost part of the prefecture, on the boundary with Hyôgo Prefecture. Mt. Hiruzen is a volcano on the boundary with Tottori Prefecture. In the Hiruzen Highland at the southern foot of the mountain, tourist facilities have been established, including a Jersey cattle ranch, a camp ground, and a horse-riding ground. In the Chûgoku mountains, which form the boundary with prefectures, a considerable number of mountain passes are to be found from 500 to 1,000 m above sea level. For example, from east to west, these are Shitosaka, Kuroo, Monomi, Ningyô, Tashiro, Inubasari, Shijûmagari, Akechidawa, and Tandadawa. Uranium ore was mined near the Ningyô Pass from the 1950s to the 1980s.

The Asahi River appears at the Hiruzen Highland, runs through the Okayama Plain, including built-up areas in Okayama city, and feeds into Kojima Bay. The bay was reclaimed by a Dutch engineer in the Meiji period. At the headwaters, there are Japanese giant salamander habitats.

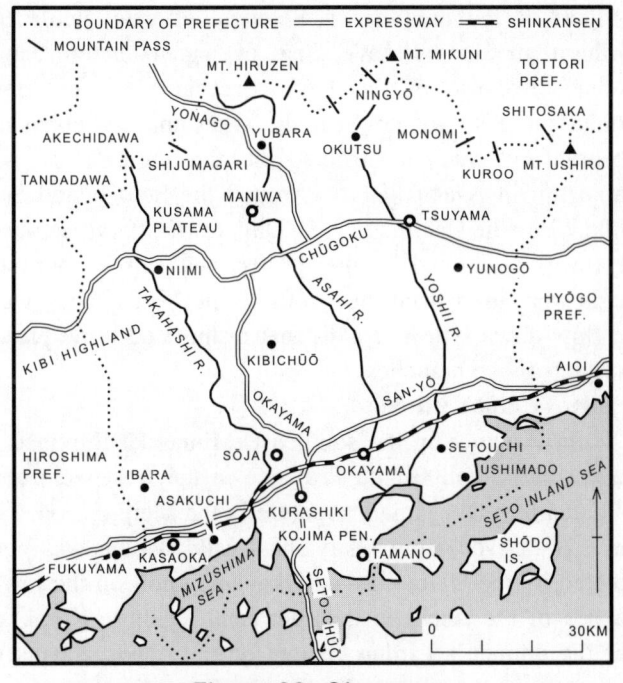

Figure 33 Okayama

The amphibians have been designated as special natural monuments. Located on the upper reaches of the river, the Yubara hot spring near Yubara Dam is one of three hot springs in the Mimasaka region, besides the Okutsu and Yunogô hot springs in the basins of the Yoshii River. The Yoshii emerges at Mt. Mikuni on the boundary with the old Mimasaka, Hôki, and Inaba provinces in the Chûgoku Mountains, and passes through in the east. On the upper reaches of the Takahashi River that runs in the west, there is a karst landscape on the Kusama Plateau. It includes Ikura and Rashômon limestone caves, and an intermittent mineral spring.

Much of the area has a Setouchi climate, while the northern mountains have Sea of Japan-central Japan climate. Because of the high percentage of fine days around the Seto Inland Sea, the Okayama Astrophysical Observatory was constructed at the summit of Mt. Chikurinji in Asakuchi city. Around the Seto Inland Sea, Kinkai Bay in Ushimado and Oku towns (now Setouchi city) was reclaimed in the 1950s, and salt evaporation ponds were used from the 1960s to the 1970s. They were the flow-down type salt pans that evaporated brine placed on fine bamboo branches.

History and Culture

Bizen Province in the southeast, Mimasaka Province in the northeast, and Bitchû Province in the west were consolidated into Okayama Prefecture in the Meiji period. The name is derived from Okayama Castle, which was constructed by the Ukita clan on Okayama knoll on the lower reaches of the Asahi in the fourteenth century. Kôrakuen was the domain's garden created on the opposite bank of the castle in the sixteenth century. It consists of one of the famed three gardens, along with Kairakuen and Kenrokuen. The Ôhara Museum of Art, which opened in 1930 in Kurashiki, is the first western art museum in the country. The streets in the neighborhood were designated as Kurashiki Bikan historical quarter in the 1960s.

In terms of food culture, specialties are *bara-zushi* and *mamakari-zushi*. The former is mixed sushi *(gomoku-zushi)* topped with boil-downed shiitake mushrooms and dried gourd shavings *(kanpyô)* on vinegared rice. It is often served during the Girls Festival in March. *Mamakari-zushi* is a kind of sushi topped with the pickled herring called *mamakari* or *zappa* on vinegared rice. The meaning of *mamakari* is fish "so delicious that people 'borrow' *(kari)* 'rice' *(mama)* from neighbors."

Population and Traffic

The population of Okayama Prefecture is 1,945,000. The main cities are Okayama (710,000), Kurashiki (476,000), Tsuyama (107,000), Sôja (66,000), Tamano (65,000), Kasaoka (54,000), and Maniwa (49,000). Okayama was assigned as an ordinance-designated city in 2009. San-yô Shinkansen, San-yô Expressway, and National Route 2 are the main routes crossing east to west in the coastal areas along the old San-yô Road. The railways in the area are the San-yô Mein Line, connecting Kôbe city and Moji in Kitakyûshû city, the Akô Line, connecting Aioi and Okayama cities, and the Ibara Line, connecting Sôja and Fukuyama cities. In inland areas, the Kishin Line connects Himeji city in Hyôgo and Niimi city, and the Chûgoku Expressway crosses the Tsuyama Basin and the Kibi Highland.

In terms of the transport infrastructure running north to south, there are the Seto-chûô Expressway and the Honshi-

Bisan railway line. The latter is operated by JR West and JR Shikoku (Shikoku Railway Company). They connect the cities of Kurashiki and Sakaide in Kagawa Prefecture across the Seto Inland Sea via the Great Seto Bridge. It is the world's longest two-story suspension bridge, carrying a road and a railroad. In inland areas, the Hakubi Line and Okayama Expressway run along the Takahashi River in the west, and the Tsuyama Line and the Yonago Expressway run along the Asahi River in the center of the area.

Primary Sector of Industry

The main agricultural commodities in terms of gross production are rice, eggs, and grapes. The main rice varieties are *Akebono*, *Akitakomachi*, and *Hinohikari*. *Akebono* was bred by Tôkai-Kinki Agricultural Experiment Station in Tsu city in the 1950s. In terms of egg production, there used to a National Poultry Experiment Station in the city of Okayama and a Harima Poultry Breeding Station in the city of Tatsuno in Hyôgo Prefecture. They contributed to the animal husbandry industry in the San-yô region (Okayama, Hyôgo, and Hiroshima prefectures), which is not very flat. Grape and peach cultivation for the fruit market is thriving in Okayama city and the town of Kibichûô. The main grape varieties are muscat and *Momotarô*, and the main peach variety is *Shimizuhakutô*. Muscat is a family of old varieties, which originated in the Mediterranean Basin. It was introduced to the Banshû government vineyard in the 1880s, whereupon its greenhouse cultivation was begun in Kaidani (now the North Ward in Okayama city). The fruit became a local specialty because of its specific fragrance and vivid green color.

Other Industries

The main industrial products in terms of gross production are gasoline, heavy oil, and light oil. Mizushima Coastal Industrial Zone, facing the Mizushima Sea, was developed at a Mitsubishi Heavy Industries aircraft factory site after the company had been invited to create the new site from reclaimed land at the mouth of the Takahashi. The company's name was changed to Mitsubishi Motors Corporation, and it began to produce automobiles after 1945. Several large factories were then established in the industrial zone, for instance, Mitsubishi Oil (now JX Nippon Oil & Energy Corporation) in the 1950s, and Kawasaki Steel (now JFE Steel Corporation) in the 1960s. On the Kojima Peninsula, Mitsui Shipbuilding & Engineering Co. was established in the 1910s in the town of Hibi (now the city of Tamano). The textile industry is also thriving. For instance, chemical fibers are produced in the city of Okayama, school uniforms in Tamano city, and jeans and school uniforms in Kurashiki city. Magosaburô Ôhara, who continued developing Kurashiki Bôseki (now Kurabô Industries), established Chûgoku Hydroelectric Company (now Chûgoku Electric Power Co.) and Kurashiki Kenshoku Co. (now Kuraray Co.), and also served as the president of Daiichi Gôdô Bank (now Chûgoku Bank) in the 1920s.

34. Hiroshima

Hiroshima is located in the center of the Chûgoku region, facing the Seto Inland Sea (Figure 34).

Nature

The highest peak is Mt. Osorakan, located in the Chûgoku Mountains in the west. Most of the area has a Setouchi climate, but the mountainous areas around the

Chûgoku Mountains are categorized as having a Sea of Japan-central Japan climate, and have been designated as a heavy snowfall zone. Osorakan ski resort was opened in the 1920s on the eastern slope of Mt. Osorakan. The river systems are divided into the Ôta River, which flows from Mt. Kanmuri, and the Gônokawa River (the Enokawa), which flows from Mt. Asa. On the upper reaches of the Ôta, *tatara* ironworks, such as the Kakesumiya Iron Mine that was established in the seventeenth century, took place, making use of local iron sand and charcoal until the Meiji period. The Hiroshima Plain is an alluvial plain on the lower reaches of the Ôta. The urban center of Hiroshima

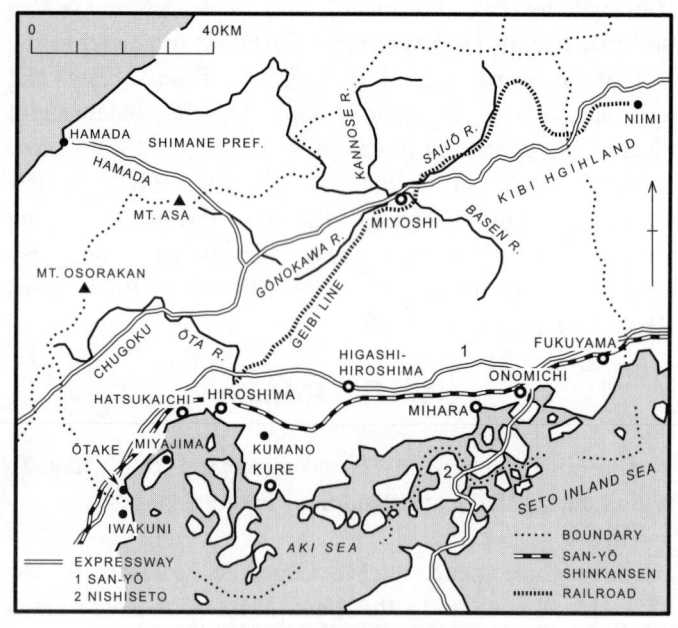

Figure 34 Hiroshima

city was developed on the deltas of the mouth, which are enclosed by mountains. In the new city residential areas that spread to the foothills, more than 70 people died as a result of the debris flows caused by the torrential downpour in 2014. The Miyoshi Basin between the Chûgoku Mountains and Kibi Highland is a river juncture in which the Saijô, the Basen, and the Kannose join the Gônokawa. The area also was a traffic node that connected the San-in and San-yô regions.

Miyajima Island (Itsukushima Island) in Hiroshima Bay is one of three such scenic sites in the country. Itsukushima Shrine, with its planked floors on the sea shore, was dedicated by Kiyomori Taira in the twelfth century. It was listed as a World Heritage Site in 1996. Tomonoura Bay in Fukuyama city was designated as the national "Tomo Park" scenic site in 1925, and designated as part of Setonaikai National Park in 1934, the first national park in the country. Red-throated loon *(abi)* was designated as a prefectural bird. Fishing with red-throated loons was conducted in the Geiyo Islands in the Aki Sea. In the process, a flock of red-throated loons chased the sand lances, and fishermen caught the sea bass and red sea bream that chased the sand lances.

History and Culture

With the abolition of the domain system in 1871, Aki Province, under the Ritsuryô code, became Hiroshima Prefecture, and Bingo Province became Fukuyama Prefecture (later Fukatsu Prefecture). They were merged into Hiroshima Prefecture with the integration of prefectures in 1876. The name is derived from Hiroshima Castle, which was built by Motonari Môri in 1589. The castle's name is derived from a delta in the Ôta River. During World War

II, the Fifth Division of the Imperial Army was stationed at the castle and a supply base was established at the Port of Ujina (now the Port of Hiroshima). An atomic bomb was dropped on Hiroshima at the end of the war. The Atomic Bomb Dome was listed as a World Heritage Site as Hiroshima Peace Memorial in 1996.

In terms of food culture, the best-known local food is cabbage pancakes *(okonomi-yaki)*. This is actually a wheat pancake with cabbage, Chinese noodles, egg, and pork, and seasoned with a thick sauce that does not soak into the dough. This current variation was established by the stalls in the 1950s. The origin of it was "one penny Western food" *(issen-yôshoku)* in the prewar years. *Okonomi-yaki* stalls were run also by war widows after the war. Onomichi is known as a history and movie city. Since fine weather prevails in summer, movies of some repute have been filmed in the city, such as *The Girl Who Leapt Through Time*. Beginning with the scene "the plow reaches heaven," *The Naked Island* was also filmed in Mihara Bay in the Seto Inland Sea.

Population and Traffic

The population of the prefecture is 2,861,000. The main cities are Hiroshima (1,174,000), Fukuyama (461,000), Kure (240,000), Higashihiroshima (190,000), Onomichi (145,000), Hatsukaichi (114,000), and Mihara (101,000). Hiroshima, the prefectural capital, was assigned as an ordinance-designated city in 1980. Hiroshima University moved out of the city to Saijô town in the 1980s (now Higashihiroshima city), and Hiroshima Airport was moved to the town of Hongô (now Mihara city) in the 1990s. The main traffic crosses east and west along the Seto Inland Sea. It consists of National Route 2, the San-yô Main Line, the San-yô Shinkansen, and the San-yô Expressway. In inland areas, the Geibi Line and the Chûgoku Expressway cross along the southern foot of the Chûgoku Mountains. Among the transport infrastructure running north to south, the Nishiseto Expressway (Shimanami Expressway) connects the cities of Onomichi and Imabari via the islands of Mukai, Innoshima, and Ikuchi in Hiroshima Prefecture, and of Ômi, Hakata, and Ôshima in Ehime Prefecture.

Primary Sector of Industry

The main agricultural commodities in terms of gross production are rice, eggs, beef cattle, and citruses. Terraced paddy fields were constructed in mountainous areas and islands. The main rice varieties are *Koshihikari* and *Hinohikari*. The former is cultivated in the north including, in mountainous areas. The latter was bred in the Kyûshû region, and is cultivated mainly in the south. Cultivation of citruses is flourishing on the island. In particular, lemon production accounts for 50 percent of the country's total. It is cultivated in the cities of Onomichi and Kure. In other agricultural and marine products, arrowheads produced in Fukuyama accounts for 60 percent of the country's production. The oyster production of the prefecture also accounts for 60 percent of the total in the country.

Other Industries

The main industrial products in terms of gross production are automobiles, automobile parts, and sheet steel. Those are produced mostly in the Seto Inland Sea Industrial Zone. Mazda Motor Corporation's main assembly point is located in the town of Fuchû, whose area is surrounded by Hiroshima city. The company has also set up other plants in the city of Miyoshi, as well as in Hôfu city in Yamaguchi Prefecture. The gross industrial output of

Fukuyama is the second largest in the prefecture after Hiroshima. In the city, Nippon Kokan K.K. (now JFE Steel Corporation) was established in the 1960s on coastal reclaimed land, and Fukuyama Transporting Co., which deals in freight, was founded in the 1940s. Shipbuilding and steel industries were developed at a naval arsenal site in the city of Kure. Other industries include shipbuilding in the city of Onomichi in the east and chemical fibers in Ôtake city in the west, contiguous to Iwakuni city in Yamaguchi Prefecture. Regarding traditional crafts, Kumano calligraphy brushes are crafted in the town of Kumano, and sake is brewed in Higashihiroshima city.

35. Yamaguchi

Yamaguchi is located in the west of Chûgoku region (the westernmost part of Honshû Island), facing the Seto Inland Sea and the Sea of Japan (Figure 35).

Nature

The highest peak is Mt. Jakuchi (1,337 m) in the Kanmuriyama Mountains in the east, near the boundary with Shimane and Hiroshima prefectures. Akiyoshi Plateau at the center is the largest karst site in the country. Among the over 400 limestone caves in the basement, the most extensive, Akiyoshi Cave, was designated as a special natural monument. At the east of the plateau, shriveled grass is burned at the end of winter in order to maintain the landscape and enable the practicing of doline agriculture. Limestone is quarried in the Shûhô and Isa mines in Mine city in the south of the plateau. A cement industry was developed in the cities of Onoda (now San-yô Onoda), Ube, and Mine using the limestone.

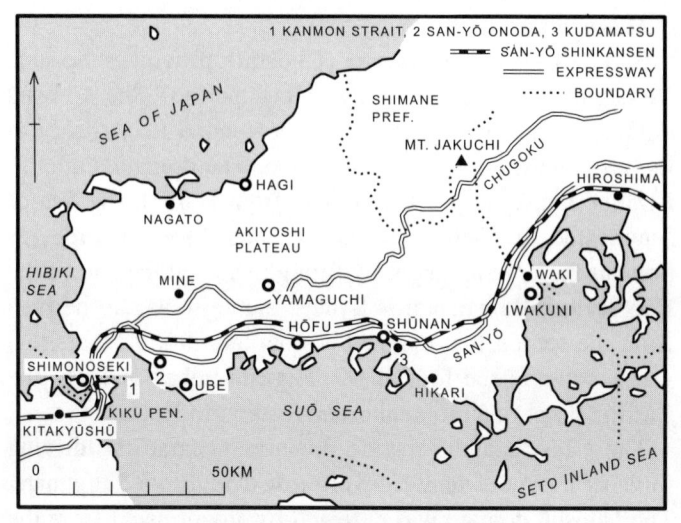

Figure 35 Yamaguchi

The Kanmon Strait connects the Hibiki Sea in the Sea of Japan with the Suô Sea in the Seto Inland Sea. It is known for the Battle of Dan no Ura in the twelfth century, in which the Taira clan was defeated, and also for the Duel of Ganryû Island by a sword master Musashi Miyamoto in the seventeenth century. The Kanmon tunnel on the San-yô Main Line was the first undersea tunnel in Japan, and was opened in 1942. The area from the city of Hagi to the former town of Yuya (now Nagato city) is a scenic site embracing sea cliffs, floating islands off the coastline, and singular sunsets over the Sea of Japan. It has been designated as Kita-Nagato Kaigan Quasi-National Park. The climate ranges from a Setouchi one to a Sea of Japan-central Japan one to a "southern Japan climate" (warm in summer, slightly cold in winter, much rainfall in the rainy

179

season, and less snowfall in winter).

History and Culture

Suô (Bôshû) and Nagato (Chôshû) provinces became Yamaguchi Prefecture in the Meiji period. The Chôshû domain, ruled by the Môri clan, extended its territory to the provinces in the Sengoku period. The domain's administrative headquarters was moved from Hagi at the Sea of Japan side to Yamaguchi in an inland area in order to prevent the bombardment by foreign ships at the end of the Edo period. Yamaguchi is a place name in Nagato derived from the terrain that denoted a mountain mouth, that is, it was located at the foot of Mt. Higashi-hôben and was the starting point of a mountain road leading to Hagi.

The Chôshû and Satsuma domains became the driving force of the movement to overthrow Tokugawa Shogunate. The Chôshû domain was defeated by a contingent from the United Kingdom, France, the Netherlands, and United States during the Shimonoseki Campaign in 1864, and changed its policy from one of expelling foreign countries to overthrowing the Shogunate. Many politicians who were active in the Meiji periods were educated at Shôkason-juku, a private school in the castle town of Hagi. These include Hirobumi Itô (the first, fifth, seventh, and tenth prime minister) and Aritomo Yamagata (the third and ninth prime minister).

Population and Traffic

The prefecture's population is 1,451,000. The main cities are Shimonoseki (281,000), Yamaguchi (197,000), Ube (174,000), Shûnan (149,000), Iwakuni (144,000), Hôfu (117,000), and San-yô Onoda (65,000). Yamaguchi city is located in the center of the Yamaguchi Basin. Although the area the city covers is the largest in the prefecture after the great merger of municipalities in the Heisei period, since the flatlands available for housing and industries are narrow, it is one of the most sparsely-populated capitals, along with Tottori city. Shimonoseki city is located at the western tip of the prefecture. The city is included in Kitakyûshû metropolitan area on the opposite shore of the Kanmon Strait. National Route 2 and the San-yô Main Line lead to the Kiku Peninsula in Fukuoka Prefecture through the Kanmon tunnels. The San-yô Shinkansen also leads to the peninsula through the New Kanmon tunnel. An old name of Shimonoseki was Akamagaseki, which is associated with the reddish rock strata. Among the traditional crafts produced there are Akama inkstones that were made from reddish brown tuffs quarried in Shimonoseki.

Primary Sector of Industry

The main agricultural commodities in terms of gross production are rice, vegetables, and eggs. Paddy rice farming has thrived since the Edo period because the Chôshû domain encouraged Bôchô *san-paku* (three white products in Bôshû and Chôshû), namely, rice, paper, and salt. The main rice varieties are *Koshihikari*, bred in Fukui Prefecture, *Hitomebore*, bred in Miyagi Prefecture, and *Hinohikari*, bred in Miyazaki Prefecture. Perennial crops cultivated include *unshû* mandarins and tea alongside Seto Inland Sea. Deciduous fruits, such as Japanese pears and apples, are cultivated in inland areas, and *natsu-mikan* (*Citrus natsudaidai*) are cultivated alongside the Sea of Japan. The original location for *natsu-mikan* is Ômi Island in Nagato city. Its cultivation began in the Meiji period as a remedy for the former samurai (incidentally, the guardrails of national roads in the prefecture are painted in *natsu-*

mikan orange). In the fishing industry, the sales of blowfish at Shimonoseki fishing port are the largest in the country. The port used to be a base for whaling.

Other Industries

The main industrial products in terms of gross production are gasoline, automobiles, and medicines. Gasoline is produced by Idemitsu Kôsan Co.'s Tokuyama refinery, at a petrochemical complex in Shûnan city, and by JX Nippon Oil & Energy Co.'s Marifu refinery in the town of Waki. Automobiles are produced by Mazda Motor Corporation in Hôfu city, and rail vehicles are produced by Hitachi Ltd., in the city of Kudamatsu. Medicines are produced by Takeda Pharmaceutical Co. in Hikari city, and by Kyôwa Hakkô Kirin Co. in Ube city. These heavy and chemical industries were developed on coastal reclaimed lands facing the tranquil inland sea. Uniqlo Co. is a fashion company, whose head office is located in Yamaguchi city (the headquarters is in Minato Ward in Tokyo). It is modeled after The Gap in the United States, and sells low-priced, highly functional products. Supplying clothes for wintry weather, it expanded its branches nationwide in the 1990s, then became a multinational company in the 2000s.

36. Tokushima

Tokushima is located in the east of the Shikoku region, facing the Kii Channel (Figure 36).

Nature

The highest peak is Mt. Tsurugi (1,955 m) in the Tsurugi Mountains, which constitute the highest massif in the eastern Shikoku Mountains. The annual precipitation levels on the mountain exceed 3,000 mm, and Tsurugi ski ground was constructed on the hillside. The Sanuki Mountains from 300 to 800 m above sea level cross the prefecture's northernmost part. They are also denoted as the Asan Mountains since they divide Awa and Sanuki provinces.

The east-flowing Yoshino River crosses the Tokushima Plain along the Median Tectonic Line between the Sanuki Mountains and Shikoku Mountains. The river is also called Shikoku Saburô (the third in Shikoku) as it consisted of three majestic rivers, besides Bandô Tarô (the first in Kantô: the Tone River) and Tsukushi Jirô (the second in Kyûshû: the Chikugo River). The Yoshino courses north to south through gorges, including Ôboke and Koboke in the western tip of the prefecture. There are stations with switchback rails on the JR Shikoku Dosan Line at the gorges. The basin of the Iya River, a tributary of the

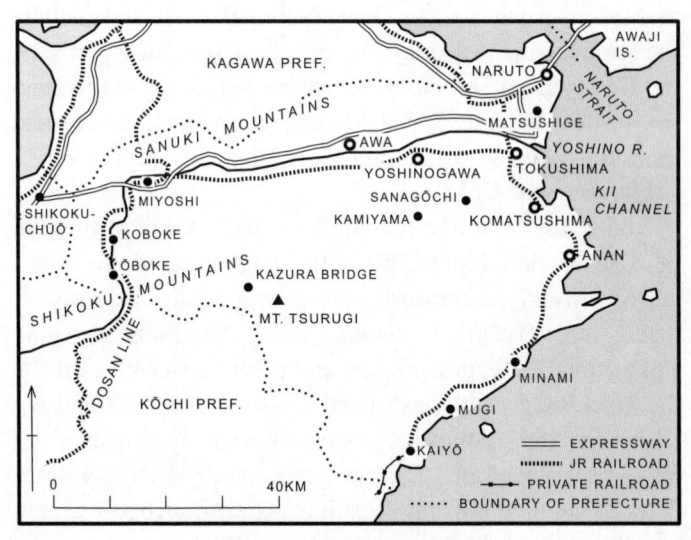

Figure 36 Tokushima

183

Yoshino, is known for the legend of the fleeing Taira clan. Kazura Bridge, a pair of precarious suspension bridges, in the inner Iya region is regarded as one of three peculiar-shaped bridges, along with Saru Bridge in Ôtsuki city and Kintai Bridge in Iwakuni city.

The Naruto Strait is a narrow stretch of water that connects the Kii Channel in the Pacific Ocean and the Harima Sea in the Seto Inland Sea. After the Ônaruto Bridge was opened across the Naruto Strait in 1985, Tokushima city strengthened ties with the Hanshin region. The opposing currents of the strait under the suspension bridge create one of the largest three whirlpools in the world, besides Messina and Seymour straits. The climate is categorized as a Pacific Ocean-central Japan one. Scenic sites and preservation areas relating to the climate continue from Anan city to Cape Muroto, which have been assigned as Muroto-Anan Kaigan Quasi-National Park, and include the tropical plant displays in Benten Island in Anan city, the Senbakaigai sea cliffs, a nesting beach for loggerhead sea turtles, Hiwasa Turtle Museum in Minami town, and thousand-year-old coral on Ôshima Island in Mugi town.

History and Culture

Under the Ritsuryô code, Awa and Awaji provinces became Myôdô Prefecture in the beginning of the Meiji period. Shortly afterwards, the Awaji area was consolidated into Hyôgo Prefecture, and Awa area became Tokushima Prefecture. At the end of the sixteenth century, the Hachisuka clan constructed Tokushima Castle and established the Tokushima domain on the orders of Hideyoshi Toyotomi. The castle's name is derived from a delta at the mouth of the Yoshino. After the Kôgo Incident revolt in the early Meiji period, the Hachisuka clan (the lord) and the Inada clan (the chief retainer) were moved respectively to Uryû and Shizunai (now Shinhidaka town) in Hokkaidô. *Awaodori* is a big *bon* dance that is known for a song that goes, "dancers are fools, watchers are fools, both are fools, why not dance?" Although it began in the era of the Tokushima domain, it became popular after the war and spread to Kôenji district of Suginami Ward in Tokyo in the 1950s.

Population and Traffic

The population of the prefecture is 785,000. The main cities are Tokushima (265,000), Anan (76,000), Naruto (62,000), Yoshinogawa (44,000), Komatsushima (41,000), and Awa (39,000). Tokushima city is the terminal of various non-electrified railroads, namely, the Tokushima Line that comes from Miyoshi city, the Kôtoku Line that comes from Takamatsu city in Kagawa Prefecture, and the Mugi Line that goes to the town of Kaiyô. The Tokushima Expressway, which opened in the 1990s, starts in Naruto city, runs along the Yoshino River, and finishes at Shikokuchûô city in Ehime Prefecture. Tokushima's airport is located on a delta at the mouth of the Yoshino in Matsushige town. It was constructed on a naval air base, and named Tokushima Awaodori Airport.

Primary Sector of Industry

The main agricultural commodities in terms of gross production are vegetables, rice, fruit, and broilers. Vegetable production is thriving on the Tokushima Plain. The vegetables are shipped mostly to the Keihanshin region. The main rice varieties are *Koshihikari* and *Kinuhikari*, both of which were bred in the Hokuriku region. The former is cultivated mainly in the city of Anan as an early-ripening variety that is harvested in late August. The production of *sudachi (Citrus sudachi)*, a small green citrus native to the prefecture, is the largest of all the prefectures. It is cultivated in hilly areas near the capital, such as in the town of Kamiyama and the village of Sanagôchi. *Sudachi* jelly, which was also created in the prefecture, is served in school lunches in elementary and junior high school in the graduation season since the fruit is a homophone of "leaving the nest." The area specializes in chicken and indigo production. Awa-*odori* is a local breed of long-tailed chicken bred in the 1990s (it is categorized as a broiler). As for indigo cultivation, the basin of the Yoshino River used to be the main indigo producing center because of the encouragement of the Tokushima domain. The indigo cultivation decreased dramatically in the twentieth century because of the increase in imports from India and the influx of synthetic dyes. Indigo cultivation and indigo-dyed goods production are mainly industries at tourism today.

Other Industries

The main industrial products in terms of gross production are medicines, light emitting diodes, and lithium ion batteries. Ôtsuka Pharmaceutical Co. was established in the prefecture (the headquarters is in Chiyoda Ward in Tokyo). It has been producing popular products such as Oronine-H Ointment since the 1950s, Oronamin-C Drink since the 1960s, and Pocari Sweat and Calorie Mate since the 1980s. The production of light-emitting diodes and the lithium ion batteries is the largest of all the prefectures. Nichia Corporation in Anan city commercialized the world's first blue light-emitting diode. Sanyo Electric Co. has the world's largest lithium ion battery factory in the town of Matsushige. It was moved from Awaji Island so as to avail of a larger lot. JustSystems Corporation, which is known for its input software technologies, such as Ichitaro and ATOK, is headquartered in Tokushima city.

37. Kagawa

Kagawa is located in the northeast of the Shikoku region, facing the Seto Inland Sea (Figure 37).

Nature

The highest peak is Mt. Ryûô (1,060 m) in the Sanuki Mountains, which run east to west in the south of the prefecture. The Sanuki Plain extends to the north of the mountains. The plain has seven inselbergs, which are called the Sanuki Seven Fuji. Among them, Mt. Iino (422 m) in the west of the plain is an imposing sight from the Dosan Line and the Takamatsu Expressway (Illustration 12). The climate is categorized as a Setouchi one, and the precipitation levels are low in summer. Since the rivers running from the Sanuki Mountains are small-scale ones, more than 14,000 reservoirs were built in the Sanuki Plain. The largest one is Mannô Pond on the west foot of the Sanuki Mountains. The pond was constructed in the eighth century, and renovated in the ninth century by Kûkai, the founder of Shingon Buddhism. To deal with water shortages, a Kagawa Canal across the plain was completed in 1974. It takes water from the Ikeda Dam at the Yoshino River in Tokushima Prefecture.

Shôdo Island is the second largest island in the Seto Inland Sea after Awaji. It is the sole olive-producing center in the country. The huge granite stones, weighing more than 100 tons, used in Ôsaka Castle were cut on the island. The shipping method used for the immense stones is

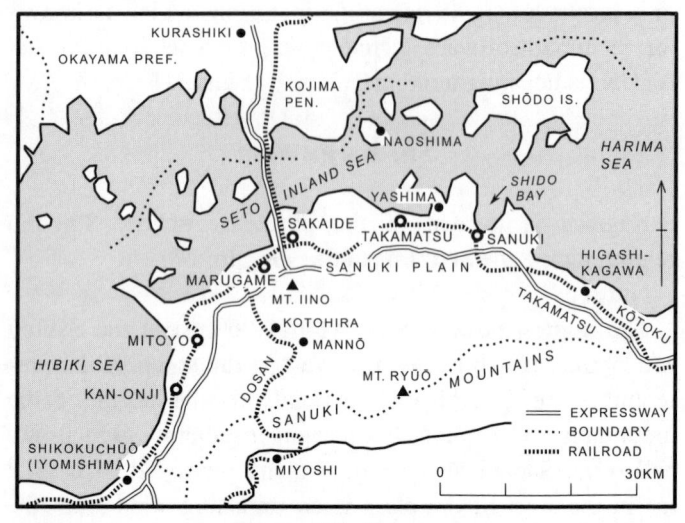

Figure 37 Kagawa

unknown. Granite is currently quarried at Aji town in the city of Takamatsu, on the opposite shore of the island, across Shido Bay. The Law Concerning Special Measures for Conservation of the Environment of the Seto Inland Sea was enacted in 1973 to regulate ocean dumping of industrial waste and human sewage that was causing eutrophication. Following that, the Akashiwo Research Institute of Kagawa Prefecture was established in Takamatsu to curtail the damage to the fishing industry caused by red tides.

History and Culture

Under the Ritsuryô code, Sanuki Province was divided into the Takamatsu domain in the east and the Marugame domain in the west during the Edo period. They were merged into Kagawa Prefecture in the Meiji period. The name came from Kagawa county, which contained the prefectural capital, and the county name might be derived from the scent of the birch tree ("ka-gawa" literally signifies a sweet-smelling river). Mt. Yashima, in a suburb of Takamatsu city, is an ancient battlefield site that is known for the episodes "a folding fan as the target" of Yoichi Nasu and the "floating bow" by Yoshitsune Minamoto. Taking advantage of the warm climate, the Takamatsu clan devised local specialties called Sanuki *san-paku* (three white products), namely, the salt produced in the salt fields utilizing tidal action *(irihama-shiki enden)*, the sugar made from local sugarcane *(wasanbon-tô)*, and the cotton plant.

The god of maritime traffic is worshipped at Kotohiragû Shrine in the town of Kotohira. It is affectionately nicknamed Konpira-san, although visitors toil up more than 1,000 steps to the shrine. Even an annual stone stepping marathon is held there. In food culture, the prefecture has received the epithet the "udon prefecture." Udon noodles are close to people's lives. Many Sanuki udon shops provide udon bowls at low prices. *An-mochi zôni* is also a local food of white miso soup and rice cakes with sweet bean jam.

Population and Traffic

The population of Kagawa is 996,000. The main cities are Takamatsu (419,000), Marugame (110,000), Mitoyo (69,000), Kan-onji (63,000), Sakaide (56,000), and Sanuki (53,000). The Great Seto Bridge, which was opened in 1988, connects Sakaide and Kurashiki city. It is a series of two-tiered suspension bridges whose length reaches 13 km. Seto-chûô Expressway, which starts from Hayashima interchange in Okayama Prefecture, runs on the upper deck and the Honshi-Bisan railway line, on the lower deck. The Takamatsu Expressway starts in the city of Naruto in

Tokushima Prefecture, crosses the Sanuki Plain, and leads to Shikokuchûô city in Ehime Prefecture. The JR Shikoku's Yosan and Kôtoku lines, and the Takamatsu-Kotohira Electric Railroad Co.'s Kotohira Line extend east to west on the plain.

Primary Sector of Industry

The main agricultural commodities in terms of gross production are vegetables, rice, and eggs. Lettuces are harvested in winter and shipped to wholesale markets in the Keihanshin region. Onions are harvested in early summer, the pre-harvest season of other prefectures, and shipped mainly to the Keihin (from Tokyo to Yokohama) region. Among the main rice varieties, the *Hinohikari*, bred in Miyazaki Prefecture, accounts for 43 percent of the paddy rice-cultivation area, and the *Koshihikari*, bred in Fukui Prefecture, accounts for 37 percent. Once wheat production thrived in the dry weather of the Seto Inland Sea; hence, Kagawa comprised the top three wheat producers besides Hyôgo and Okayama. After suffering competition from imports, the cultivated wheat area declined greatly, and is now less than one seventieth of Hokkaidô Prefecture's, the largest wheat producer at present. Marugame Udon, a nationwide Sanuki udon chain, is also managed by a company outside the prefecture.

In the fishing industry, young yellowtail *(hamachi)* and laver cultivation, and cultural fishery by discharging of fries of Japanese Spanish mackerel *(sawara)* are thriving. Young yellowtail cultivation was started at Ado Pond in the former town of Hiketa (now Higashikagawa city) in the 1920s, although the main cultivation center shifted to Kagoshima Prefecture during the outbreak of red tides in summer and the low water temperature in winter.

Other Industries

The main industrial products in terms of gross production are cargo ships, gasoline, and gold bullion. In terms of number of establishments, the main categories are Japanese noodles and stone masonry products. Shipbuilding and oil manufacturing are operated by Kawasaki Heavy Industries and Cosmo Oil Co. at Bannosu Coastal Industrial Park, which was built at a salt field site in Sakaide city. Gold bullion production is the largest of all the prefectures. It is produced at a Mitsubishi Materials Corporation smelter on Naoshima Island. A copper smelter was established on the island in the early twentieth century for reducing the environment problems caused by copper smelting in Honshû Island. In terms of light industry, fans are made in Marugame city and gloves, in Higashikagawa city, accounting for the largest production of these items in the country. Fan manufacturing was started as a sideline by farmers and clansmen in the Marugame clan. Glove manufacturing was brought from Ôsaka Prefecture in the end of the nineteenth century, and substituted for the declining salt industry.

38. Ehime

Ehime is located in the northwest of the Shikoku region, facing the Seto Inland Sea and the Bungo Channel (Figure 38).

Nature

Mt. Ishizuchi (Mt. Tengu: 1,982 m) at the Ishizuchi mountain range in the west of the Shikoku Mountains is the highest peak in western Japan. A chain field was installed to climb up to the vicinity of the steep summit. It has been worshiped as a sacred place of Shugendô since ancient times. Mountain roads and a ropeway were provided after the mountain was designated as Ishizuchi Quasi-National Park in the 1950s. The Dôzan is a Class A river, and the largest tributary of the Yoshino. The Besshi Copper Mine on the upper reaches was operated by the House of Sumitomo from the 1690s to the early 1970s. It became the basis for the house advancing as one of Japan's three conglomerates (zaibatsu) in modern times. The Niihama Plain (the Dôzen Plain) stretches from Niihama to Saijô cities. The plain waters were shallow enough for a

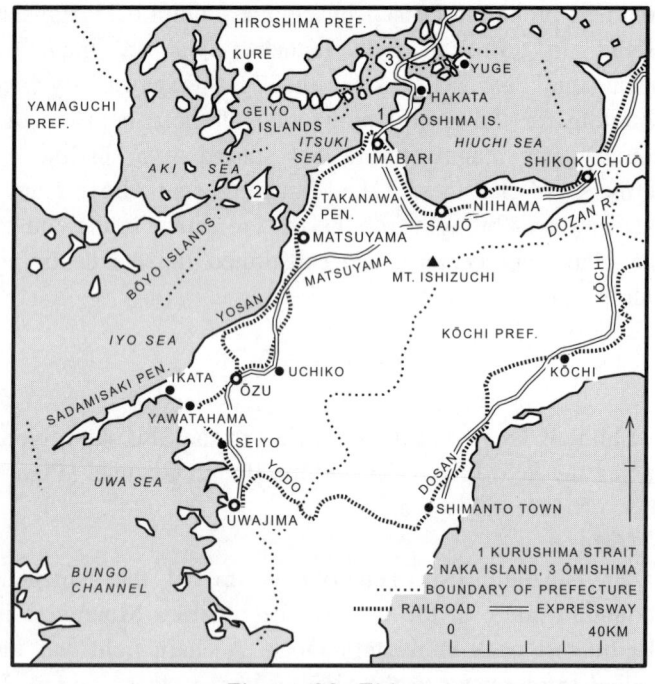

Figure 38 Ehime

192

good distance for constructing industrial parks by land reclamation. Dôgo hot spring of Matsuyama city on the Matsuyama Plain (the Dôgo Plain) has non-volcanic hot water. There are no volcanoes on Shikoku Island, hence the heat source is the Median Tectonic Line fault.

The Seto Inland Sea inlets are divided into the seas of Hiuchi, Itsuki, Aki, and Iyo from east to west. The Hiuchi Sea, at the east of the Takanawa Peninsula, was named after the flints that it once yielded. The Itsuki Sea, at the west of the peninsula, was named after Itsuki Island, one of the Geiyo Islands of Kure city. A winding boundary between Ehime and Hiroshima prefectures runs between the Geiyo and the Bôyo Islands since it was delimited based on traditional fishing villages and fishing grounds. The Sadamisaki Peninsula is stretched along the Median Tectonic Line. The Iyo Sea to the north of the peninsula was the epicenter of the Geiyo earthquakes in 1905 and 2001. The Uwa Sea to the south of the peninsula is the water source for the aquaculture farming of red sea bream, white trevally, and pearls. In the warm temperatures of the Setouchi climate, citrus cultivation is also thriving on the sloping hills along the ria coastline of the sea.

History and Culture

Under the Ritsuryô code, Iyo Province became Matsuyama (Ishizuchi) and Uwajima (Kamiyama) prefectures, and they were merged into Ehime Prefecture in the Meiji period. Ehime was named after a place mentioned in the Ancient Matters Records that was edited in the eighth century. Regarding the religious culture, 26 of the 88 holy places *(fudasho)* of the Shikoku Pilgrimage, which is associated with the Buddhist monk, Kûkai, are found in the prefecture (the largest of the Shikoku four prefectures).

In terms of food culture, sea bream bowls and *jakoten* (local fish paste) in Uwajima city were selected for the 100 Local Cuisines by the Ministry of Agriculture, Forestry and Fisheries. Furthermore, the *unshû* mandarins in the Nishiuwa region (Yawatahama and Seiyo cities, and Ikata town), the fragrant orange-colored olives at Oshimori Temple in Saijô city, and the Japanese candles in the town of Uchiko were selected as some of the 100 Aromatic Landscapes by the Ministry of the Environment. In terms of literature, *Botchan* is a famous novel written by Soseki Natsume. He became a teacher of English in Ehime *Jinjô* junior high school in Matsuyama city in 1895.

Population and Traffic

Ehime's population is 1,431,000. The main cities are Matsuyama (517,000), Imabari (167,000), Niihama (122,000), Saijô (112,000), Shikokuchûô (90,000), Uwajima (84,000), and Ôzu (47,000). The Kurushima Channel Bridge, on the Nishiseto Expressway, is a triad suspension bridge that connected Ôshima Island and Imabari city in 1999. The Matsuyama Expressway, which partly opened in 1985, was the first expressway in the Shikoku region. It runs east to west, and connects Shikokuchûô and Matsuyama cities in a straight line. JR Shikoku's Yosan Line connects Takamatsu and Uwajima cities. It leads to Matsuyama city via Imabari city in the north of the Takanawa Peninsula.

Primary Sector of Industry

The main agricultural commodities in terms of gross production are fruit, vegetables, rice, and swine. The citrus production, including *unshû* mandarins, *iyokan* mandarins, and *ponkan* mandarins, is the largest of all the prefectures. Citruses are cultivated on well-drained slopes in coastal areas along the Uwa Sea, such as Yawatahama and Uwajima cities, and on islands such as Naka and Ômi. The citrus harvest peaks in December, although because of greenhouse cultivation, there are harvests all year round. The local agricultural cooperative embarked on orange juice processing in 1952. It is distributed nationwide under the Pon Juice brand. In the city of Matsuyama, avocado trees were planted as substitutes for *iyokan* mandarins.

Other Industries

The main industrial products in terms of gross production are cargo ships, copper products, and gasoline. In terms of number of establishments, the main categories produced are towels and ready-mixed concrete. In the shipbuilding industry, Imabari Shipbuilding Co. has dockyards in the cities of Imabari and Saijô. A long spell of fair weather under a Setouchi climate is suitable for outdoor works such as painting and drying hulls. As for oil manufacturing, the Taiyô Oil Co. oil refinery, which was founded in Kôchi Prefecture, is located in the former town of Kikuma (now Imabari city). Imabari is the largest producer of towels in the country. Towel production was started by machine weaving in the Meiji period. In Matsuyama city, chemical fibers are produced by Teijin and agricultural machinery, by Iseki Co. At a coastal industrial zone in the former city of Iyomishima (now Shikokuchûô city), modern paper mills have been established by Daiô Paper Corporation and Unicharm Corporation. Ôzu-*washi* is the Japanese paper produced in traditional paper mills in the west Iyo province. The previous Iyo-*hôsho* produced in the east Iyo Province was used by ukiyo-e (traditional woodblock prints) print masters, as it was of high quality and competitively priced.

Salt production once flourished on the islands of Hakata, Yuge, and Ômi. The monopoly in salt held by Japan Tobacco and Salt Public Corporation (now Japan Tobacco) was amended in the early 1970s. Afterward, although extensive salt fields were abandoned, Hakata Salt Mfg. was established. The company's factory on Ômi Island began to sell imported salt blended with the bittern of the Seto Inland Sea. When the consumption of natural salt boomed in the 2000s, it resulted in a revival of the flow-down type salt fields that made use of natural drying. Incidentally, the monopolization was continued until the late 1990s.

39. Kôchi

Kôchi is located in the south of the Shikoku region, facing the Pacific Ocean (Figure 39).

Nature

The proportion of the prefecture's area given over to forestry comes to 84 percent, the highest of all the prefectures. The highest mountain, Mt. Miune (1,893 m) in the east has been designated as Tsurugisan Quasi-National Park including Mt. Tsurugi in Tokushima Prefecture. The Yoshino River originates at Mt. Kamegamori in Ishizuchi Quasi-National Park in the north, whose summit lies in Ehime Prefecture. It runs in the north of the prefecture, and crosses the Shikoku Mountains along a transverse valley. Japan Water Agency's multi-purpose Sameura Dam and Shikoku Electric Power Co.'s Ômorigawa, Nagasawa, and Ôhashi dams build for power generation were constructed on the upper reaches of the river. Shikoku Karst, at about an altitude of 1,400 m, is located in the west of the Shikoku Mountains, at the boundary with Ehime Prefec-

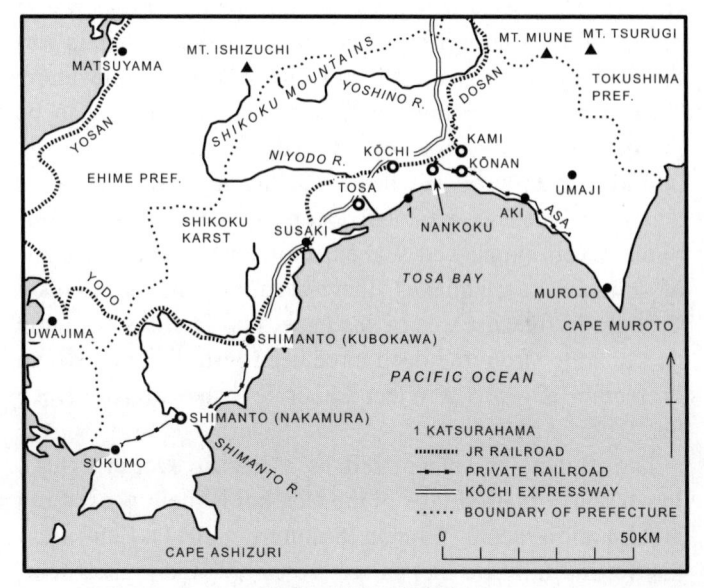

Figure 39 Kôchi

ture. The plateau's landscape has grazing dairy and beef cattle on grassland, and the scattered white Karrenfelds are a tourism attraction. The Shimanto (Watari) River, one of the 100 Exquisite Water, rises around Shikoku Karst and flows into the Pacific Ocean from the Nakamura Plain. The Niyodo river emerges from Mt. Ishizuchi, crosses the Shikoku Mountains, and flows into Tosa Bay from the Kôchi Plain. Both rivers are known for clear streams, having low-water crossings, and fisheries of freshwater prawns (the so-called *kawa-ebi*) and glass eels.

Mt. Torigata (1,220 m) is located on the east of Shikoku Karst. As the Chichibu Paleozoic strata in the mountain contain high-quality limestone, Nittetsu Mining Co. acquired a mining right in 1966, and embarked on mining from 1971. It was developed as an open-pit mine whose output was the largest in the country, and the mountain was reduced by more than 200 m from its original elevation. That mountain and the neighboring Mt. Irazu used to be protected *(otome-yama)* by the Tosa domain in the Edo period. Cape Muroto divides Tosa Bay and Kii Channel. It was designated as a Global Geopark because of the turbidite layers (upheaved seabed sediment) and the imprints of massive earthquakes that occurred in the Nankai Trough. In the east side of the cape, two facilities to pump up sea water from the deep have been installed, i.e., Kôchi Prefectural Deep Sea Water Laboratory and Muroto Deep Sea Water Aqua Farm.

The climate is categorized as a Pacific Ocean-central Japan one. Umaji village in the east holds the highest daily precipitation record in Japan (852 mm in 2011). Ekawasaki district in Shimanto city in the west holds the highest temperature record (41.0 °C in 2013). Gales were observed at the tapered Muroto and Ashizuri capes. The fastest wind of the country on flat ground (69.8 m/s) was recorded at Muroto cape by Typhoon No. 23 (Shirley) in 1965. More than 650 people were killed or went missing as a result of the 1946 Nankai earthquake (so called Shôwa Nankai earthquake) and its tidal wave, which hit the cities of Nakamura (now Shimanto), Susaki, and Kôchi.

History and Culture

Tosa Province under the Ritsuryô code became Kôchi Prefecture in the Meiji period. The name is derived from Kôchi Castle, which was constructed by the Yamauchi clan in the early Edo period. The castle, meanwhile, was named after Mt. Kôchi between the Kagami and Enokuchi rivers. Harimaya Bridge is located in the downtown area of Kôchi city, to the east of the castle. It is described in a *yosakoi* song as follows: "A Buddhist monk bought a hair ornament at Harimaya Bridge." Katsurahama beach in Urado Bay, which the two rivers enter, is known for its bronze statue of Ryôma Sakamoto, a political activist at the end of Edo period. His thousand rifles were used in the Boshin War after his death.

The *Yosakoi* festival was started by the Kôchi City Chamber of Commerce and Industry in the 1950s. The festival has spread, including the derivative *Yosakoi Sôran* festival, and dancer teams have been organized throughout the country since the 1990s. In some festivals, dancers follow trucks carrying sound speakers. The style resembles a parade of street carnival in Brazil. Other cultural specialties include the Tosa breed of fighting dog, which was bred from the English Mastiff and Great Dane in the Meiji period. The Kôchi Prefectural Makino Botanical Garden was established in the memory of Tomitaro Makino, who is known as the father of Japanese botany.

Population and Traffic

The prefecture's population is 764,000, the third smallest after Tottori and Shimane prefectures. The main cities are Kôchi (343,000: 45 percent of the population), Nankoku (49,000), Shimanto (36,000), Kônan (34,000), Kami (29,000), and Tosa (29,000). Regarding the railroad infrastructure, JR Shikoku operates the Dosan and Yodo lines and Tosa Kuroshio Tetsudo Co. the Asa, Nakamura, and Sukumo lines. The Asa Line extends to the east from the Dosan Line, and the Nakamura and the Sukumo lines extend to the south from the Yodo Line. Those JR and private railroad companies run decorated *Anpanman* trains in homage to a popular cartoonist from the prefecture.

Primary Sector of Industry

The main agricultural commodities in terms of gross production are vegetables, rice, and fruit. The amounts of aubergines, gingers, *myôga* gingers, leeks, and *shishitô* peppers produced are the largest of all the prefectures. Cucumber and green pepper production is also thriving. Aubergines and cucumbers are grown mainly in greenhouses on paddy fields in the Kôchi Plain. Regarding the rice production, double cropping on paddy fields prospered until the enactment of the policy of reducing rice production in the 1970s. Rice farming was changed to early-ripening cultivation, whose harvest starts from the end of July. As for fruit production, the amounts of *yuzu* and pomelos grown are the largest of all the prefectures. The *yuzu* producing center is located in mountainous municipalities in the east, including Aki city and Aki country, whereas pomelos are cultivated in the city of Tosa in the Kôchi Plain and in Sukumo city in the southwest.

In the fishing industry, pole-and-line fishing of bonito flourishes. That pelagic fish is caught by means of the deep-sea and coastal fisheries that operate continuously for about 10 months. The fishing boats unload at fishing ports all around the country. Annual bonito consumption per resident in Kôchi is the largest of all the prefectures. Popular bonito foods include *tataki* (lightly roasted bonito) and *sawachi-ryôri* (a feast of bonito sashimi served on a large plate). Formerly, sashimi was consumed mostly in coastal areas.

Other Industries

The gross output of industrial products is the lowest of all the prefectures. The main products are paper, cement, and dental materials. In terms of number of establishments, the main categories are ready-mixed concrete and lumber. As for paper production, Nippon Kôdoshi Corporation's factories produce separators for capacitors in the cities of Kôchi, Aki, and Nankoku. In the vicinity of Nankoku interchange of the Kôchi Expressway, there is an Ortus Technology Co. factory, which produces small and medium-sized liquid crystal displays. The factory is a spin-off from Casio Computer Co., whose founder was from Nankoku city.

40. Fukuoka

Fukuoka is located in the north of the Kyûshû region, facing the Sea of Japan, the Seto Inland Sea, and the Ariake Sea (Figure 40).

Nature

The highest peak is Mt. Shakadake (1,231 m) on the boundary with Ôita Prefecture. At the foot of the mountain, shaded green tea *(gyokuro)* is cultivated in the villages of Hoshino and Yabe (now part of Yame city). Hoshino village has steep terraced fields made of stonework for paddy rice cultivation. During the rice harvest season, the terraced fields are surrounded by cluster-amaryllises and many people take pictures of the scenes. Such masonry fields are to be found in western Japan. At the west foot of the Minô (Mizunawa) Mountains, Yame Central Tea Garden is to be found, and the area has been turned into the main Yame-tea producing center. The Hirao Plateau in the north is counted as one of the largest three karst areas in the country, besides Akiyoshi Plateau and Shikoku Karst. The amount of limestone that is quarried around the plateau is the fourth largest of all the prefectures, after

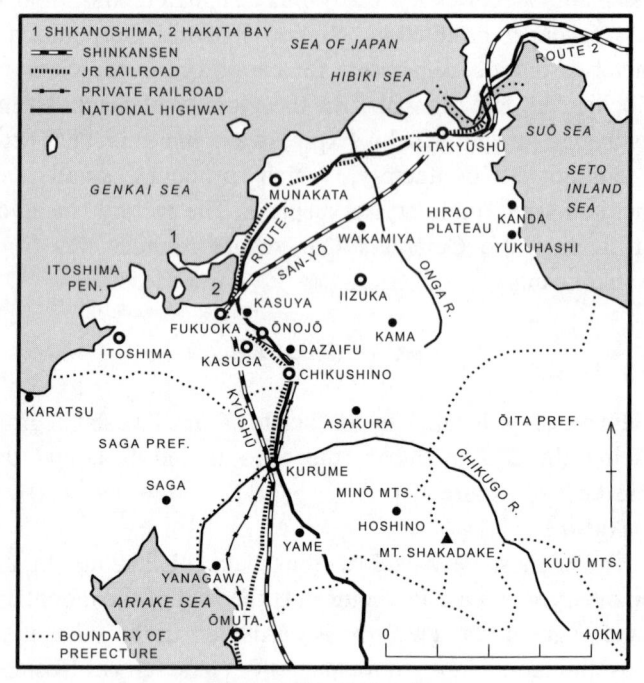

Figure 40 Fukuoka

Ôita, Yamaguchi, and Kôchi.

The Chikugo River begins the Senomoto Highland between Mt. Kujû and the outer rim of Mt. Aso, crosses the Tsukushi Plain, the largest plain in the Kyûshû region, and flows into the Ariake Sea. On the middle reaches of the river, water wheels are preserved, including the triad water wheel in Asakura city. The Onga River appears in Kama city, runs through the Nôgata Plain, and flows into the Hibiki Sea. In the basin, the Chikuhô Coalfields once produced the largest output of coal in the country. The coal was supplied to the Yahata Steel Works, which opened in

Yahata village (now Kitakyûshû city) in 1901, and to households as a daily necessity until the energy revolution in the 1960s. In addition to the Chikuhô Coalfields, there were Kasuya (Fukuoka) coal mine in the Fukuoka Plain and the Mitsui Miike coal mine in the city of Ômuta.

The Itoshima Peninsula faces the Genkai Sea and Hakata and Karatsu bays. Keya no Ôto in the west of the peninsula is a sea cave made of columnar joints of basalt. Genkô Bôrui (stone walls for the attack of the Yuan dynasty) was assembled in the east of the peninsula in the late thirteenth century. Shikanoshima Island in the city of Fukuoka on the northeast of Hakata Bay is a land-tied island in which a gold seal was excavated in the Edo period. Judging from the five characters inscribed on the seal, "the king of Na of Wa (Japan), Han," it was sent from the Han dynasty to the Na state that existed around Fukuoka from the first to the third centuries. With respect to the climate, the whole area is categorized as a southern Japan one. It is warm in terms of the annual average temperature, and receives considerable rainfall during the rainy season. The primeval forest of camphor laurel in Fukuoka city and Kasuya county and of the Japanese boxes in Asakura city are designated as special natural monuments.

History and Culture

The name Kyûshû is derived from the nine provinces of the island that were named under the Ritsuryô code, namely Chikuzen, Chikugo, Buzen, Hizen, Higo, Bungo, Hyûga, Ôsumi, and Satsuma. Besides them, Tsushima and Iki provinces were included in Saikaidô. Among the provinces, Chikuzen and Chikugo, and a part of Buzen became Fukuoka Prefecture in the Meiji period. The name is derived from the hometown of Nagamasa Kuroda, the first castellan of the Fukuoka domain, who had come from Fukuoka manor in Bizen Province (now Setouchi city in Okayama Prefecture). Dazaifu was the provincial office in ancient times, and Hakata-*tsu* was the outer harbor. Hakata merchants flourished from the trade with the Song dynasty from the tenth to the thirteenth centuries, and with the Ming dynasty *(Kangô-bôeki)* from the fifteenth to the sixteenth centuries. The Dazaifu Tenmangû Shrine, known as the god of study, was dedicated to Michizane Sugawara who had been relegated to Dazaifu from Kyôto in the tenth century. Regarding food culture, Hakata râmen with pork soup, which sometimes is served with an extra ball of noodles *(kae-dama)*, was pioneered by the street stalls in Kurume city. Spicy *mentaiko* is marinated roe of Alaska pollock with red pepper, which became famous as a souvenir of Hakata Station after the San-yô Shinkansen was extended to the prefecture in the mid-1970s.

Population and Traffic

The prefecture's population is 5,072,000. The main cities are Fukuoka (1,464,000), Kitakyûshû (977,000), Kurume (302,000), Iizuka (131,000), Ômuta (124,000), Kasuga (107,000), Chikushino (100,000), Itoshima (98,000), Munakata (96,000), and Ônojô (95,000). Kitakyûshû was assigned as an ordinance-designated city in 1963, and Fukuoka, in 1972. At that time, Kitakyûshû was regarded as one of the four major industrial zones in Japan, besides Keihin, Chûkyô, and Hanshin. It became the sixth ordinance-designated city by merging with the neigh-boring municipalities, including Yawata, Kokura, and Moji cities. In the city of Fukuoka, Tenjin and Hakata districts are the largest downtown areas in the Kyûshû region. Nakasu is an entertainment district on the sandbar of the

Naka River that separates the downtown areas. JR Kyûshû's (Kyûshû Railway Company) Kagoshima Main Line and National Route 3 run through Kyûshû Island along the old Nagasaki and Satsuma roads. In parallel with those routes, the Kyûshû Expressway was completed in 1995 and the Kyûshû Shinkansen, in 2004. On Nishi-Nippon Railroad Co.'s Tenjin Ômuta Line a melody of Red Sweet Pea (a hit song of a singer from Kurume city) was played when they approach stations.

Primary Sector of Industry

The main agricultural commodities in terms of gross production are vegetables, rice, fruit, and flowers. Among the vegetables, strawberry production in the prefecture is the second largest of all the prefectures after Tochigi (strawberry is categorized as a vegetable in agricultural censuses). The main strawberry varieties, such as *Toyonoka* and *Amaô*, were bred by the Kurume branch of the National Research Institute of Vegetables, Ornamental Plants and Tea (now the National Agricultural Research Center for Kyûshû Okinawa Region). As they were advertised on TV commercials in Tokyo metropolitan area, the prefectural strawberries grew in popularity. Cultured chrysanthemums are one of the special products in Yame city. Although flower cultivation started as a suburban agriculture, following the development of expressway networks and truck transportation, the distribution extended to the whole country, mainly to the Tokyo and Ôsaka metropolitan areas.

Other Industries

The main industrial products in terms of gross production are automobiles, automobile parts, and cigarettes. As Kyûshû is expressed as a "car island" (car-producing island), major companies branched out of the prefecture: Toyota Motor Corporation to Wakamiya city and Kanda town, Nissan Motor Co. to Kokuraminami Ward in Kitakyûshû, and Daihatsu Motor Co. to Kurume city. Regarding the cigarette industry, Japan Tobacco's Kyûshû plant in the city of Chikushino has increased the amount of its exports to Asian countries. In tire and rubber shoe manufacturing, Bridgestone Corporation, MoonStar Co., and Asahi Corporation were founded in the city of Kurume. A ceramics manufacturer, Tôyô Tôki (now Tôtô), was founded in Kiku county (now Kitakyûshû) in 1917, taking advantage of the availability of raw materials, such as coal from the Chikuhô coalfields and kaolin from the Korean Peninsula and Amakusa Islands.

41. Saga

Saga is located in the north of the Kyûshû region, facing the Iki Channel in the Sea of Japan and the Ariake Sea (Figure 41).

Nature

The highest peak is Mt. Kyôgatake (1,076 m) in the south at the boundary with Nagasaki Prefecture. It is a volcano that is included in the utmost point of the Hakusan volcanic belt along with neighboring Mt. Taradake, although there are no records of them erupting. They were active between 400,000 and 800,000 years ago. Ureshino and Takeo hot springs to the north of the mountain were founded around the third century. A tower gate *(rômon)* for the hot spring has been designated as an important cultural property. It was built in the 1910s by Kingo Tatsuno, an architect from the prefecture who also designed Tokyo

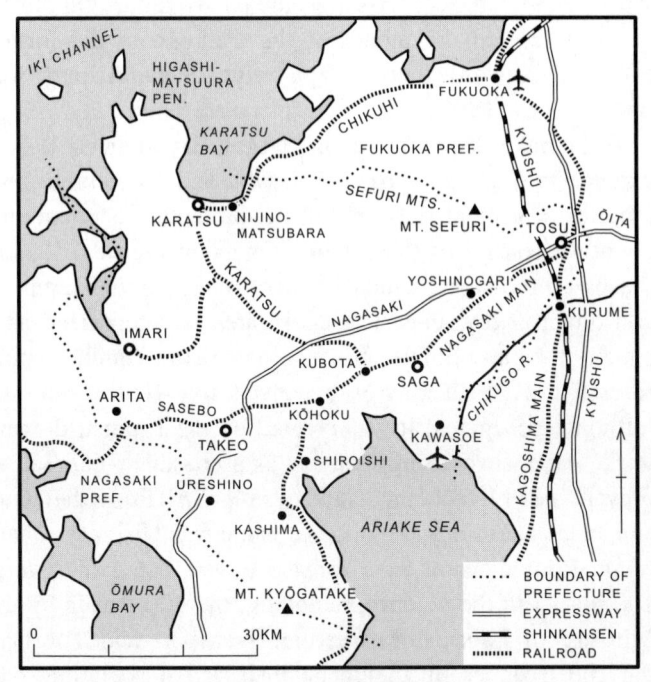

Figure 41 Saga

Station. The Sefuri Mountains, ranging from 800 to 1,000 m above sea level, are located in the western portion of the Tsukushi Mountains, and form a boundary with Fukuoka Prefecture. They are fault-block mountains made of granite, and have steep slopes on the Fukuoka side, and gentle ones on the Saga side.

The Saga Plain comprises a part of the Tsukushi Plain on the west of the Chikugo River. In the plain, paddy fields extend to coastal areas along the Ariake Sea as a result of reclamation works conducted in the Edo period. In the south of the plain, near the urban areas of Saga city, waterways called "creeks" crisscross the paddy fields. On the re-claimed land at the mouth of the Chikugo in the former town of Kawasoe (now Saga city), Saga Airport was opened in the 1990s.

The Ariake Sea is the second largest bay after Ise Bay. It extends to Saga, Fukuoka, Nagasaki, and Kumamoto pre-fectures. The tidal flats area in the prefecture accounts for about 40 percent of the country. On extensive tidal flats in the bay, blue-spotted mud hoppers *(mutsu-gorô)* jump up and down at low tide. The entire area is categorized as a southern Japan climate. Niji no Matsu-bara (rainbow pine forest) at Karatsu Bay is a coastal forest of about one million black pines. It was created by the Karatsu domain in the early seventeenth century as a coastal windbreak to prevent newly reclaimed lands *(shin-den)* from the wind and sand. Therefore, the original name was Niri matsu-bara (eight kilometers of pine forest). It was listed in several 100 places in the country, including, the 100 Roads by the Ministry of Land, Infrastructure, Transport and Tourism, the 100 Beaches by the Japan Fisheries Association, and the 100 Aromatic Landscapes.

History and Culture

Under the Ritsuryô code, the east of Hizen Province became Saga Prefecture in the Meiji period. The name is derived from Saga county, in which the Saga domain was based, and the county name was documented in the *Fudoki* (reports on provincial geography edited in the eighth century). There was a moat village in the Yayoi period on the site from Yoshinogari town to Kanzaki city. Replicas of a watchtower and pit dwellings were installed when the site was restored as a park in the 1990s. Nagoya Castle at the tip of the Higashimatsuura Peninsula was a base for the

Japanese invasions of Korea *(Bunroku no eki and Keichô no eki)* in the late sixteenth century. At the end of Edo period, the Saga domain ruled by the Nabeshima clan constructed reverberatory furnaces to build iron cannons. The Saga Rebellion in 1874 was the first uprising by ex-samurai against the Meiji government. Several uprisings ensued, namely, the Shinpûren Rebellion in Kumamoto Prefecture, the Akizuki Rebellion in Fukuoka Prefecture, the Hagi Rebellion in Yamaguchi Prefecture, and the Satsuma Rebellion (the Southwestern War) in Kumamoto, Kagoshima, Ôita, and Miyazaki prefectures.

Population and Traffic

The population of the prefecture is 850,000. The main cities are Saga (238,000), Karatsu (127,000), Tosu (69,000), Imari (57,000), and Takeo (51,000). Tosu city is a junction of railroads and roads in the east of the prefecture. As terms of railroad infrastructure, the Kagoshima Main Line, the Nagasaki Main Line, and the Kyûshû Shinkansen cross the city. The major road network comprises National Route 3 and National Route 34 (the old Nagasaki Road), which cross the city, and Tosu junction, which connects the Kyûshû, Nagasaki, and Ôita expressways. In the west of the Saga Plain, two railroads diverge from the Nagasaki Main Line, namely, the Karatsu Line from Kubota Station in the former town of Kubota (now Saga city), and the Sasebo Line diverges from Hizen-Yamaguchi Station in the town of Kôhoku. Prior to the opening of Hizen-Kashima Station on the Nagasaki Main Line in 1930, the Yûtoku rail track carried worshipers from Takeo to the Yûtoku Inari Shrine in Kashima at the north foot of Mt. Kyôgatake. Because of the increase in the number of new year worshipers coming by train, a large red building was constructed in the 1930s, and became a symbol of the *inari* shrines.

Primary Sector of Industry

The main agricultural commodities in terms of gross production are vegetables, rice, fruit (mainly *unshû* mandarins), and beef cattle. In terms of rice production, the double cropping of rice and wheat (or barley) at paddy fields still exists on the Saga Plain. Although it is in the warm climate of the Kyûshû region, for the double cropping, the planting season (June) and the harvest season (October) in the paddy rice cultivation are the latest in the country. Onion and strawberry production was increased after the implementation of a policy of reducing rice production. Onions are cultivated in the west of the Saga Plain, and harvested from April to May.

In the fishing industry, the laver cultivation that takes place in the Ariake Sea is the largest of all the prefectures. On the tidal flats, pushing planks were used for catching crab, shellfish, and goby, including blue-spotted mud hoppers. Suko-*zushi* is a local food in the Suko district of Shiroishi town. It is made with grilled blue-spotted mud hoppers. In the Genkai Sea, the main catches are horse mackerel, mackerel, squid, octopus, and prawns. The sliced raw squid dish served in the Yobuko area of Karatsu city has been selected as one of the 100 Local Cuisines.

Other Industries

The main industrial products in terms of gross production are silicon wafers, medicines, and cargo ships. Silicon wafer production is the largest of all the prefectures. The wafers are used as raw materials for integrated circuits, and produced in the town of Kôhoku, and the cities of Takeo and Imari. In medicine production, Hisamitsu Pharmaceutical Co., which is known for its poultices, is located in Saga, and Yutoku Pharmaceutical Co., known for its sticking plasters, is located in Kashima city. In ship-building, bulk cargo ships and tankers are assembled in Imari city. In terms of number of establishments, the main category of production is porcelain tableware. Porcelain ornament production in Saga is the largest of all the pre-fectures. Porcelain was fired in Arita for the first time in the country in the seventeenth century. Arita ware is also called Imari ware after it was shipped to Europe from the Port of Imari by the Dutch East India Company.

42. Nagasaki

Nagasaki is located in the north of the Kyûshû region, facing Tsushima Strait and the East China Sea (Figure 42).
Nature
The highest peak is the Heisei-shinzan (1,483 m) in Mt. Unzen (Unzendake), an active volcanic complex in the Shimabara Peninsula. The highest peak used to be Fugen-dake (1,359 m) in the mountain prior to the eruptions in the 1990s. More than 40 people, including firefighters and foreign geologists, were killed or went missing in the py-roclastic flow of 1991. Although the area is 37th in size of the 47 prefectures, since it consists of many islands, penin-sulas, and rias, the coastline stretches for 4,200 km, the second longest after Hokkaidô (4,500 km). The Kita-matsuura Peninsula, Hirado Island, and the Gotô Islands have been designated as Saikai National Park. The penin-sula features a ria coastline and the Kujûku Islands, which consist of more than 200 islands. The Nishisonogi Penin-sula to the north of Nagasaki city extends between Ômura

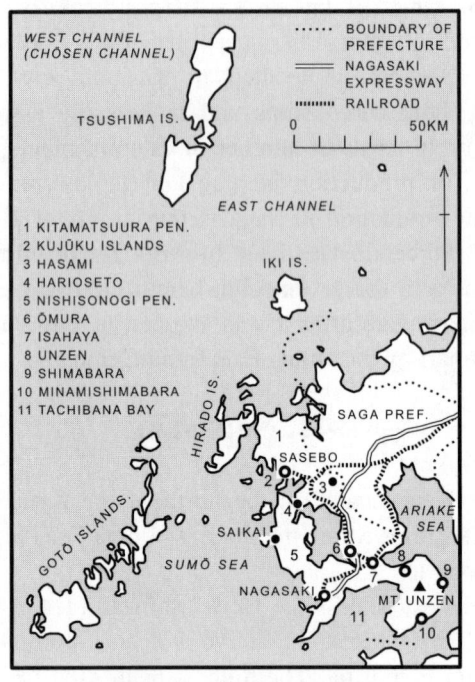

Figure 42 Nagasaki

Bay and the Sumô Sea. The Harioseto Strait, which separates Ômura and Sasebo bays, is a torrent that creates
eddying currents. As for the climate, the whole area is categorized as a southern Japan one.

The prefecture has about 70 inhabited and 520 unin-
habited islands. Tsushima Island between the West and the
East Channels in Tsushma Strait is the largest of the
islands. It is located about 150 km (around five hours) from
the Port of Hakata by ferry via Iki Island. The island is
inhabited Tsushima leopard cats, an endangered species
that moved from the Asian continent some 100,000 years

ago. At a ria coastline on the island, Kaneda Castle was constructed in the seventh century as a defense against the Silla kingdom and the Táng dynasty. The Gotô Islands are located about 100 km west of the Port of Nagasaki. On the islands, Catholic churches were built by the Jesuits in the sixteenth century. Besides the coastal and farming fisheries, tourism is a significant industry, replacing to some extent the pelagic fishery, which is in decline, and the churches have become popular tourist attracts there.

History and Culture

The west of Hizen Province and the provinces of Tsushima and Iki became Nagasaki Prefecture in the Meiji period. The name is derived from Nagasaki city. There are opinions about the origin of the name. It may refer to "a long promontory" or "ruler's family name." On Hirado Island, British and Dutch mercantile houses were built in the beginning of the seventeenth century, although they were closed before long as a result of the isolation policy of the Tokugawa Shogunate. Only the Netherlands among other European countries could retain trade with the Shogunate on an artificial Dejima Island in Nagasaki because it was not involved in Christian missionary work. The Shimabara Rebellion took place in the seventeenth century by the Catholics in the Shimabara Peninsula and Amakusa Island. The leader of the rebellion was Shirô Amakusa, who was in his mid-teens. His head was exhibited on Dejima Island after the rebellion's defeat. In the Meiji period, Sasebo city was developed as a naval base, and battleships were built in the city of Nagasaki. A large air raid took place on Sasebo, and an atomic bomb was dropped on Nagasaki at the end of World War II.

Population and Traffic

The prefecture's population is 1,427,000. The main cities are Nagasaki (444,000), Sasebo (261,000), Isahaya (141,000), Ômura (91,000), Minamishimabara (50,000), Shimabara (47,000), and Unzen (47,000). The Port of Nagasaki was opened at the end of the Tokugawa Shogunate, and the foreign settlement adjacent to the port evolved into Shinchi Chinatown. Popular tourist destinations are to be found in the city of Nagasaki. For instance, Glover Garden is the former residence of a British merchant, Dutch Slope (Oranda-zaka) has well-preserved western houses, and Ôura Tenshudô is the oldest church in the country. Nagasaki is also known as a city with slopes, as referred to in a verse of an old song, "–saka no Nagasaki zabon uri" (a pomelo vender in sloped Nagasaki). In the Nagasaki Flood in 1982, which was caused by a torrential downpour, about 300 people were killed or went missing. Nagasaki Airport, on Minoshima Island, Ômura Bay, was opened in 1975 as the first offshore airport in the country. The airport serves regular flights to Tsuhima, Fukue in Gotô Islands, and Iki.

Primary Sector of Industry

The main agricultural commodities in terms of gross production are beef cattle, rice, swine, potatoes, and fruit. Livestock grazing thrives on the islands and peninsulas. The main rice varieties are *Hinohikari* and *Nikomaru*. The latter was bred in the National Agricultural Research Center for Kyûshû Okinawa Region. It has been designated as an encouraged variety by the prefecture in the 2000s because of its tolerance to high temperatures. The prefecture's cultivated potato area is the third largest of all the prefectures after Hokkaidô and Kagoshima. Since the potatoes can be harvested twice in spring and autumn in the prefecture, they are called *nido-imo* (twice potatoes). Potatoes are cultivated mainly in the Shimabara Peninsula and Gotô Island. Their main seed varieties are *Nishiyutaka* and *Dejima*, which were bred for adaption to the warm climate. Regarding fruit production, Nagasaki's cultivated loquat area is the largest of all the prefectures, and its orchards are distributed around Tachibana Bay. In terms of the fishing industry, the sea around Iki Island is a reliable fishing ground as the warm Tsushima Current meets the cold Liman Current. The catches of horse mackerel and yellowtail are the largest of all the prefectures, and the total catches are the second largest after Hokkaidô now. The number of fishing ports, at around 280, is also the largest.

Other Industries

The main industrial products in terms of gross production are cargo ships, digital cameras, and integrated circuits. Mitsubishi Heavy Industries, in Nagasaki city, Sasebo Heavy Industries Co. in Sasebo city, and Ôshima Shipbuilding Co. in Saikai city run shipyards. They produce not only cargo ships and tankers but also passenger liners and navy ships. Digital cameras are made by Nagasaki Canon in the town of Hasami and integrated circuits, by Sony Semiconductor Manufacturing Corporation in Isahaya city. In terms of number of establishments, the main production categories are Japanese noodles and fish paste products. Japanese-style thin noodles are produced in the Shimabara Peninsula, where the quantity produced is the second largest of all the prefectures after Hyôgo. The dried noodles are made in winter and sold in summer. On Hario Island, facing Harioseto Strait, Hario Industrial Park was built on reclaimed land, but invitations for companies to set up there were not successful. Instead of factories, Huis Ten Bosch, a Dutch theme park, was established in 1992. Hashima Island off the Nagasaki Peninsula is termed a battleship island because of its appearance. It was a coal mine that closed in 1974, and, in 2015, it was listed as one of the "Sites of Japan's Meiji Industrial Revolution," which collectively form a World Heritage Site.

43. Kumamoto

Kumamoto is located in the center of Kyûshû Island, facing Shimabara Bay and the Yatsushiro Sea (Figure 43).
Nature
The highest peak is Mt. Kunimi (Kunimidake: 1,739 m) in the Kyûshû Mountains on the boundary with Miyazaki Prefecture. There are more than 30 mountains in the country that have been named Kunimi. Even in the prefecture, there are seven Kunimi mountains in the Kyûshû, the Kunimi, and the Chikuhi Mountains. Mt. Aso is an active volcano, whose central crater, Nakadake, emits smoke. It is located in the center of Kyûshû Island, and composes the northernmost part of the Kirishima volcanic belt. Aso caldera extends 25 km north to south, and 18 km east to west. It is the second-largest caldera in the country after Kussharo caldera in Hokkaidô. Aso caldera contains not only agricultural land but also built-up areas, such as Aso city, as well as other ones around Aso county. National highways and railroads cross the caldera, namely, National Route 57, JR Kyûshû's Hôhi Main Line in Aso Valley, and Minami Aso Railway Co.'s Takamori Line in Nangô Valley. Near the summit of Mt. Aso, there is a large colony of Kyûshû azalea *(miyama kirishima)*. Kusasenri, at around

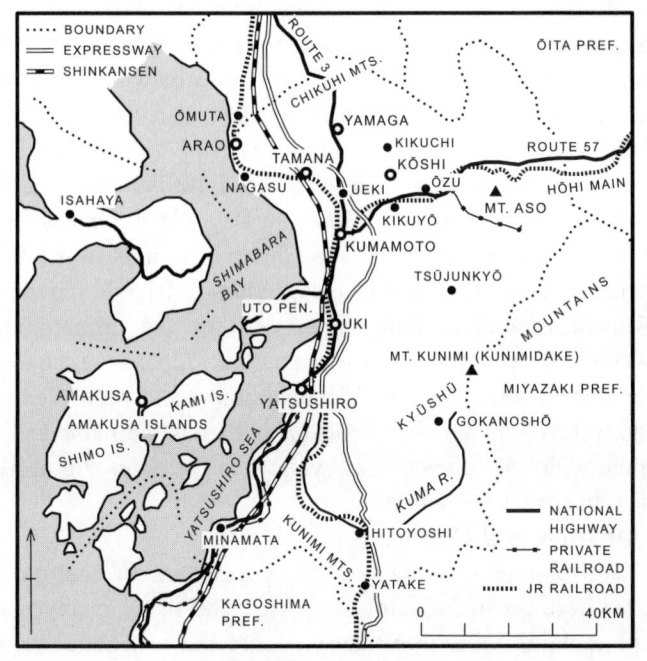

Figure 43 Kumamoto

1,100 m above sea level, is a wide pasture used for grazing beef cattle and horses (Illustration 13). Horseback riding has become popular among tourists.

The Kuma River starts from the Kyûshû Mountains, crosses the Hitoyoshi Basin and the Yatsushiro Plain, and flows into the Yatsushiro (Shiranui) Sea. It comprises one of three fast flowing rivers in the country, besides the Mogami and the Fuji rivers. On the upper reaches of the Kawabe, a tributary of the Kuma, the Gokanoshô community is based. The area is known as a secluded place to where, according to legend, the Taira clan fled. The Shirakawa (white river), Kurokawa (black river), and

217

Midorikawa (green river) stream from Mt. Aso, and enter Shimabara Bay from Kumamoto Plain. The Tsûjunkyô Bridge on the upper reaches of the Midorikawa was chosen as an important cultural property, and also as one of the 100 Irrigation Canals by the Ministry of Agriculture, Forestry and Fisheries. The Amakusa Islands in front of the Uto Peninsula separate Shimabara Bay and the Yatsushiro Sea. They were known as the Christian islands in the Edo period. One of the islands, Shimo Island, contains Amakusa pottery stone mines. As for the climate, the whole area is categorized as a southern Japan one, characterized by year-round mild temperatures and high precipitation levels in summer. *Matsubori-kaze* is the name of the local wind that blows across valleys at the outer rim of Mt. Aso in spring and autumn.

History and Culture

The prefectural area was titled Hinokuni (a country of fire) because of belching Mt. Aso. The name changed to Higonokuni under the Ritsuryô code, and to Kumamoto in the Meiji period. The prefectural name is derived from Kumamoto Castle, which was built by Kiyomasa Katô at the end of the sixteenth century. The castle's name refers to the meandering of the Shirakawa River. The fifth High School (*Gokô*, one of the old number schools) was established in Kumamoto ward in 1887. It was dissolved after World War II, and absorbed into Kumamoto University. Arao city, facing the Ariake Sea, developed its economy based on the mining of Mitsui Miike Coal Mine, along with the neighboring city of Ômuta in Fukuoka Prefecture. The Manda Shaft in Arao city, which operated from 1902 to 1951, has been listed as one of the "Sites of Japan's Meiji Industrial Revolution" that collectively are a World

Heritage Site. In terms of the local food culture, *karashi-renkon* and *basashi* are famous. The former is lotus loots that are filled with miso mixed with mustard. The latter is raw horse meat that was a local food derived from the tradition of horse grazing. Meanwhile, the shôchû distilled from rice is produced in the Kuma region in the southeast.

Population and Traffic

The population of the prefecture is 1,817,000. The main cities are Kumamoto (734,000), Yatsushiro (132,000), Amakusa (89,000), Tamana (70,000), Uki (62,000), Yamaga (55,000), Arao (55,000), and Kôshi (55,000). Kumamoto is the latest ordinance-designated city assigned in 2012. The city was developed on the west of the outer rim of Mt. Aso. It is the only prefectural capital whose tap water is supplied by groundwater. National Route 3 and the Kyûshû Shinkansen run through the coastal areas and enter the Satsuma Peninsula. They were constructed along the Izumi course of the old Satsuma Road. The Hisatsu Line and the Kyûshû Expressway were constructed along the Ôkuchi course of the Satsuma Road. These railroads and expressways go inland from Yatsushiro and cross the Hitoyoshi Basin and the Kunimi Mountains. The Yatake Pass, which can be seen on the Hisatsu Line between Kumamoto and Miyazaki prefectures, was considered by the former Japan National Railways to be one of the three prime views from a train window.

Primary Sector of Industry

The prefecture's gross agricultural production is the fifth largest of all the prefectures. The main commodities are tomatoes, rice, beef cattle, and raw milk. Kumamoto devotes more areas to the cultivation of tomatoes and watermelons than any other prefecture. They are cultivated mainly in greenhouses. The tomato producing regions are located on the Yatsushiro and the Kikuchi Plains, and also at the foot of Mt. Aso. Although the peak harvesting time is May, tomatoes can be harvested all year round as they are cultivated in a variety of areas, from lowlands to high-altitude, cool climate areas. Watermelons are cultivated mostly in the former town of Ueki (now Kumamoto city) on the Kikuchi Plain.

Citrus production is the third largest of all the prefectures after Ehime and Wakayama. Kawachi-*mikan* and *dekopon* are brands of oranges. Due to a rise in temperatures, the quality of the oranges grown in orchards at low altitude has decreased. This manifests itself by as an uneven coloring of the rind. Therefore, there has been a shift to new varieties that are resistant warmer temperatures. Regarding industrial crops, the cultivation areas devoted to rushes and tobaccos are the largest of all the prefectures. More than 90 percent of domestic rushes are produced in the prefecture. The deep-green rush fields are distributed among the paddy fields on the Yatsushiro Plain.

Other Industries

The main industrial products in terms of gross production are integrated circuits and motorcycles. In terms of number of establishments, the main categories are cut timber and planks. Kyûshû Island is known as the silicon island, and Kumamoto Prefecture as a whole also prospers from integrated circuit production. Examples include Sony Semiconductor Manufacturing Corporation in Kikuyô town and Renesas Semiconductor Manufacturing Co. in Kumamoto city. Regarding motorcycle production, Honda Motor Co.'s Kumanmoto factory is located in the town of Ôzu in Kikuchi county. It was opened in 1976 as a forerunner of the automobile industry in the Kyûshû region. In other industries, Nippon Paper Industries Co. operates a paper mill in the city of Yatsushiro, and a Japan Marine United Corporation dockyard in Nagasu town. Minamata disease, associated with mercury poisoning in the 1950s, as counted as one of four major pollution diseases, besides Yokkaichi asthma, Second Minamata disease in Niigata Prefecture, and *itai-itai* disease.

44. Ôita

Ôita is located in the east of Kyûshû Island, facing the Seto Inland Sea and the Bungo Channel (Figure 44).

Nature

Nakadake (1,791 m) on the Mt. Kujû is the highest peak in Kyûshû Island (the second highest in the Kyûshû region after Mt. Miyanoura). Mt. Kujû is a volcanic complex in the Hakusan volcanic belt that crosses western Japan. It has been designated as Aso Kujû National Park along with the Iida Highland at the north foot of the mountain. Kujû Forest Park Ski Resort and Hatchôbaru Geothermal Power Plant were constructed at the west foot. The former is the largest ski ground in the Kyûshû region, and the latter is the largest geothermal power plant in the country. The Median Tectonic Line runs to the southwest as the crow flies between the Saganoseki Peninsula and Mt. Aso in Kumamoto Prefecture. There are volcanoes to the north of Median Tectonic Line, for instance, the Kujû Mountains, Mt. Hane, Mt. Yufu, and Mt. Tsurumi. Beppu hot spring at the foot of Mt. Tsurumi and Yufuin hot spring at the foot of Mt. Yufu are famous for their abundant hot water wells and rich discharges of water.

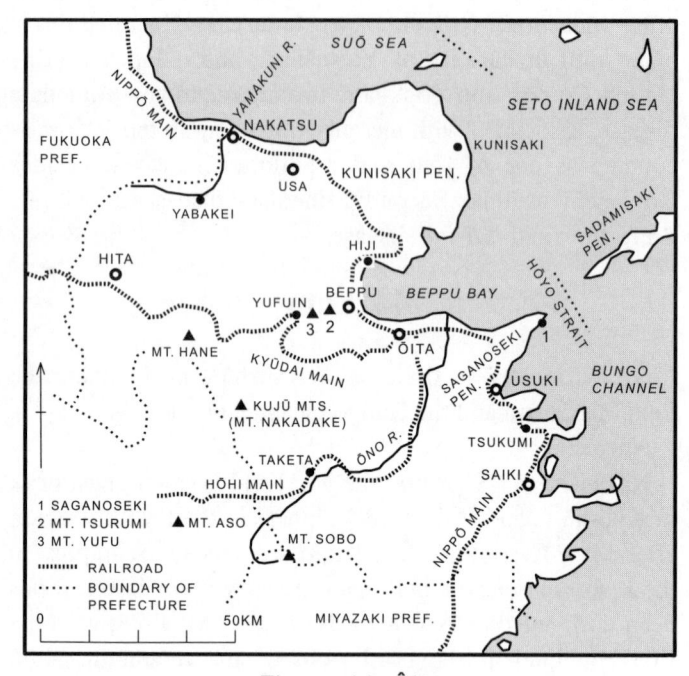

Figure 44 Ôita

The prefecture's limestone production is the largest of all the prefectures. It is quarried from the mines in Tsukumi city, and shipped from the Port of Tsukumi facing the Bungo Channel (Japan is self-sufficient in limestone, which is used as a material for construction, electric poles, fertilizers, sugar refining, and steel manufacturing). In Usuki and Saiki cities, neighboring the city of Tsukumi, there are Fûren and Onagara limestone caves that have been designated as special natural monuments. In the former village of Nakatsue (now Hita city) in the northwest, an underground museum was opened at the Taio

222

Gold Mine site.

The Ôno River flows from Mt. Sobo in Miyazaki Prefecture, and feeds into Beppu Bay from the Ôita Plain. The headwaters of the river have been designated as Sobo-Katamuki Quasi-National Park. The Yamakuni River marks the boundary with Fukuoka Prefecture, and flows into the Suô Sea from the Nakatsu Plain. On the upper reaches of the river, Yabakei gorge, a scenic site known for its Aonodômon (a hand-carved tunnel), is to be found. A ria coastline extends from Usuki and Saiki bays to the Nippô Coast in the south. In the calm bays, flounder and yellowtail aquaculture farming are thriving. The climate ranges from a southern Japan one in the north to a Setouchi one in the south.

History and Culture

Bungo Province and the southeast of Buzen Province became Ôita Prefecture in the Meiji period. The name is derived from Ôita city, whose origin was *ôki-ta* (lots of fields). The cultural assets include the carved stones distributed in the prefecture, for instance, the Usuki *magaibutsu* (stone carvings of the Buddha) in Usuki city, which is designated as national treasures, the Kumano *magaibutsu* in the Kunisaki Peninsula, assigned as an important cultural property, and the arched stone bridges in the former town of Innai (now Usa city) and other municipalities. The one-village, one-product movement was started in 1980. It was a policy aimed at local development based on agriculture, forestry, and fisheries. As a result of the movement, more than 300 specialties were developed, including shiitake mushroom, house-*mikan* (kinds of mandarin oranges grown in greenhouses), *kabosu (Citrus sphaerocarpa*, a close variety of *sudachi)*, flowers, and beef. In terms of the production of spirits, *mugi*-shôchû, which is distilled from barley, is thriving. One of the producers, Sanwa Shurui Co. in Usa city, is known for using the catch phrase, "Napoleon of the people" (*Shita-machi no* Napoleon), and Nikaidô-Shuzô in Hiji town is known for its nostalgic TV commercials broadcast in the Tokyo metropolitan area.

Population and Traffic

The prefecture's population is 1,197,000. The main cities are Ôita (474,000), Beppu (125,000), Nakatsu (84,000), Saiki (77,000), Hita (71,000), Usa (59,000), and Usuki (41,000). The Kyûdai Main Line connecting Kurume and Ôita cities runs along two river systems, namely the Kusu River in the Chikugo River system and the Ôita River that goes into Beppu Bay. The Mizuwake Pass near Yufuin Station forms the divide between the rivers. In 1971, Ôita Airport was moved to the Kunisaki Peninsula from the vicinity of the Ôita River's estuary so as to be able to handle jetliners.

Primary Sector of Industry

The main agricultural commodities in terms of gross production are rice and beef cattle. The main rice variety is *Hinohikari*, which is bred in Miyazaki Prefecture. The *Hitomebore* bred in the Tôhoku region is also cultivated to a great extent in hilly and mountainous areas (*chû-sankan-chi*) more than 300 m above sea level. In the Kyûshû region, *Hitomebore* is cultivated only in the prefecture. The variety is shipped to Fukuoka city, as well as being consumed locally. In animal husbandry, the Japanese Black cattle grazed in the prefecture are sold under the brand of Bungo beef. Among the local specialties, the production of *kabosu*, log-cultivated shiitake mushrooms, and dried shiitake mushroom is the largest of all the prefectures. As for marine products, Seki horse mackerel and Seki mackerel, both of which are landed at Saganoseki fishing port, are sold as prime fish. The fish is fatty and firm as they inhabit the rapids of Hôyo Strait (Hayasui no Seto), where there is abundant plankton.

Other Industries

The main industrial products in terms of gross production are sheet steel, light cars, and digital cameras. In the Ôita Coastal Industrial Zone, Nippon Steel Corporation's main factory opened in 1972. A Daihatsu Motor Co. factory was moved to Nakatsu city in 2004, and began producing light cars. Ôita produces more digital cameras than all of the other prefectures. Its main factory is Ôita Canon in Kunisaki city, adjacent to Ôita Airport. Japan Sun Industries is a social welfare organization supporting the independence of people with disabilities. It was founded in the city of Beppu in 1965. It manages factories and offices that employ people with disabilities in collaboration with large companies such as Honda Motor Co., Omron Corporation, Sony Corporation, Fujitsu Fsas, Denso Corporation, and Mitsubishi Corporation.

45. Miyazaki

Miyazaki is located in the southeast of Kyûshû Island, facing the Pacific Ocean's Hyûga Sea (Figure 45).

Nature

The highest peak is Mt. Sobo (1,756 m) on the boundary with Ôita and Kumamoto prefectures. It was discovered to be the highest peak in Kyûshû Island when Walter Weston, an English missionary, climbed it in 1890. The Gokase

River streaming at the south foot of the mountain cuts through Takachiho gorge, a chasm surrounded by a procession of columnar joints. The name of Takachiho relates to a myth as well as a peak on Mt. Kirishima. On the upper reaches, the wafting smell of grilled sweetfish at *yana* fish traps, has been listed in the 100 Aromatic Landscapes. Gokase Highland ski resort is to be found at the east foot of Mt. Kunimi, the highest peak of Kumamoto Prefecture. It is the southernmost ski resort in the country, at an elevation of 1,400 to 1,600 m. On the southeast of the mountain, there are remote hamlets, which, legend has it, were made

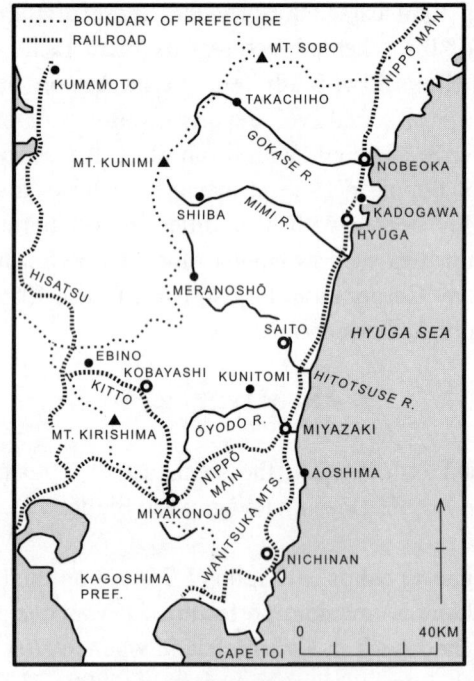

Figure 45 Miyazaki

by the exiled Taira clan, namely, the Shiiba community on the upper reaches of the Mimi (Mimitsu), and by the Meranoshô community on the upper reaches of the Hitotsuse. In the south of the Miyazaki Plain, the Ôyodo River crosses the downtown of Miyazaki city, and flows into Hyûga Sea.

The climate ranges from a Setouchi one on the plains to a southern Japan one in inland areas. Mountainous areas receive considerable rainfalls. For instance, the precipitation levels in Ebino city reach 4,390 mm per year, which is the second largest in the country after Yakushima Island. Subtropical plants grow in coastal areas under the warm climate, such as *binrô* (betel palm) in the town of Kadogawa in the north, *yakko-sô* (*Mitrastemon* Makino: a genus of parasitic plant) in the clumps of *suda-jii* (*Castanopsis sieboldii*: a species of chinquapin) on the Nichinan Coast, and *sotetsu* (fern palm) in Cape Toi. On Aoshima Island, in Nichinan Kaigan Quasi-National Park, the parallel stratum consisting of sandstone and mudstone is a scenic site known as the "demon's washboard."

History and Culture

Under the Ritsuryô code, Hyûga Province became Mimitsu and Miyakonojô prefectures by the abolition of the domain system in the Meiji period, and they were merged into Miyazaki Prefecture. It was merged into Kagoshima Prefecture in 1876, a year before the Satsuma Rebellion, and then separated from it in 1883. The prefectural name is derived from Miyazaki county at the boundary with Mimitsu and Miyakonojô prefectures. Miyazaki literally means "a place in front of a shrine." The Nichinan Coast encompassed an image of a subtropical resort for Phoenix Boulevard (rows of *Phoenix canariensis* palms). It was a mecca for honeymooners until the floating exchange rate regime started in 1973. Formerly, one US dollar was exchanged for 360 yen.

Population and Traffic

The prefecture's population is 1,135,000. The main cities are Miyazaki (401,000), Miyakonojô (170,000), Nobeoka (131,000), Hyûga (63,000), Nichinan (58,000), Kobayashi (48,000), and Saito (33,000). The Nippô Main Line connecting Kokura in Kitakyûshû city to Kagoshima city runs along National Route 10 (the old Hyûga Road). In the prefecture, it goes through coastal areas from Nobeoka city to the Miyazaki Plain, and runs in inland areas from Miyazaki city to Miyakonojô city. The Kitto Line travels in parallel with the Miyazaki Expressway. It severs the Hisatsu Line in Kagoshima Prefecture, detours Mt. Kirishima (Kirishimayama) at the north foot, runs through the Kobayashi Basin, and enters the Miyakonojô Basin. The second-largest city in the prefecture, Miyakonojô, used be annexed to the Satsuma domain, and is located between the Wanitsuka Mountains and Mt. Kirishima. Its animal husbandry production, mainly, swine, beef cattle, and broilers, is the largest of all the municipalities in the country.

Primary Sector of Industry

The main agricultural commodities in terms of gross production are broilers, vegetables, beef cattle, swine, and rice. The prefecture's broiler production is the second largest of all the prefectures after Iwate. Beef cattle production is the third largest of all the prefectures after Hokkaidô and Kagoshima. The production of cucumber is the largest of all the prefectures (its cultivated area is the second largest after Gunma). The cucumbers produced in the Miyazaki Plain are harvested all the year round, with combinations of cultivation methods used, such as early-ripening, retarding, forcing, and semi-forcing cultures in greenhouses, and open-field culture. The main rice variety is the *Hinohikari* that was registered in 1990 by Miyazaki Agricultural Research Institute. It became the main variety not only in the prefecture but also in Kagawa, Nagasaki, Kumamoto, Ôita, and Kagoshima prefectures. Mango production is the second largest of all the prefectures after Okinawa. Mangos are cultivated in the cities of Saito, Miyazaki, and Nichinan. The mangos are known for their good quality, and are sold throughout the country, with a former governor, who had been a TV personality at one stage, being used for advertising purposes.

Other Industries

The main industrial products in terms of gross production are shôchû, chicken, and tires. Regarding the distillation of shôchû, Kirishima Shuzô Co. in Miyaknojô city is one of the largest liquor companies in the country, whose main offerings are made from sweet potatoes. As for tire production, there is a Sumitomo Rubber Industries factory in Miyaknojô, which was invited to the city in the 1970s. Hitachi Ltd. once produced plasma displays in the town of Kunitomi. The factory was transferred to Solar Frontier K.K. (*Kabushiki Kaisha*, a corporation) to produce solar cells. Nobeoka in the north of the prefecture is a company town of Asahi Kasei Corporation, a producer of Saran Wrap. It started as Nicchitsu Konzern (conglomerate) that manufactured chemical fertilizers before the war.

Miyazaki Seagaia Resort in the north of Miyazaki city was opened in 1994. It has high-rise hotels going to 43 stories and all-weather pools. It was designated as a first resort by the Comprehensive Resort Areas Development Law (the so-called resort law). Although the resort was bankrupted in 2001, it was re-opened as Phoenix Seagaia Resort, managed by Ripplewood Holdings, an investment company in the United States.

46. Kagoshima

Kagoshima is located in the south of Kyûshû Island. It comprises the mainland and a number of islands (Figure 46).

Nature

The highest peak is Mt. Miyanoura (Miyanouradake: 1,936 m) on Yakushima Island, part of the Ôsumi Islands. Yakusugi cedars, whose ages exceed 1,000 years, are grown on Yakushima Island. The oldest one, named Jômon Sugi, is approximately 3,000 years old. The entire island was listed as a World Heritage Site in 1993. Although the botany of the island is protected, the soil-embedded cedars can be processed and sold as ornaments. Mt. Sakurajima (1,117 m) in Kagoshima Bay (Kinkô Bay) is a volcano that comprises the Kirishima volcanic belt. The volcanic ash sometimes falls on the ground of Kagoshima city. *Shirasu* plateaus consist of accumulated volcanic ash, and the pyroclastic lands comprise more than 50 percent of the mainland in area. The largest one is the Kasanohara Plateau in Kanoya city. Mt. Kaimon (Kaimondake: 924 m) is a symmetric stratovolcano in the southernmost place of the Satsuma Peninsula. It is the second lowest mountain in the 100 Mountains of Japan after Mt. Tsukuba. At the mountain's foot are Ikeda Lake (a caldera lake) and Ibusuki hot spring. Visitors to the hot spring enjoy basking

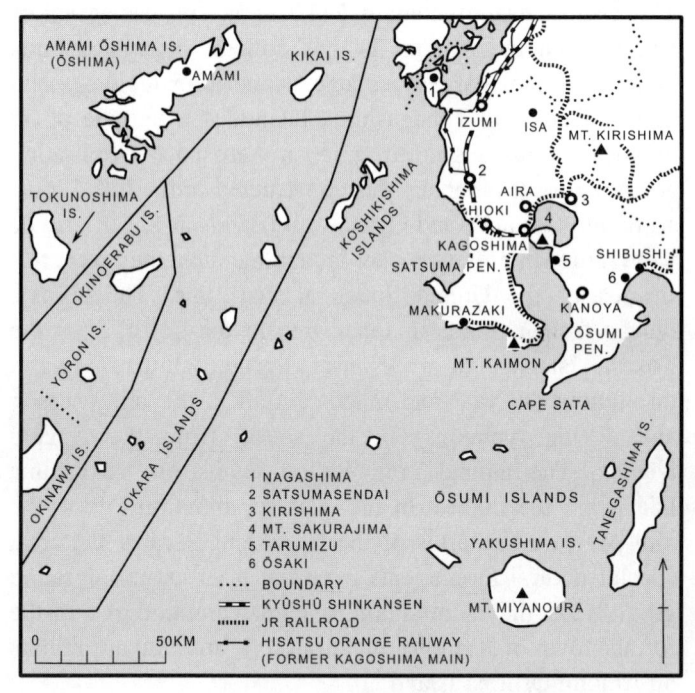

Figure 46 Kagoshima

in the sand steam baths. The lighthouse of Cape Sata in the southernmost spot of the Ôsumi Peninsula was built at the end of the Edo period as a result of the amended trade agreement with the United States, England, France, and the Netherlands. It was selected as one of the 50 Lighthouses in Japan by the Maritime Safety Agency.

The total area taken up by the islands (2,485 km²) is the largest of all the prefectures (c.f., Okinawa Prefecture is 2,276 km²). The Satsunan Islands consist of the Ôsumi Islands, the Tokara Islands, and the Amami Islands. The Koshikishima Islands are part of the city of Satsumasendai.

231

The Ôsumi Islands contain Yakushima and Tanegashima islands, and the Amami Islands contain Amami Ôshima Island, the third-largest isolated island after Okinawa and Sado islands. On Tanegashima Island, at a latitude of 30 degrees 24 minutes north, a Japan Aerospace Exploration Agency rocket launcher was constructed in the late 1960s. Although Okinawa and Ogasawara islands at lower latitude were more suitable as rocket launching sites, they were territories of the United States at that time. The climate ranges from a southern Japan one in the north, from the Tokara Islands, to a "Nansei Islands climate" (warm throughout the year and much rainfall in the rainy season and during typhoons) in the south, from the Amami Islands. The annual precipitation levels on Yakushima Island are the highest in the country, amounting to 4,480 mm per year. In terms of the fauna and flora of the area, special natural monuments exist, such as crane migration grounds on the Izumi Plain, a giant camphor tree in the former town of Kamô (now Aira city), and Amami rabbits on Amami Ôshima Island.

History and Culture

Satsuma and Ôsumi provinces and a part of Hyûga Province became Kagoshima Prefecture in the Meiji period. The name is derived from an old name of Sakurajima Island. The Satsuma Rebellion in 1877 (Meiji 10) was the last civil war in the country. Takamori Saigô in the Satsuma domain was one of the leading figures of the Meiji Restoration. At the rebellion, he led the ex-samurai who were dissatisfied with the Meiji government. Even head-on crashed bullets were excavated at the fierce battle site in Tabaruzaka in Ueki town (now Kumamoto city). Several Prime Ministers have made appearances in the prefecture, namely, Kiyotaka Kuroda (the second), Masayoshi Matsukata (the fourth and sixth), and Gonbee Yamamoto (the sixteenth and the twenty-second). Kiyotaka Kuroda also became Director General of Hokkaidô Development Commission, and led the reclamation of Hokkaidô. Masayoshi Matsukata reclaimed Senbonmatsu ranch in the Nasunogahara Plain. In terms of food culture, molded and fried fish paste is known as *satsuma-age*, which is also regarded as fried *kamaboko* in some regions.

Population and Traffic

The prefecture's population is 1,706,000. The main cities are Kagoshima (606,000), Kirishima (127,000), Kanoya (105,000), Satsumasendai (100,000), Aira (75,000), Izumi (56,000), and Hioki (51,000). Prefectural airlines fly from Kagoshima Airport in Kirishima to the islands of Amami Ôshima, Yakushima, Tanegashima, Okinoerabu, Kikai, and Yoron. Kagoshima Chûô Station is the terminal of the Kagoshima Main Line and the Kyûshû Shinkansen. The former Nishi-Kagoshima Station was known as the terminal of limited expresses and the longest line of sleepers (blue trains).

Primary Sector of Industry

Kagoshima's gross agricultural production is the fourth largest of all the prefectures after Hokkaidô, Ibaraki, and Chiba. The main commodities are beef cattle, swine, and broilers. In terms of numbers of livestock, swine (1,012,000 heads) are the largest of all the prefectures, beef cattle (292,000 heads) are the second largest after Hokkaidô, and broilers (85,400,000 heads) are the third largest after Iwate and Miyazaki. The Kagoshima Black is the brand of pork whose breed is the Berkshire, which originated in England. The sweet potato production is the largest of all the prefectures. Its main seed varieties are for processing. They are processed not only into shôchû but also into starch. Sweet potatoes are the native to tropical America, and they were called Kara-*imo* (the potato from the Táng dynasty) or Ryûkyû-*imo* (the potato from the Ryûkyû Kingdom) in Kagoshima Prefecture, and Satsuma-*imo* (the potato from Satsuma Province) in the other prefectures. Since rice was hardly ever cultivated in the *shirasu* plateaus, sweet potato cultivation and swine raising using the fodder of sweet potatoes started in the Satsuma domain. In terms of other primary products, the cultivated tea area is the second largest of all the prefectures after Shizuoka. Sakurajima radishes are known for their size, and weigh from 10 to 30 kilograms.

In the fishing industry, the hauls of eel, young yellowtail, amberjack, and bluefin tuna are the largest of all the prefectures. Shibushi city and Ôsaki town on the Ôsumi Peninsula are the main cultivation areas for eel, the former town of Azuma (now Nagashima town) and Tarumizu city for young yellowtail, Kanoya and Tarumizu cities facing Kinkô Bay, for amberjack, and Amami Ôshima Island for bluefin tuna.

Other Industries

The main industrial products in terms of gross production are compound feeds, frozen meat, and shôchû. In terms of number of establishments, the main categories are unprocessed tea and seafood processing. Although shôchû production had been the largest of all the prefectures, because of an increase in shôchû consumption in recent years, the prefecture was relegated to third position since the latest factories were constructed in Chiba Prefecture by Takara Shuzo Co., and in Ôita Prefecture, by Sanwa Shurui

Co. Satsuma *kiriko* cut glass was a traditional craft that was commenced by the Satsuma domain as a Western-style industry. Although it had been extinct through the Anglo-Satsuma War, the Meiji Restoration, and the Satsuma Rebellion, it was revived in the 1980s after a 100-year interregnum. Ôshima pongee and Amami shôchû, made from brown sugar, are traditional crafts on the Amami Islands. On the islands, tourists take advantage of the nature amenities, such as coral reef diving, whale watching, surfing, and canoe tours through mangrove forests.

47. Okinawa

Located in the westernmost part of the country, Okinawa faces the East China Sea to the north and the Pacific Ocean to the south (Figure 47).

Nature

The Ryûkyû Islands in the southern section of the Nansei Islands consist of the Okinawa Islands (including the Kerama Islands), the Sakishima Islands (including the Miyako, the Yaeyama, and the Senkaku Islands), and the Daitô Islands. The highest peak is Mt. Omoto (526 m) on Ishigaki Island, one of the Yaeyama Islands. The built-up areas on Ishigaki Island are based in the south of the mountain. The island is located 410 km from the prefectural capital, Naha city, and 270 km from Taipei. Adjacent to Ishigaki Island is Iriomote Island, on which the Iriomote wild cat was discovered in 1965. The highest peak of Okinawa Island is Mt. Yonaha (503 m) in the north. At the foot of the mountain, Okinawa rail *(Gallirallus okinawae)* was discovered in 1981.

The whole area is categorized as a Nansei Islands

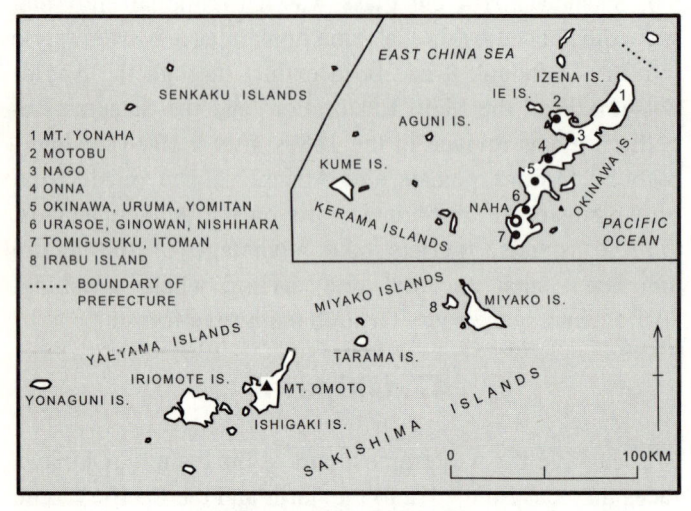

Figure 47　Okinawa

climate. According to climatic observation data from 1981 to 2010, the Sakishima Islands (such as Miyako, Ishigaki, and Iriomote islands) are classified as an Af climate (tropical rainforest) according to the Köppen climate classification system, whereas the former classification was a Cfa climate (humid subtropical-hot summer). The islands are considered to be a typhoon alley. The maximum instantaneous wind speed of 85.3 m/s, the fastest record on flat ground in Japan, was observed on Miyako Island with typhoon No. 18 (Cora) in 1966. Traditional houses are single-storied with thickly stuccoed red roofing tiles. They are surrounded by a fence made of coral reef or *fukugi* trees *(Garcinia subelliptica)*. Reinforced concrete houses with a water tank on the roof in preparation for any water shortages are now the norm.

History and Culture

The Ryûkyû Kingdom, which was a tributary of the Satsuma domain, became the Okinawa Prefecture in the Meiji period. It was named after Okinawa Island. The island's name signifies "offshore fishing grounds," which is derived from a document, *Tôdaiwajô tôseiden*, written in the eighth century. The Gusuku sites and related properties of the Kingdom of Ryûkyû have been classified as historical sites of the kingdom and listed as a World Heritage Site. It features the castles of Shuri, Nakagusuku, Katsuren, and Nakijin, and the ritualistic location of Seefâ Utaki (Illustration 14). Okinawa Island was a battleground between the Empire of Japan and the Allies at the end of World War II. After the war, it was ruled by the United States until 1972. Some battle sites are preserved, such as Okinawa Senseki Quasi-National Park and the Tower of Himeyuri in the south of the island. The area under the control of the Unites States Forces extends to about 18 percent of the island. There has been a big economic impact by the military bases on land rents. Problems with land ownership at military bases arose after the war, since a lot of emigrants left the prefecture for South America.

In terms of the food culture, local specialties are *sôki* soba (soup Chinese noodles with boneless pork ribs), *gôyâ chanpurû* (sautéd bitter melon with Okinawa tôfu), and the *sâtâ andagii* (a sugar confectionery). Unique foodstuffs are sold at the Makishi Public Market in the city of Naha, such as Knobsnout parrotfish *(irabuchâ)*, sea snakes *(irabû)*, and pork head skins *(chiragâ)*.

Population and Traffic

The prefecture's population is 1,393,000. The main cities are Naha (316,000), Okinawa (130,000), Uruma

(117,000), Urasoe (110,000), Ginowan (92,000), Nago (60,000), Itoman (57,000), and Tomigusuku (57,000). The prefecture's airports provide regular flights to Naha, Ishigaki, Miyako, Kume, Aguni, Yonaguni, Tarama, Kitadaitô, and Minamidaitô (the Daitô Islands are located about 350 km east of Naha). Naha Airport also serves international regular flights to Taipei, Shanghai, Hong Kong, and Seoul. No railroads operated in the postwar prefecture except for a light railroad that was once operated by a sugar mill in Minamidaitô Island, and a monorail that opened in 2003 between Naha Airport and Shuri in the city of Naha.

Primary Sector of Industry

The main agricultural commodities in terms of gross production are industrial crops, beef cattle, vegetables, swine, and flowers. It is difficult to find paddy fields in Okinawa Island at present. In terms of industrial crop production, sugar cane production is the largest of all the prefectures. Eighteen sugar factories remain on the islands of Ishigaki, Okinawa, Irabu, Minamidaitô, and Tarama. The factories operate from December to April, which is the sugarcane harvest season. Regarding beef cattle production, several Japanese Black beef cattle brand names (Ryûkyû, Ishigaki, Yanbaru, Miyako, and Ie) gave been consolidated into Okinawa Wagyû. In floriculture, cultured chrysanthemums are shipped to metropolitan areas by airplane. Chrysanthemums are short-day plants, and grown with light treatment. Besides the cut flowers, tropical horticultural crops are cultivated, such as pineapples, bananas, mangos, papayas, and dragon fruit.

Other Industries

The main industrial products in terms of gross production are heavy oil, gasoline, and light oil. In terms of number of establishments, the main categories are printing, ready-mixed concrete, and Western-style fresh cakes. As for oil manufacturing, the largest company is Nansei Sekiyu K.K., a subsidiary of Petróleo Brasileiro S.A. (*Sociedade Anônima*, a corportaion). It is located in the town of Nishihara in Nakagami county. In alcohol production, an Orion Breweries factory is located in Nago city, whereas local distilleries that produce *awamori* (the liquor made from rice) are distributed among the islands. Traditional crafts from the area include Kumejima pongee, Yuntanza Hanaui (silk or cotton fabric) in Yomitan village, and Tsuboya ware in Naha. Ryûkyû glasses originated in the bottles that were discarded from the U.S. bases.

As a tertiary sector industry, tourism is growing. Large resort hotels are distributed in the village of Onna. The Manza and Moon artificial beaches in the village were listed in the 100 Comfortable Beaches by the Ministry of the Environment. The Okinawa Churaumi Aquarium, which has whale sharks, is based at Expo '75 (Okinawa *kokusai kaiyô hakurankai*) site in Motobu town. Within remote island industry, the beaches of Eef on Kume Island, Futamigaura at the village of Izena, and Sawadanohama on Miyako Island have been listed as among the 100 Beaches *(nagisa)*. Iriomote Island is one of the original places for eco-tourism in the country, along with Yakushima Island. Tourists enjoy mangrove kayaking and slow ox cart tours on the island.

Conclusions

As Japan is a mountainous country, mountains have functioned as landmarks and boundaries for prefectures and municipalities. Through the lens of cultural stratigraphy at a prefectural level, mountains can be viewed the basis of culture, since rivers supply water to paddy fields, and mountains supply water to rivers. The Japanese penchant for mountains can be observed even in small gardens in which people keep trimmed trees. This is compared to the Anglo-Saxon gardens in North America that are covered with well-groomed lawns modeled after the plains over which people can gaze into the distance.

Most plains in the country were created by rivers' sedimentation, and comprise a significant space for food production. Simultaneously, parts of the plains were developed as consumption centers in which people, traffic, and economic activities were concentrated. The coastal plains close to metropolitan areas turned into ideal sites for heavy and chemical industries, since in the present day, large quantities of raw materials are shipped from foreign countries. Meanwhile, the coasts along suburbs and remote areas have provided leisure spaces for beach resorts, sporting activities, and fishing. Climatically, snow-covered lands constitute unique landscapes. The mountains are covered with snow reserve water, which creates the conditions for the rice cultivation quality in their surrounding areas. The general warming tendency is expected to result in a decrease in snowfall, which will lead to substantial daily energy loss in the summer, and increased natural disasters caused by torrential downpours.

In terms of food culture, local foods have been developed, which has proved to be a tourist attraction. The Japanese preference for rice has weakened since they began to import huge amounts of wheat, and Western foods entered society. For instance, the consumption of rice per person per year used to amount to 120 kilograms (2 *hyô*); currently, it amounts to 60 kilograms (1 *hyô*). Regardless, rice is still deemed a staple in local foods. With regard to traditional religious culture, the shrines and temples assume the role of sacred places. Concurrently, they provide spaces for recreation, environmental preservation, and refuge. In this sense, religion has become intertwined with local tourism.

The country's agricultural regions can be roughly divided into rice paddy areas and upland field areas. Even in rice paddy areas, agricultural land use has diversified through the spread of horticulture following the implementation of a policy to reduce rice production. Double cropping of rice and wheat (or barley) creates diversity in some rice paddy areas. As agriculture reflects regional uniqueness, so does the branding of agricultural commodities. In the fishing industry, the branding of fish products is based mainly on the unloading grounds rather than the catching grounds. For example, tuna landed in the town of Toi (now Hakodate city) is not as expensive as tuna landed in Ôma, located on the opposite shore of the Tsugaru Strait.

The distribution of the secondary industry sector can be explained not only by previous locational theories, but also by human affairs, such as the abilities of local government personnel tasked with inviting prestigious companies to set up new facilities, and the location of entrepreneurs' hometowns. Local industry traditions have also influenced current industrial locations. The tertiary sector of industry involves the essence of regional geography (nature, history, culture, population, transportation, and the primary and secondary industries). In particular, tourism operates according to its regional uniqueness. Therefore, accurate figures in regional geography will be helpful for subjective tourism experiences, by which individuals come to enjoy their own discoveries.

Epilogue

The idea of writing about the geography of Japan in English occurred to me in autumn 2014. At that time, a year had passed since the determination of the Tokyo Olympics had been made, and I was editing an obituary booklet for my supervisor who had been in charge of regional geography. On the campus, I was teaching an English seminar course on geography using the textbook "Discovering Japan" (Teikoku Shoin, 2009). It explains Japan's regional geography by seven regions. I then reflected on friends who came from faraway places and enjoyed talking about their hometowns, from which I developed the concept and began to write a Japanese draft in February 2015. The draft and the original 48 figures were completed in April 2016, and an English draft was proofread by Scientific Language Co. in February 2017. After I finished writing about the diversity of prefectures, I made a thumbnail sketch (an outline) and concluding remarks. This endeavor can be regarded as "comprehending the entity *after* assembling minute parts."

Writing takes time and human phenomena move swiftly. On being published, the contents of a publication age, and come to be regarded as information "of that time." Looking at atlases published in different years, I recall an old phrase *shogyô mujô* (the impermanence of worldly things). Not only place names and traffic networks but also the local products dealt with in atlases have changed with the lapse of time. Recent atlases illustrate information on industrial products instead of crops and mines, which were covered by the former ones. The changeable world, therefore, implies a profusion of subjects for human geography.

Better writing in the area of regional geography will be an issue for the next work. When that time arrives, the cultural stratigraphy viewpoint I have sought to express here will be worth considering, though it would be difficult to single out a topic among the profusion of information. A hint is to choose a subject that is distinct in space and moderate in terms of its time sensitivity. Such a description may be boring vis-à-vis sensational news, but a firm grasp of reality will not reduce its value even after time passes. To figure a causal relationship between topics in a spatio-temporal context, perhaps, large scale maps such as topo-graphic maps I use in field excursions will be helpful for the readers who seek discoveries.

Maps are of value in geography since they are spatial renderings. They used to be hand drawn with ink, taking time, however, the method changed to digital mapping after the mid-1990s. At present, open source software such as Inkscape and QGIS play an important role in the creation of maps for their usability.

Bibliography

Arai, Y., Kagami, M., Sato, T., Kojima, Y., Oguchi, T., Tsutumi, J., Nihei, T., Matsumoto, J. and Ikeya, K. 2013. *High school: new geography A [Kôtô gakkô: shin chiri A]*. Tokyo: Teikoku Shoin. (written in Japanese)

Beikoku Data-bank 2014. *Rice map 2015 [Kome map '15]*. Tokyo: Beikoku Data-bank. (written in Japanese)

Fujita, Y. and Tabayashi, A. eds. 2007. *Regional geography of Japan 7: central Japan [Nihon no chishi 7: Chûbu-ken]*. Tokyo: Asakura Shoten. (written in Japanese)

Geospatial Information Authority of Japan 2013. *GSI maps [Chiriin-chizu]*. https://maps.gsi.go.jp/ (last accessed in November 2017)

Inoue, T. and Matsumoto, J. 2005. Climatic division of Japan based on seasonal transition patterns of precipitation. *Proceedings of the General Meeting of the Association of Japanese Geographers*, 67, 296. (written in Japanese)

Kikuchi, T. ed. 2011. *Regional geography of the world 1: Japan [Sekai chishi series 1: Nippon]*. Tokyo: Asakura Shoten. (written in Japanese)

Nihei, T. 2004. *Database of offprints in geography: a collection of Nihei laboratory*. http://www.labo-geo.jp/cgi-bin/journal2.cgi (last accessed in November 2017)

Nihei, T. 2010. Commodification of rural space and changes in the main varieties of paddy rice in the Tohoku region. *Geographical Review of Japan, Series B*, 82, 49-59.

Saito, I. ed. 2006. *Regional characters of central Japan: cultural stratigraphy in the Matsumoto Basin [Chûô-nihon ni okeru bonchi no chiikisei: Matsumoto bonchi no bunkasôjo]*. Tokyo: Kokon Shoin. (written in Japanese)

Saito, I., Ishii, H. and Iwata, S. eds. 2009. *Regional geography of Japan 6: metropolitan area II [Nihon no chishi 6: shutoken II]*. Tokyo: Asakura Shoten. (written in Japanese)

Tabayashi, A., Yagasaki, N., Kikuchi, T., Nihei, T., Kaneko, J. and Waldichuk, T. 2016. Commodification of rural space in British Columbia, Canada. *In* D. W. Edgington, N. Ota, N. Sato and J. F. Steele eds. *Japan and Canada in comparative perspective: economics and politics; regions, places and people.* Japan Studies Association of Canada, 96-109.

Taniuchi, T. and Kagami, M. eds. 2016. *Social studies: geography of junior high school: the world and Japan [Shakaika: chûgakusei no chiri: sekai no sugata to nihon no kokudo].* Tokyo: Teikoku Shoin. (written in Japanese)

Teikoku Shoin editorial board 2009. *Discovering Japan: a new regional geography.* Tokyo: Teikoku Shoin.

Teikoku Shoin editorial board 2010. *Teikoku's atlas [Shinshô kôtô chizu].* Tokyo: Teikoku Shoin. (written in Japanese)

Teikoku Shoin editorial board 2013. *Teikoku Shoin geography series: figures of Japan 7: Hokkaido region [Nihon no sugata 7: Hokkaidô chihô].* Tokyo: Teikoku Shoin. (written in Japanese)

Yamamoto, S., Taniuchi, T., Kanno, M., Tabayashi, A. and Okuno, T. eds. 2006. *Regional geography of Japan 2: general remarks of Japan II [Nihon no chishi 2: nihon sôron II].* Tokyo: Asakura Shoten. (written in Japanese)

Index

Utsunomiya (city), 52-54

W
Wakayama (city), 156-157,
 159

Y
Yamagata (city), 27, 34,
 36-37, 41
Yamaguchi (city), 167, 180,
 182
Yamizo (Mt), 44
Yatsushiro (city), 219, 221
Yokkaichi (city), 125, 127,
 129
Yokohama (city), 78-80, 123
Yokote (city), 32, 34
Yonago (city), 162-163
Yoshino (river, Shikoku),
 183-187, 192, 196

Z
Zaô (Mt), 24, 34